Studies in Classical History
and Society

AMERICAN PHILOLOGICAL ASSOCIATION

AMERICAN CLASSICAL STUDIES

Volume 45

Series Editor
HARVEY YUNIS

Studies in Classical History and Society
MEYER REINHOLD

Studies in Classical History and Society

Meyer Reinhold

OXFORD
UNIVERSITY PRESS
2002

OXFORD

UNIVERSITY PRESS

Oxford   New York

Athens   Auckland   Bangkok   Bogotá   Buenos Aires   Calcutta   Cape Town
Chennai   Dar es Salaam   Delhi   Florence   Hong Kong   Istanbul   Karachi
Kolkata   Kuala Lumpur   Madrid   Melbourne   Mexico City   Mumbai   Nairobi
Paris   São Paulo   Shanghai   Singapore   Taipei   Tokyo   Toronto   Warsaw

and associated companies in
Berlin   Ibadan

Copyright © 2002 by the American Philological Association

Published by Oxford University Press, Inc.
198 Madison Avenue, New York, New York 10016

Oxford is a registered trademark of Oxford University Press

Library of Congress Cataloging-in-Publication Data
Reinhold, Meyer, 1909–
Studies in classical history and society / Meyer Reinhold.
p. cm.—(American classical studies)
Includes index.
ISBN 0-19-514543-7
1. Greece—History—To 146 B.C.   2. Rome—History.
3. Civilization, Classical.   I. Title.
II. Series.
DE86 .R45 2001
938—dc21   00-051671

$$DE$$
$$86$$
$$.R45$$
$$2002$$

1   3   5   7   9   8   6   4   2

Printed in the United States of America
on acid-free paper

In memory

Diane Reinhold, my wife,
who kept the window into
today's world always open
for me

Robert Reinhold, my son,
who reported the events
of our times

Foreword

Meyer Reinhold's active career spans sixty-five years, comparable in length and energy to Gildersleeve's. He began in an age when towering Roman historians like Rostovtzeff (1870–1952), Tenney Frank (1876–1939), and Lily Ross Taylor (1886–1969) were at work in America, and he emulated their control of sources and clear exposition in his first love, the history of Augustan Rome. Most of the articles collected in this volume date from the latter part of his career but result from the methods and interests he developed in its first phase. The second phase of his career came after World War II and was in some part a response to the huge numbers of students coming to college under the GI Bill and in need of new kinds of textbooks and study guides. The third phase began after the painful interruption of a decade. Perhaps because he had been away from academia for so long, he had sufficient vigor in his late fifties to develop a new discipline, what William M. Calder III called "the scientific study of classics in early America."[1] When most colleagues had retired, he founded an institute unique in this country, organized a large international membership to support it, and planned enough projects for the near future to fill another half century. To all three phases of his work he brought an indefatigable energy, a scrupulous accuracy, and a reliance on documents to speak for themselves.

He was born in New York City on 1 September 1909 to Joseph and Ethel (Rosen) Reinhold, who had emigrated from Europe. A precocious student, he was debarred from the Ivy League education he was qualified for by the *numerus clausus* most of these institutions maintained for the admission of Jews. Like many similar overqualified students, he attended a public institution in New York City, City College (now the City University of New York) where he would share classes with his lifelong friend and collaborator Naphtali Lewis (1911–), who entered a year later. An interest in ancient history was encouraged at City College by the now-forgotten Emory Bair Lease (1863–1931), an exciting and popular teacher of language and culture who published on Livy and on numerology. After receiving his A.B. in 1929, Reinhold found that the Ivy League was not so restrictive in admissions to its graduate schools when he was accepted at Columbia University, the eldest of a remarkable trio that included Lewis and Moses I. Finkelstein (later Sir M. I. Finley) (1912–1986). All three were intent on working with William Linn Westermann (1873–1954), the leading ancient historian at Columbia and one of the founders of the American study of papyrology. Thanks to Westermann they learned the principles of the new science and even had a memorable dinner with Rostovtzeff. So highly did Westermann regard them that one day when the three were walking along the street, Westermann caught up with them, and as he walked along, said, "You are the three ablest students I have ever had."

But as Westermann's career declined, he turned increasingly bitter and unhelpful. He torpedoed both a Guggenheim grant that he had encouraged Lewis to apply for and a publication of Finkelstein's at Rutgers University Press. Reinhold was scarcely treated better.

In common with others of his social background and personal experience, Reinhold (at least in his youth) held economic and political views that were considerably to the left. Seeing the enormous disparity between rich and poor in the 1920s exacerbated by the Depression and being himself a victim of a restrictive Establishment, he early formed an interest in social and economic history that would lead to his studies of wealth and status in antiquity. After receiving the A.M. in 1930, Reinhold hoped to write his dissertation with Westermann, but even as a young man his eyes were not good enough for papyrology. When he asked his mentor if he could write a dissertation on ancient economic history, he was told he had to study economics for three years before Westermann would even consider the idea. Discouraged, Reinhold turned to a much lesser light, Charles Knapp, who directed his dissertation, a biography of Marcus Agrippa.[2] Agrippa appealed to Reinhold as "a self-made man" who by hard work and intelligence rose to advise an emperor. Reinhold's stated goal was "to include every piece of evidence which bears on the life of Agrippa" and establish a chronology. Agrippa's military career may be slighted, but the work on constitutional law and history as well as the study of his writings and personality are extraordinarily researched and, for a twenty-three-year-old, maturely expressed. G. W. Richardson praised its "high level of scholarship and historical judgment," while Allen B. West, amid his praise, said that there were perhaps "traces of hero worship" that might be pardonable in a young man who so admires his subject.[3] One sour review notwithstanding, particularly painful as it came from Arnaldo Momigliano, his dissertation is still considered the standard work on the subject.[4]

Reinhold had the Ph.D. in hand in 1933, but he had few prospects in Depression America. At the encouragement of the young Moses Hadas (1900–1966), he received a two-year fellowship at the American Academy at Rome in 1933. Westermann, who had just come off a ten-year term as trustee of the academy, characteristically discouraged him from going.

On 1 September 1933, as Reinhold shared the crossing to Europe with Richmond Lattimore and a half-dozen other fellows, President Roosevelt took the country off the gold standard, effectively cutting the fellows' $4,000 stipend in half. For this and other reasons, Reinhold's experience at the academy was not a pleasant one. The drabness of the building, the inadequacy of the library (he preferred the Deutsches Institut), and particularly the class arrogance of the faculty and many of the fellows discouraged him to the point that he longed to return home to New York, though he knew there would be no job waiting for him. He was insulted by the professor-in-charge, Allen Chester Johnson (1881–1955) of Princeton, for the trivial offense of having given a talk from memory rather than reading it off a paper. He was already a published author and he continued to pursue his interest in the great fortunes of the Augustan Age by writing some articles for *Classical Weekly*, then edited by his *Doktorvater* Knapp. He also wrote a long article that Tenney Frank declined for the *American Journal of Philology*, calling it "a good beginning, but [not] satisfactory." The article was never published.

In his second year at the academy, he got on better with the professor-in-charge, Lily Ross Taylor, than he had with Johnson. His friend Lewis, with a fresh Ph.D. from the Sorbonne, joined him, and he also made friends with Frederic M. Wheelock (1902–1987), who was visiting Rome and accompanied him on a trip to Sicily and Greece. He found far less class prejudice and anti-Semitism among the Italians than at the academy and happily got out among the locals. He also met Rostovtzeff and Momigliano (1908–1987). Nevertheless, he was still miserable and eager to get home. He left in the spring of 1935 with Lewis, who had completed only one year of his fellowship.

On his return Reinhold was so dispirited with the lack of opportunities in his profession that he virtually abandoned the notion of getting a job. He nevertheless sent out nearly one hundred applications. He received only one positive response, a letter from a school welcoming him to its faculty but stating that as the school was a lay brotherhood, it paid no salaries. Reinhold sent his regrets. This lay brotherhood later became Dickinson College.

Within three years, Finley, who was an instructor at City College, had introduced him to Joseph Pearl, the chairman of the classics department at Brooklyn College. In 1938 Reinhold joined the faculty as an instructor in classics, rising to associate professor in a department with his friends Wheelock (1938–1952) and Lewis (1947–1976). Around the time that "Mo" Finley introduced Reinhold to Brooklyn College, Finley's wife, Mary F. Thiers, introduced Reinhold to Diane Roth, an executive medical secretary. They had their first date at a meeting of the New York Classical Club and were married on 29 September 1939. They would have two children, Robert, who became a reporter for the *Los Angeles Times* and the *New York Times*, and Helen, who became a university administrator. The marriage lasted fifty-nine years, until Diane's death in 1998.

The depressing years of the academy now put behind him, Reinhold resumed his study of Augustan wealth in earnest. Heavy and diverse teaching loads restricted the amount of time he could spend on research. In the year after the war, his efforts were directed at a comprehensive review of Rostovtzeff, reprinted here as chapter 8. He then turned to a large project on the documentary history of Rome with Lewis that would be of use for students in the burgeoning classics-in-translation courses. The result was *Roman Civilization: Selected Readings*[5] in two volumes: the first, treating the Republic to 27 B.C., was published in 1951; the second, on the Empire, in 1955. Modeled on Botsford and Sihler's *Hellenic Civilization*, it is divided into chapters on historiography, legal sources, inscriptions, papyri, coins, and so forth. Americans like Finley recognized the value of the project—"a first-rate source book," he called it[6]—while some Europeans were mystified.[7] J. A. O. Larsen said, "It is likely to remain the standard source book for Roman history for a generation and to be widely used." He was right: the book has remained in print and in use in classrooms throughout the country for nearly fifty years.

In 1955, Reinhold was one of the promising young (age forty-six) American historians of Rome. He had made his name with well-crafted, highly researched articles more reliant on meticulous and irrefutable research than interpretation. Unfortunately this was also the period referred to by Lillian Hellman as "scoundrel time." Having examined the Manhattan Project, the State Department, and the Army for Communists, real or imagined, the House Un-American Activities Committee turned in earnest to an examination of the faculties of the nation's universities and colleges. No region of the country was exempt, but the chief targets were in the Ivy League (Harvard and Cornell especially), and New York City. Finley had already testified before investigating committees twice and had lost his job at Rutgers in 1952. He felt the climate was so hostile that he immigrated to England in 1955 to become a lecturer and eventually professor of ancient history at Cambridge. Reinhold felt himself under such severe pressure at Brooklyn College that he resigned his position at the end of the school year, seemingly ending his promising career.

Because of the pernicious effects of the McCarthy era, Reinhold was unemployable in classics for the next ten years. A lesser man with a young family to feed might have renounced his principles or abandoned the field of classics altogether. Reinhold did neither. His brother gave him the title of vice president in his firm, Richmond Advertising Service of Brooklyn, and he remained there from 1955 to 1965. After the war, the GI Bill had flooded the colleges with students and new textbooks, and translations were needed that spoke a clearer and simpler language to these students, who represented far broader ranges of American society than had been on campuses before the war. Reinhold's supporter Moses Hadas at Columbia was probably the leading writer of such volumes. In 1946 Reinhold had written a review volume for Barron's called *Essentials of Greek and Roman Classics: A Guide to the Humanities*. Now he produced seven more guides for the company between 1959 and 1967.[8]

He returned to teaching in 1965 when he became associate professor of Greek, Latin, and ancient history at the University of Southern Illinois at Carbondale. Here he began gathering up his work on status in the ancient world, and in 1970 produced *History of Purple as a Status Symbol in Antiquity*[9] and "The Generation Gap in Antiquity," followed by "Usurpation of Status and Status Symbols in the Roman

Empire" (the opening chapters of this volume). He also became interested in the study of the effect of classical learning on the founders of the American republic.

His work on the classical tradition began in earnest following his move in 1967 to the University of Missouri at Columbia, where he was named Byler Distinguished Professor of Classical Studies in 1976. Here he applied the same methods of gathering and reporting documentary evidence that he had employed in his historiography. Even before "Bicentennial fever" gripped the nation in 1976, Reinhold produced important works of deep research on the classical tradition in America: *Past and Present: The Continuity of Classical Myths*, and *The Classick Pages: Classical Reading of Eighteenth-Century Americans*. In time he published a collection of his essays on the subject, *Classica Americana: The Greek and Roman Heritage in the United States*.[10] He retired from Missouri in 1980 and became a visiting university professor of classical studies at Boston University, where he founded the Institute for the Classical Tradition, which he directed for the next seventeen years. While at Boston he published yearly bibliographies (with various collaborators) of the classical tradition in *Classical and Modern Literature*, and he contributed to Merrill D. Peterson's *Thomas Jefferson: A Reference Biography*.[11]

In the midst of this enterprise, he managed to continue his work on documentary Roman history, producing the source books *The Golden Age of Augustus* on Augustan literature, culture, and history, *Diaspora: The Jews among the Greeks and Romans*, and *Jewish Life and Thought among the Greeks and Romans: Primary Readings*, which he edited with Louis H. Feldman. In 1988 he published his long-awaited work, *From Republic to Principate: An Historical Commentary on Cassius Dio's "Roman History" Books 49–52*, which covered the period from the aftermath of Antony's dalliance with Cleopatra to Octavian's ascendancy. Widely praised as a master of the material, Reinhold was able at the close of his career as a historian to return to the figure with which he had begun, in a lucid analysis of Marcus Agrippa's debate with Maecenas in Book 52.

Reinhold mastered the field of documentary history and founded a new discipline that continues to attract scholars both in America and abroad. The essays gathered here are a faithful index to the career of a historian of antiquity who also, throughout a career spanning periods of public and private vicissitude, has significantly extended the study of "the Classick pages."

Ward Briggs
University of South Carolina

Preface

This collection of studies, culled from more than a half century of research, is derived from a multiplicity of influences. These began when I was a graduate student at Columbia University in New York City in the early 1930s. My interests in research were formed and motivated by two mentors and two friends and fellow students. Professor William Linn Westermann and Professor Charles Knapp influenced me in different directions. Professor Knapp, who was for thirty years editor of *Classical Weekly*, had an exquisite knowledge of the Latin language and Roman literature. He was a tyrant who demanded accuracy and complete documentation, and he was a perfectionist in editing. From Professor Westermann I learned the significance of Greek and Latin inscriptions and Greek papyri for a knowledge of ancient history.

My friend Naphtali Lewis shared with me his splendid knowledge of the Greek language. He is a masterful papyrologist and has been the international president of the Society of Papyrologists. From Moses I. Finley I acquired a lifelong interest in social and economic history. Finley, who immigrated to Britain and became a British citizen, was knighted and is better known as Sir M. I. Finley. Arnaldo Momigliano called Finley the greatest ancient historian of the middle of the twentieth century. The friendship of our triumvirate (as Professor Westermann called us) was commemorated in a banquet at Cambridge University on its fiftieth anniversary.

This book has been brought to the light of day by the editorial assistance of my young classicist friend Mark Anderson and by the encouragement of Susan Ford Wiltshire of Vanderbilt University, whose friendship and interest in my scholarship have been invaluable. My Boston University colleague Loren J. Samons happily provided a recent bibliography on the subjects in this volume. In addition, I owe my gratitude to historians Robert Drews and Thomas McGinn of Vanderbilt University for assistance with editing and to Tommye Corlew for her caring and careful preparation of the manuscript.

Contents

Foreword by Ward Briggs   vii

1   The Generation Gap in Antiquity   3

2   Usurpation of Status and Status Symbols
in the Roman Empire   25

3   Human Nature as Cause in
Ancient Historiography   45

4   The Declaration of War against Cleopatra   54

5   Augustus's Conception of Himself   59

6   Cassius Dio's *History of Rome*:
From Republic to Principate   70

7   In Praise of Cassius Dio   77

8   Historian of the Classic World:
A Critique of Rostovtzeff   82

Notes   101

Index   139

Studies in Classical History
and Society

1

The Generation Gap in Antiquity

HOW UNIVERSAL IS GENERATIONAL CONFLICT? WAS THE younger generation in all past societies in a state of tension with the older generation because of Oedipal hostility of sons against fathers, or political and socioeconomic ambitions of the rising youth against gerontocratic power structures? Dare we say even of the Greeks on historical grounds that "to the ancients the primacy of generational struggle in history was entirely familiar and obvious. Every form of government seemed to breed its own distinctive form of generational contradiction. Generational conflict seemed to them an everlasting threat to political stability"?[1] Can we find in antiquity a generational consciousness among the youth as a result of competition or disillusionment with the older generation? A consciousness reflecting deep psychological cleavage between fathers and sons and "deauthoritization" of the older generation?

The peoples of the ancient Near East could not have conceived of the possibility of generational tensions or disequilibrium. The concept of a generation gap is irrelevant and unthinkable in such societies, whose basic ideological principle of the flux of society is that change in any form is a threat to the well-being and security of all. Given a pragmatically successful pattern of affairs—political, social, religious, technological—society's aim, nay duty, was to maintain this structure in every possible manner. Accordingly, every mode of human and animal behavior, every natural phenomenon, every significant event that was believed to have contributed to the establishment and continuity of the "good society" was cherished. Hence the diligence in isolating the archetypal happenings of the culture, and the validating of the present through constant repetition of the same rituals, periodic retelling of ritual myths, and inculcation of behavior patterns through paradigmatic myths of heroes. Hence also their "terror of history" and the rejection of any concept of the uniqueness of past events. For Near Eastern cultures the past was regarded as a repository of significant precedents for present success; occurrences in the past had value only as criteria by which to test the validity of each new event for the continuity of society. For example, the Akkad dynasty in Mesopotamia, notably the reign of Sargon I, served as the paradigm for future rulers and future events; and among the Jews the concept of their selection by Jehovah as the people chosen to act as the vehicle of history colored their evaluation of all events that affected them subsequently.[2]

Against this ideological complex, the concept of change by human agency was inconceivable. The younger generation, moreover, was in so close a dependency relationship with the family, even where large urban complexes existed, that, as an elementary matter of survival, the principal concern of the youth was to imitate their parents and train themselves for speedy absorption into the life patterns of their elders. Fear of insecurity apart from the family or tribal organization was so basic that the younger generation strove in every way to obtain the approval of the older generation, submitting to often arduous discipline and initiation ceremonies. In short, insecurity and fear of change served to maintain basic generational harmony as being mutually advantageous to both younger and older generations. This generational equilibrium was directed from the top, for the elders controlled not only the mechanisms and mysteries by which order and continuity were assured, but also the apprenticeship systems and career ladders which the younger generation had to master and climb in order to attain the tools of survival and advancement.[3]

Yet the older generation in such patriarchal and gerontocratic societies did not assume that generational balance would automatically ensue because of economic dependency of the youth. It methodically, as a matter of social policy, indoctrinated the youth with obedience to and respect for elders, in regard to both their superior wisdom and ways of doing things. For example, as early as 2450 B.C., in "the earliest formulation of right conduct in any literature," Ptah-hotep, a vizier of the Fifth Dynasty of Egypt, in his popular and famous pamphlet of advice to young aspirants for high status in Egypt, proclaimed the necessity to "hearken," to heed "the thoughts of those who have gone before." "If you are held in high esteem," Ptah-hotep advises parents,

> and have a household, and beget a son who pleases the god—if he does right, and inclines to your nature, and hearkens to your instructions, and his designs do good in your house, and he has regard for your substance as it befits, search out for him everything that is good. . . . But if he does wrong and trespasses against your designs, and acts not after your instructions, and his designs are worthless in your house, and he defies all you say, then drive him away, for he is not your son, and he is not born to you.

Further, "How good is it when a son hearkens to his father, and how happy is he to whom this is said! A son who is good as a master of hearing, namely one who has heard, he is honored of his father." "If a son accept it, when his father says it, not one of his plans miscarries."

> A son who has heard . . . prospers after he has heard. When he has grown old and has attained honor, he talks in like manner to his children and renews the instruction of his father. And everyone who is so instructed should talk to his children, and they again to theirs. May the people who shall see them say: "He is as that one was."[4]

Thus it is obvious that as early as twenty-fifth century B.C., the older generation in authoritarian Egypt had to work to mold the younger generation in its own image. Ptah-hotep assumes the possibility of rebellious sons; the control is the threat of exclusion from the family hearth. Isolated instances of rebellious children do not, of course, constitute generational disaffection. For generational consciousness to exist, there must occur some traumatic generational event that is shared by the youth, leading to disillusionment with and opposition to the older generation.[5]

Our first historical record of such generational conflict comes also from Egypt. About 2100 B.C. the aging pharaoh Wahkare-Achthoes II, of the Ninth/Tenth Dynasty, prepared for his son and heir a document of "Instruction for King Meri-ka-re." This dynasty, with its capital at Heracleopolis, came to power in a time of troubles for Egypt, the massive political and social crisis in the transition period between the Old and New Kingdoms. Though our sources are extremely fragmentary, it is clear that some sort of generational tension affecting the youth existed. The pharaoh warned against the danger: "The contentious man is a disturbance to citizens; he produces two factions among the younger generation."[6] The future pharaoh Meri-ka-re was advised to "foster thy younger generation . . . and increase thy adherents with recruits" to "increase the younger generation of thy followers." Wahkare was pessimistic: "Generation will oppress generation, as the ancestors prophesied about it." It is perhaps as a result of Meri-ka-re's restoration of generational balance that an era of peace was brought to Egypt for several decades.[7]

Despite the societal conditions fostering generational harmony and the managerial techniques employed to assure dynamic equilibrium between the younger generation and their elders, the theogonic myths current in the Near East in the second millennium B.C. contain significant stories of generational conflict. It is indeed surprising that authoritarian, ideologically static societies that value mythicohistorical precedents as paradigms for present behavior should place father-son conflict at the very summit of the divine origins. The Hittite theogony of 1400–1200 B.C., from the royal archives at Hattusas (translated or adapted from Hurrian myths of the fifteenth century B.C., whose roots lie in earlier Babylonian-Sumerian traditions), depicted the divine succession as a struggle for kingship in the sky, involving a three-generational conflict characterized by cruelty of the heavenly fathers against their children and their displacement by rebellious sons. This story, involving mutual violence and cruelty between older and younger generations of gods, is an age-old cosmogonic myth. In the now-famous Hittite version, the Kumarbi "Kingship in Heaven" text, Alalu is dethroned by his son Anu, god of heaven. Anu, representing the forces of the past holding back youth, then oppresses his son Kumarbi, presumably originally a vegetation god. Kumarbi arms himself with a *harpe* (the common reaping tool of the Near East), castrates his father and seizes control of heaven. But Kumarbi fears his son Teshub (the Hittite-Hurrian weather god) and seeks to control him by swallowing him, but a stone is substituted in place of Teshub. Eventually, Teshub overthrows Kumarbi and brings order to the cosmos.

A Ugaritic text of ca. 1400–1350 B.C. tells of a similar dynastic struggle involving El (who is equated with Kumarbi); and an age-old Phoenician myth deriving from theogonic literature of the second millennium B.C., preserved in the *Phoenician History* of Sanchuniathon, contains a similar tradition of generational struggle among the gods.[8]

Such Near Eastern theogonic concepts, involving divine succession through violence and generational conflicts for power, found their way—the route is not certain—into Greek mythology. Our prime source is the great theogonic poem of Hesiod. The recovery of Near Eastern antecedents of the myth of divine succession in heaven compels us to regard the parallel stories in Hesiod's *Theogony* as an adaptation to Greek mythic and cultural patterns of widely diffused theogonic literature current from the second millennium B.C. Echoes of the Kumarbi text resound in the stories of the cruelty of the Greek sky god, Uranus, toward his children by Gaea; the revolt of his son Cronus (a vegetation god); Cronus's castration of Uranus with a *harpe*, and his seizure of control of the kingdom in the sky; his own fear of and cruelty toward his children, whom he swallowed; the substitution of a stone for his son Zeus; and the overthrow of Cronus by Zeus, a weather god. The generational conflict depicted in the Greek myth is an age-old tradition rather than new mythic creations reflecting awareness of intergenerational power struggles in Greek society.[9]

Yet the Greeks did incorporate in this way the concept of generational conflict in their myths. To halt the pattern of divine succession, Zeus swallowed his consort Metis, because of fear of a rebellious child. The subsequent birth of Athena out of his own head brought him instead a dutiful daughter. Even after the final victory of Zeus against all the forces of chaos (notably Typhon and the Aloades), Zeus's reign was challenged by a palace plot involving his children Poseidon and Athena and his wife, Hera, who sought unsuccessfully to throw him into chains. Civil war on Olympus was averted by the intervention of the Nereid Thetis, who brought about the release of Zeus.

Conflict between divine son and divine mother is recorded in the myth of Hephaestus's hostility to Hera. In exile from Olympus, Hephaestus sent his mother a magic throne; when she sat in it, she was unable to move, bound by invisible chains. Efforts to persuade Hephaestus by threats to return to Olympus and release Hera failed. Finally, Dionysus made him drunk, escorted him back to Olympus, and induced him to unchain his mother.

Other Greek myths authenticated the reality of conflict between young and old, between fathers and sons. For example, in the *Iliad*, Phoenix, tutor of Achilles, tells how he left his home "fleeing from strife against my father, Amyntor." In this case the cause of the tension between father and son was sexual rivalry: at the urging of his jealous mother, Phoenix seduced his father's concubine. In consequence, Amyntor invoked a curse upon his son, as the result of which, Phoenix believed, he remained childless.[10] It was Phoenix who preached to Achilles the disasters stemming from youthful pride and passion, citing also the conflict between the Aetolian hero Meleager and his mother, Althaea. Because of the deaths of her brothers in the war between Calydon and the Curetes of Pleuron in Aetolia,

Althaea cursed her son and prayed for his death.[11] In the opening scenes of the *Iliad*, aged Nestor reminds the younger kings Agamemnon and Achilles that it is proper to be guided by elders. "Nay, hearken to me; you are both younger than I am."[12]

Can it be that in the period when Homer wrote, an innovative time when many basic changes were in process of emerging, age-old patterns of social cohesion were breaking apart, and that the stories of Phoenix and Meleager reflected contemporary dislocations? At any rate, Hesiod, writing at the end of the eighth and early seventh century B.C., was sensitive to generational imbalance in his time. In characterizing the last of the five ages of man, the Iron Age, he proclaimed the end of harmony between father and children, and bemoaned a time when "men dishonor their parents," carping at them and denying them support in their old age.[13]

The Greek mythological tradition preserved more than a few father-son conflicts. It is likely that in their primitive form these myths recorded struggles for power within royal dynasties. But in the later Greek rationalized versions that have survived, they appear as efforts of fathers to avert dread oracular pronouncements that the son would kill the father. The most famous of these myths is, of course, the unwitting slaying by Oedipus of his father, Laius, as the result of which he succeeded to the throne of Thebes. A similar myth was told of Minos's son Catreus, king of Cnossus, who was warned by an oracle that he would be killed by one of his children. To avoid accomplishing this fate, his son Althaemenes fled to Rhodes. But later Catreus was unwittingly killed by Althaemenes, who was so horrified by the deed that he prayed to be swallowed up by the earth, and so atoned for his patricide. So also did Odysseus's son by Circe, Telegonus, unknowingly kill Odysseus. Premeditated patricide in mythical royal families is also recorded: Carcabus killed his tyrannical father, King Triopas of the Perrhebeians, in order to deliver the people; Temenos, a Heraclid, king of Argos, was murdered by his sons to ensure that the royal power would pass to them rather than to his favored son-in-law, Deiphantes.

While such cases are simply by-products of typical palace intrigues, they do, nevertheless, afford precedents for unfilial behavior. To guard against the dangers of generational cleavage and discontinuity, one of the prime social controls was the age-old injunction, inculcated in the young everywhere, but first elevated into a divine commandment by the Jews: "Honor thy father and mother."[14] In the Near East, as well as among the Indo-Europeans, the patriarchal family was the keystone of stability in society. Jewish law proclaimed the solidarity of the family as a cornerstone of the community by placing respect due to parents under the surveillance of Jehovah. Religious fears of divine punishment for disrespect of parents, and by extension of the older generation, were supplemented by legislation making violence or curses against father or mother crimes punishable by death.[15] In the traumatic crisis of the Babylonian captivity, at a time when separation from the ancestral cult center in Jerusalem and disillusionment with the elders endangered generational continuity, the family was accorded a new importance for the solidarity of the Jewish people in exile; moreover, in the post-exilic period, protective laws were sharpened against the disruptive force of conflicts between parents and children.[16] For example, in *Deuteronomy* extraordinary provisions were made for disciplining the incorrigible son: "If a man have a stubborn and rebellious son, that will not obey the voice of his father, or the voice of his mother, and though they chasten him will not hearken unto them," the son is to be hailed before a council of the elders of the city, and if convicted is to be stoned to death by all the men of the city, "so shalt thou put aside the evil from the midst of thee, and all Israel shall hear, and fear."[17] Against rebellious children was hurled the imprecation, "Cursed be he that setteth light by his father or his mother."[18] Mockers and scorners of parents were subject to capital punishment, and disrespectful children were also threatened with refusal of proper burial.[19] As a corollary to the injunction to honor father and mother was the principle of respect due to elders. When Job, for example, complains[20] that in his fall from wealth and station some of the youth[21] mocked him, there is almost stunned disbelief: "They abhor me, and keep at a distance from me, and they spare not to spit in my face." Job's friends are compassionate, but it is from the mouth of one of them, Elihu son of Barachiel, the Buzite, that we hear not only the conventional respect for elders, but for the first time, by way of challenge to the older generation, the demand by the youth to be heard if they possess wisdom and understanding:

> I am young in days, whereas you are aged. Therefore was I in dread and afraid to declare my knowledge to you. . . . It is not the aged that are wise, nor is it the old who understand right, therefore I say listen to me; I also will declare my knowledge.[22]

But such expressions of generational consciousness on the part of Jewish youth were negligible. The continuity of the family and the people remained overriding forces throughout Jewish history in antiquity and, indeed, until modern times.

No less so did the Greek culture area anchor family solidarity and generational harmony upon the injunction "Honor thy father and mother." Stobaeus has preserved for us a large collection of quotations from earlier Greek writers which ring the changes on the theme.[23] They extend over a period of about seven hundred years, and include Theognis, Pythagorean doctrine, Sophocles, Euripides, Agathon, the tragic poet Dicaeogenes (a contemporary of Agathon), Plato, the writer of Middle Comedy Antiphanes, Isocrates, Anaximenes of Lampsacus (rhetor and Sophist of the second half of the fourth century B.C.), the three leading writers of New Comedy Philemon, Menander, and Diphilus, Neopythagorean literature, and the late Stoic Hierocles. Besides the general concept of the duty to honor one's parents, we find such specific exegesis as: "It is a duty of children to obey the commands of a father" (Euripides); "it is necessary for children to obey the father, and it is just to think as he does" (Euripides); "it is proper not to say or do evil to one's parents, but to obey them in both little and important matters . . . , in well nigh everything, even in madness" (from a Neopythagorean work attributed to Perictyone).[24]

Aside from such moral instruction inculcated in the youth, in the Greek city-states the laws prescribed the precise obligations of children to their aged parents and grandparents: provision of food, lodging, and burial. In Athens the law appears to have originated in the legislation of Solon in the early sixth century B.C. Filial duty was accorded such weight that in the scrutiny of newly chosen officials they were questioned about their treatment of their parents. Athenians who did not fulfill their filial obligations were subject to indictment under the law concerning mistreatment of parents (γραφὴ γονέων κακώσεως). Conviction of breaking this law carried with it as punishment partial loss of civic rights. A similar law at Delphi, fragmentarily preserved, reads, in part:

> If anyone does not feed his father and mother, when this is reported to the council, if the council shall find the person guilty, they shall bind him and conduct him to the civic jail.[25]

Further weight was given to the honor and duties owed to parents by religious sanctions of various kinds. Parents were often equated with the gods, so that disrespect, violence, or neglect of obligations to them was equated with impiety. Accordingly, Olympian Zeus and the Erinyes of the underworld take the lead in punishing such violations.[26] The insecurity of the older generation must have been considerable in some periods, for sinners against parents were even threatened with punishment in Tartarus in the afterlife.[27] More fearful was the threat to the younger generation that violence to or thwarting of a parent might let loose the dread curse of the father or mother upon the child. Impressive in the mythic tradition were the effective curse of Amyntor on his son Phoenix, of Theseus upon the innocent Hippolytus, Althaea upon Meleager, Oedipus upon his sons Polynices and Eteocles, and Pelops upon his sons Atreus and Thyestes. "Countless other parents," says Plato, "cursed countless other sons, and regarding such curses of parents upon children it is clearly proved that the gods listen to parents; for a parent's curse upon children is as no other man's curse upon any other, and quite justly so."[28] Is there any wonder, then, that we find Greeks confessing to guilt feelings in relations with their parents?[29]

Besides such control mechanisms that must have imposed on most of the youth a self-censorship motivated by guilt and fear, the city of Athens made provisions for generational continuity through an early "coming of age" of youths (the eighteenth year), which extinguished the father's paternal authority over his son, and two years of civic and military training among the ephebes.[30] In Sparta the bridging of the generations was the aim of attaching in close personal relationship each young Spartan in his mess to an older citizen. It is interesting to find in early Spartan history, before the rigors of the Lycurgan system were imposed, a notorious incident involving a clash of generations. After the long First Messenian War, in the last quarter of the eighth century B.C., the younger generation of Spartans which had grown up during the war was excluded from distribution of the conquered lands on the grounds that they had not participated in the war. When these "war babies" stirred up a confrontation in protest, they were designated *partheniae* ("bastards") or half-breeds, and declared legally ineligible for full Spartan rights. After a threatened coup d'etat on the part of these youths was thwarted, they were rounded up and shipped overseas, in 705 B.C., to form the nucleus of the only colony ever established by Sparta, Taras (later Tarentum).[31]

One wonders to what extent the numerous other colonies planted in the western Mediterranean and around the shores of the Black Sea were constituted in their origins of the younger generation of the mother cities. We are ill informed about the incidence of generational tension in the critical period in the Greek city-states that experienced the enormous increase of land hunger as a result of great population increases in the eighth through sixth centuries B.C. and the resort to the safety valve of overseas colonization.[32] While the *patria potestas* of Greek fathers was originally as strong as that among other ancient peoples, it was mitigated much more rapidly than at Rome through the weakening of the authority of the patriarchal families and the clans as the result of the priorities given to the polis.[33] This reordering of societal priorities, together with the unprecedented discontinuities with tradition in all fields, was accompanied by visible gaps in the generational balance of Greek cities, emergent generational conflict, generational anxiety on the part of the older generation, and guilt feelings on the part of the youth.[34]

These incipient dislocations in generational harmony were not likely to wither away as sociological aberrations, given the growing tendencies toward egalitarianism among citizens in Greek cities, and the increasing redirection of allegiances from the patriarchal family to the city-state. Indeed, it was as a result of such an evolution that in Athens in the fifth century B.C. there occurred the first massive challenge to the older generation in the history of mankind. The causes of a decisive cleavage between the generations were complex. First and foremost was the very nature of Athenian democracy under the Periclean dispensation, which elevated all individual Athenian citizens to the highest human dignity the world had ever known. In this time of rapid change, respect for tradition, the age-old concept of honor to parents and elders were in sharp conflict with civic institutions, which placed fathers and sons (from their eighteenth year in Athens) on a level of political equality.

In the fluid, "quick turnover society" of Athens,[35] there came to the surface a polarized two-generational pattern (there is no word for "middle-aged" people in Greek),[36] the νεώτεροι or νέοι and the πρεσβύτεροι, and the tension between them mounted. The age level that separated the generations must have been somewhat fluid, though in one source the cutoff point is thirty, "below which a man is to be accounted young."[37]

In Athens, as in most other Greek cities, a peculiar psychological mechanism, characteristic of slave-owning societies, was operative. Many of the youth, particularly in well-to-do families, were reared by trusted slaves. Such a system is bound to create unclarity as to where authority is centered, because there is a separation between the source of paternal power and the actual exercise of it. Not only does the child not continue to adulthood in respect for his social inferior, but the slave, caught between two masters as it were, is vacillatory in the exercise of his surrogate paternal power. As a result, in the rearing process, while the child may idealize the father and fear his authority, he learns to circumvent it when exercised by a slave.[38] Add to this conflict the confusion engendered in the Greek value systems by the high estimation placed upon the superior wisdom of the older generation and the idealization of youth in Greek art.[39]

But it was above all the growth in respect for reason that increasingly led to the "deauthoritization" of the fathers and the older generation. Aristotle's dictum is applicable to the classical period: "In general all men seek not their forefathers' way, but what is good."[40] In the middle years of the fifth century B.C. the polarization of the generations is explicit. While in the *Persians* Aeschylus put into the mouth of the ghost of Darius the charge of "youthful recklessness" against his son Xerxes as the cause of the disaster at Salamis,[41] in the *Suppliant Women* the chorus implores King Pelasgus, who is "aged in knowledge," to "learn from one of younger birth."[42] It is particularly in the *Eumenides* that we see in a dramatic reversal the traditional dichotomy of the right of authority in the hands of the older generation and the duty of obedience on the part of the younger generation turned on its head—on the grounds of reason, justice, and the welfare of the city of Athens. The rigid Erinyes, representing an outmoded system of tribal justice and social organization based upon clan and family, are pitted against younger gods—Zeus, Apollo, Athena—who are promoters of civic justice, moderation, reason. Aeschylus explicitly stresses the conflict between the older and the younger generation of gods. The Erinyes assail οἱ νεώτεροι for trampling upon the authority of the ancient traditions. It is noteworthy that in this generational conflict on a cosmic level, the younger generation is victorious. "You trample on me, your elder, young as you are," say the Erinyes. The reply of Athena might have become the manifesto of the younger generation of Athens in the Periclean Age: "I will bear with your anger, since you are my elder. And in that respect indeed you are wiser than I am. Yet Zeus hath granted to me, too, no mean understanding."[43]

Sophocles, upholder of traditional piety and patterns, has an illuminating picture in the *Antigone* of intransigent challenge on the part of idealistic youth against the arbitrary authority of the state. While his rebellious Antigone may represent age-old religious traditions and the solidarity of the family, in his characterization of her and her fiancé, Haemon, Sophocles was reflecting a growing consciousness of independence and self-confidence among the younger generation in Athens at the time. The challenge hurled by Haemon against the authority of his father, King Creon, is unmistakable. Sophocles has depicted in this play a double-barreled attack on the authority of the state and on paternal authority. Creon clearly asserts the authority of the father and the obedience due to elders:

> Yes, my son, you should bear this in your heart—in all respects to obey your father's will. It is for this that men pray to have dutiful children grow up in

their homes—that they may requite their father's enemies with evils and honor, as their father does, his friend. But he who begets unprofitable children—what shall one say that he hath begotten, but troubles for himself, and much laughter for his enemies.[44]

Creon speaks here like Ptah-hotep two thousand years before. Haemon's formal respect for his father's wisdom and authority[45] is tempered by a demand for the claims of justice and for respect to wisdom in the younger generation. "Nay, forgo your anger," urges the young Haemon to his father,

permit yourself to change. For if I, a young man, have a right to a view, it is best, I say, that man should be endowed by nature with all wisdom; otherwise—and it is not likely to happen so—it is good also to learn from those who speak aright. . . . If I am young, you should look to my merits, not my years.[46]

Creon can only fall back upon assertion of his authority as ruler and father,[47] and demand respect as an elder. "Men of my age—are we indeed to be taught wisdom by a man of his age?"[48] In the duel between Creon and Haemon we hear for the first time in history (the cautious observations of Elihu to Job along these lines may have been written under the influence of Greek rationalism)[49] the voice of the younger generation demanding respect for the individuality of its contributions to society, even if at variance with the wisdom of the older generation.

Curiously, Euripides, whose philosophy was iconoclastic, gives us, in the extant plays, no picture of the revolt of the youth. In the *Alcestis*, written in 438 B.C., the quarrel between a father and son takes the bizarre form of King Admetus berating his aged father, Pheres, for his refusal to die in order to save his son's life. Pheres's angry words are based on the traditional relations of the generations: "You are very arrogant," he tells his son, "and, though a youth, you hurl words at me."[50] Admetus reverses traditional legal process by formally disowning his father.[51] Even so, Euripides, like his great contemporaries Aeschylus and Sophocles, all of them perceptive surveyors of the shifting values of contemporary Athens, reflects the changing status and claims of the younger generation.

This generational consciousness and aggressiveness produced under the dramatic circumstances that convulsed the Greek world in the second half of the fifth century B.C. a degree of devaluation of the older generation and of generational disequilibrium unparalleled in the previous history of mankind. The evidence is unmistakable. Increased awareness of an antithesis between the generations took form in Athens.[52] This cleavage was widened and supplied with a rationale by the Sophists, who elevated the conflict of generations to a vigorous and conscious opposition in Athenian society. Their tendency to analyze phenomena in bipolarized form, their sanctioning of reason and natural rights (*physis*) over legal and traditional institutions (*nomos*), which they held up to critical examination, their advocacy of *arete* in knowledge rather than in obedience, of egalitarianism and relativity in morals—all these heightened a generational consciousness on the part of the youth. Thus there emerged for the first time the claim of the younger generation to a "natural right" to disobey and disregard fathers and elders.[53] Such vigorous critique and assault on tradition and the customary authority of the fathers and the older generation were accelerated also by the growth of democratic institutions, the weakening of the ties toward the polis, and the rise of individualism in Athens.[54] It is, however, important to recognize that the generation gap in Athens was not motivated by revolutionary political views of the youth, despite realization on the part of many, as a result of the traumatic experience of the Peloponnesian War, that the older generation had failed. Their unrest and agitation were not directed toward thrusting themselves forward as the "self-anointed bearers of authority"[55] and the establishment of a juvenocracy in place of their deauthoritized elders. The fathers were, indeed, more devoted to the institutions of the polis and its democratic constitution than the sons, who had not only experienced disillusionment but, with growing individualism, were likely to repudiate democratic institutions as restrictive, irrational, and contrary to natural law.[56]

The failures of Athens during the Peloponnesian War, the suffering, despair, turmoil, and growing brutalization of warfare and social conflict, unleashed an open critique by the younger generation of the mismanagement of affairs by the older generation. Symptomatic and highly instructive in this connection is a fragment of a political oration "On the Constitution" by Thrasymachus (a Sophist well known for his debate on justice with Socrates in the opening pages of Plato's *Republic*): "I could wish, men of Athens, to have belonged to that long-past time when young men were content to remain silent, and when events did not compel them to speak in public, while the older men were correctly supervising the city." But now because of grave mistakes, "it is necessary to speak.[57] A person either has no feeling or has too much patience who goes on offering himself up to whoever wishes as the object of their mistakes, and is ready to assume the blame for the guile and wickedness of others." As a result, instead of harmony "[we have] reached the point of hostility and conflict with one another."[58] In another context, Antiphon (about whom little is known—he was a Sophist and an opponent of Socrates) took a stance on the side of the younger generation. In an essay "On Truth," Antiphon held that blind obedience and piety toward parents were irrational and contrary to natural law, and that there was nothing morally wrong in disregarding legal restraints, so that guilt feelings toward parents, for example, were irrational.[59]

That contacts between the younger and older generation in Athens in the last quarter of the fifth century were abrasive is underlined by the crystallization of a stock motif of Old Comedy, strained relations between fathers and sons.[60] The growing friction between and changed outlooks of the generations are especially reflected in Aristophanes's *Clouds*.[61] In the debate between Right Logic and Wrong Logic it is obvious that Aristophanes's sympathies were with the older generation and its values. "Boys," proclaims Right Logic, the symbol of traditional ways, "should be seen and not heard," they should be trained in the ways of their fathers, revere their parents, show respect for elders, not talk back to fathers or call them "old Iapetus."[62] In this connection there was created in Old Comedy the stock figure of the "father beater," symbolizing the younger generation, belligerent, scornful, emancipated from restraints imposed by the fathers.[63] In *Clouds*, for example, there is a confrontation between the generations in the characters of Strepsiades and Phidippides. Young Phidippides, arguing with his father over his own preferences for modern poetic and musical styles while Strepsiades supports older modes, strikes his father. In the ensuing analysis of this unprecedented act, which the father calls unjust and illegal, Phidippides defends the right of sons to use violence against the fathers on rational and sophistic grounds. When parents act in an immature manner, reasons Phidippides, they must be chastised like children; laws permitting parents to strike children were made by the older generation. The solution is simple: "change the law so that sons may beat fathers."[64] Similarly, in the *Birds* Aristophanes comments on the belligerent attitude of the younger generation by depicting Cloudcuckooland as a place where the young are permitted by law to strike their fathers.[65]

The generational disequilibrium, hostility, and tensions in Athens are also confirmed by the growing importance and application of two intergenerational legal processes: *apokeruxis*, disownment of a son by a father, and *graphe paranoias*, charge of mental incompetence by a son against a father.[66]

In the anxiety of the older generation to restrain the youth, there developed in Athens, as a protective device, the use of the term "youth" in a derogatory sense among members of the older generation. For example, we find a politician in his fifties labeled "the most powerful of the younger scoundrels."[67] Similarly, middle-aged democratic politicians were called οἱ νεώτεροι as compared with their more conservative predecessors.[68] In the debate over the Sicilian expedition between Nicias and Alcibiades which Thucydides incorporates for the year 415 B.C., Nicias disdains Alcibiades as "still too young to command, a rash youth." "It is of youths such as these," says Nicias, "when I see them sitting here in answer to the summons of this same man that I am afraid; and I make a counter-appeal to the older men."[69] Alcibiades concedes his youthfulness, and warns against Nicias's effort to cause friction (*stasis* is the ominous term) between the younger and older generations. This, declares Alcibiades, is detrimental to civic harmony and the national imperial goals, for "just as our fathers did, young men should take counsel with older men [for] youth and old age without one another are worth nothing."[70] Thus in this illuminating Thucydidean paradox the older Nicias is depicted as exacerbating generational conflict, while the younger Alcibiades appears as a supporter of generational harmony! It is noteworthy that Alcibiades was at this time thirty-six years of age.[71] A similar instance of the term "youth" as a rhetorical cliché with derogatory implications is to be found in the debate in Syracuse in 415 B.C., in which the popular leader Athenagoras, an older man, attacks the oligarchs, whom he calls *neoteroi*, as overly ambitious for power. Though their leader Hermocrates, the anti-Athenian statesman and general, could hardly have been a young man at the time, Thucydides has simply put into Athenagoras's mouth a typical ideological association of the politician being attacked with irresponsible young men.[72]

Because Socrates was on the side of reason when he thought the sons to be right despite traditional obligations of obedience and respect, he ranged himself on the side of the sons against the fathers. It is instructive that both factions of the older generation were hostile to him: in 404 B.C. the oligarchs ordered him to cease talking with the youth (that is, those under thirty);[73] in 399 B.C., under the restored democracy, he was charged with corrupting the youth, found guilty by the democratic courts, and executed. Actually, whatever the effects of his teaching upon individual Athenian youths—and it is clear that on rational grounds his leading pupils turned to conservative political and social philosophies—Socrates had no intention to exacerbate and widen the generational gap in Athens. His views on the generations were a mixture of Pythagorean doctrine, which required veneration of the fathers, and opposition to the despotism of the elders when they thwarted fulfillment of the rational ideals of the youth.[74]

If in his teaching Socrates fostered intellectual revolt of the youth against institutionalized irrationality, he nevertheless inculcated respect for and gratitude to parents as a fundamental duty because they give children the blessings of life. Children owe their parents obligations and respect that are imposed by the laws and public opinion.[75] This did not deter Socrates's more rabid accusers from charging him with malicious intent in fomenting hostility to and contempt for fathers and tradition, causing sons to become scorners of the gods and morally degenerate.[76] This he was said to have accomplished by substituting himself as surrogate father, asserting himself to be a wiser guide for the youth in matters of proper conduct than their own fathers.[77] But, indeed, Socrates, in his concern to make respect for reason the overriding obligation, proclaimed that "unreason is unworth" and that, therefore, respect for members of one's family should not be based upon familial ties alone.[78]

Thus in substituting the criterion of reason for the traditional principle of unthinking obedience to parents, Socrates in effect contributed to the undermining of the traditional relations between the generations. It came down to this simple proposition: if the older generation acted unwisely, righteousness was on the side of the youths who disobeyed them. "If one does not obey the evil, unjust, or shameful orders of a father or official, or even, by Zeus, a despot, he does not in any way disobey," proclaimed the Stoic philosopher Musonius Rufus, one of the intellectual heirs of Socrates.[79]

With the defeat of Athens in 404 B.C., the generational tensions of the end of the fifth century B.C. took a new turn. The increasing disillusionment with the cultural and political forms of the older generation and the rapidly increasing individualism fostered by social instability did not result in confrontations or programs for reform mounted by the youths. For many, in the first half of the fourth century B.C., scorn for elders took the form of rejecting integration into the traditional political and social institutions of the elders. Instead, the energies of many educated and affluent youth were channeled into degenerate practices—dissipation of all sorts, debauchery, drinking, squandering of wealth, general idleness. Isocrates warned that such dissolute living was especially true of "the most promising young men."[80]

The reaction of the older generation in Athens was a form of backlash directed mainly against democratic institutions. The elders urged a return to more authoritarian controls. In 355 B.C. Isocrates, in the *Areopagiticus*, an "address on the public safety," attributed the intensity of class struggle in Athens to what he called "extreme democracy." Isocrates singled out as one of the significant elements of social disharmony in Athens the disaffection of the younger generation against their parents and elders. "Let no one suppose," he assures his fellow Athenians, "that I am out of temper with the younger generation." Those who were to blame for the time wasting and the excesses of the younger generation were the politicians who introduced into Athens an excess of freedom by destroying the power of the Areopagus.[81] He therefore recommended a return to the constitutional and social order of the sixth century B.C., to a time he idealized as the "old democracy" of Solon and Cleisthenes. This, he asserted, was the golden age of Athenian democracy, when the youth were obedient and modest, when the elders exercised vigilance over the youth (who require firm restraints), when the quality of citizenship was sounder.[82] Earlier, in 374–372 B.C., Isocrates had expressed his concern for the youth in the maxims he set forth for Demonicus: he reaffirmed the traditional injunction "honor thy parents," recommended to youth their special virtues of modesty and self-control, and, in one of the earliest expressions of the Golden Rule, urged them to "Conduct yourself toward your parents as you would have your children conduct themselves toward you."[83] It is in line with such thinking that Xenophon turned to less free contemporary cultures as models for harmonious relations of the generations. For example, he admired the Persian prince Cyrus, under whom he served as a mercenary soldier, as a paragon of modesty and obedience to elders.[84] Xenophon also urged a return to the ways of the ancestors, and asserted that what was especially needed was "Lacedaemonian reverence for older people, seeing that they [Athenian youth] despise all their elders, beginning with their own fathers."[85] It is perhaps as a result of the moral decay of the Athenian youth that there was created a new group of ten officials, one for each tribe, whose duty it was to superintend the training of the ephebes. They were called *Sophronistoi*—Restrainers.[86]

The backlash was given more elegant philosophical underpinnings by Plato, who advocated return to authoritarian controls, "the ancient and world-wide traditions."[87] The youth should learn honor and respect for parents, grandparents, and elders, and show no scorn for or commit acts of violence against them (except in cases of insanity).[88] Positively, to parents are due the traditional obligations, particularly in their old age, and reverence of speech and compliance always, even when parents act in anger toward their children.[89] "Everyone shall reverence his elder both by deed and by word."[90] Yet Socrates had bequeathed to Plato the paradox of respect both for elders and for reason. And so in the *Euthyphro* Plato presents the dilemma of the righteous youth who is torn by the twin duties of honoring his father and prosecuting him for murder because his father has caused the death by exposure of a hired workingman who had committed a murder. Some have thrown up to Euthyphro the charge of impiety for prosecuting his father for murder; but Euthyphro believes that it is impious not to prosecute a wrongdoer, even if father or mother, citing as support Zeus's violence against his father, Cronus, and that of Cronus against his father, Uranus.[91]

But Plato gives greater weight to the traditional deterrents against generational arrogance: inculcation of fear of punishment by the gods, both in this life and in the afterlife, of children who inflict violence upon parents and elders.[92] True, there may arise differences between fathers and sons that cannot be harmonized, in which extreme cases there may be applied legal procedures for disownment by fathers, and, on the other side, for charging mental incompetence against parents by sons.[93] But in well-ordered states, according to Plato, elders should be revered, and treated as if they were parents; "an outrage [that is, violence] perpetrated by a younger person against an older person is a shameful thing."[94] Persons convicted of assault upon parents should be treated as a defiling thing and banished from the city and all sacred places.[95] Those who neglect their parents shall be reported to magistrates charged with administering the laws. The penalties Plato would impose for neglect include whipping and imprisonment of men under thirty and women under forty. Any person who hears of such mistreatment of parents shall be obligated, under penalty of the law, to report this to the magistrates.[96]

Reflecting upon the unstable conditions of his own times, in particular the generational contradictions in Athens, Plato isolated generational disequilibrium as a significant mechanism in political change. But Lewis Feuer has concluded, erroneously, that Plato and Aristotle set forth generational struggle as a universal theme in history.[97] Extrapolating a few passages from Plato and Aristotle, Feuer would have us believe that "both . . . recognized its [generational strife] primacy as an independent factor in political change . . . virtually the basic mechanism in political change. . . . Generational conflict seemed to them an everlasting threat to political stability."[98] It is true that Plato, in his concern over the loss of respect for their elders by the younger generation of his day, did seek to analyze the relations between the generations prevailing under different types of government. Under certain forms of government, he declares, there tends to develop loss of respect for the fathers. For example, in an aristocracy affluent fathers who are excluded from political power are deauthorized in their sons' eyes in various ways. The mothers, out of status jealousy, complain to their sons that their fathers do not hold official positions because of personal weakness. Even house slaves talk to the sons in the same way. Such loss of respect for the fathers leads to generational disequilibrium and political instability, resulting in the degeneracy of aristocracy into timocracy, which opens up office holding and political power to the men of wealth.[99] Particularly in a democracy, excessive freedom, according to Plato, results in loss of respect for the older generation; attendant egalitarian concepts and leveling downward produce a generational adaptation on the part of the older generation to the manners and values of the younger generation. In a democracy, the fathers therefore do not discipline their sons, who turn to dissipation and abandon modesty and self-control, becoming rebellious, insolent, and profligate, interested only in the satisfaction of material desires.[100] Thus does equality of all destroy the authority of the older generation.

> The parent falls into the habit of becoming like a child, and the son like the father. The father is afraid of his sons, and they show no reverence or respect for their parents, in order to assert their freedom. Citizens, resident aliens, and strangers from abroad are all on an equal footing. . . . The schoolmaster is afraid of and flatters his pupils, and the pupils make light of their masters as well as their attendants. Generally speaking, the young copy their elders, and compete with them in words and deeds, while the elders, anxious not to be thought disagreeable tyrants, imitate the young, accommodating themselves to the young and filling themselves full of wit and bon mots.[101]

This condition of affairs Plato calls "anarchy"; the consequence is dictatorship. Thus Plato, in his horror of political instability, nonconformity, and pluralism, and in his efforts to validate an oligarchic and paternal social structure, advocates a return to a vigorously policed hierarchical organization of society to assure firm restraints of elders over the youth.

One of the by-products of the generational tensions of the fourth century B.C. was the study of the psychological makeup of each generation and the formulation of the characteristic ethos of each in bipolarized form.[102] The lead in this formal analysis was taken by the conservatives, who tended to characterize the youth as unstable in views, mercurial, and insolent in behavior. Aristotle laid down the classic formulation of the antithesis between the natures, values, and conduct of the older and younger generations.[103]

> The young are changeable in their desires and quickly sated; they have violent desires which are soon appeased. . . . Owing to ambition, they cannot bear to be slighted, and they become indignant if they think they are being wronged. . . . They are ambitious for honor but more so for victory. . . . These two they desire more than money because they have not yet experienced want. . . . They are not prone to evil, but rather to goodness, because as yet they have not seen much vice. . . . For the most part they live by hope; for hope belongs to the future, as memory to the past, and for young men the future is long and the past short. . . . They are rather courageous, for they are full of passion and hope, and passion keeps men from being fearful, while hope makes them confident. . . . They are shy, for as yet they have no independent standards of propriety, but have been trained by convention alone. They are high-minded, for they have not yet been humbled by life, they are inexperienced in its necessities. . . . They prefer honorable before expedient actions, for they live by their disposition rather than by calculation. . . . They are fond of their friends and their companions rather than of persons of other ages. . . . All their mistakes are due to excess and vehemence. . . . They think they know everything and are positive; this, indeed, is the cause of their excess in all things.[104]

By contrast, the older generation is materialistic and ungenerous, guided by expediency rather than principle; and so it appears temperate. "Their life is guided by calculation rather than by what is noble."[105]

All these tendencies, suggestions for controls, and theoretical formulations affirm that in the highly unstable conditions of the fourth century B.C., friction between the generations was a historical fact of life. But revolutionary programs or violent gestures on the part of the young did not develop.[106] The older generation was largely deauthoritized, but there were safety valves, such as employment in the ever growing mercenary armies of the time, escape into dissolute living, and, above all, in the last third of the fourth century, into the massive Macedonian-Greek imperialistic scheme to invade the Persian Empire, the success of which was to siphon off vast numbers of Greek youth into the great reaches of Asia.

In the new cultural patterns created by the conquests and policies of Alexander the Great, the conditions that had produced generational consciousness in the fifth and fourth centuries B.C. on the part of the youth in Athens and the tensions between the older and the younger generations were largely eliminated. In the Hellenistic world, democracy quickly withered away, the autonomy of the Greek city-states came to an end, and, despite ever increasing individualism, political despotism and authoritarian societal patterns prevailed. In this atmosphere, generational disequilibrium such as Isocrates, Plato, and Aristotle had sought to combat ceased to be a major concern.

Symptomatic of the altered relations between the generations in Athens is the social outlook of the New Comedy. In the plays of Menander the stock type of the younger generation is now the "Good Young Man," who is the worthy son of the "Good Old Man." Between father and son there exists a harmonious relationship of love, trust, and affection. True, Menander, his contemporaries Diphilus and Philemon, and their Roman imitator Terence reflected principally the lives of the rich strata of the period. Their older men—extremely wealthy, industrious, wise—are intent on preserving the conventional moral standards of the family as the nucleus of their neat, respectable little worlds. Their conventional young men, mostly of the leisure class, sure to succeed to their father's estates, feel nothing but the highest respect for their fathers; they may occasionally deviate from the rules in their amorous adventures, and the fathers may generously indulge their sons' peccadilloes. But the aims of both the older and the younger generation are identical: adherence to respectability and maintenance of familial harmony.[107] "How sweet is harmony of parents and children" wrote Menander,[108] epitomizing the ideals and practices of the Hellenistic Age.

It was in the Hellenistic Age, nevertheless, that the first efforts in world history took place to organize the youth into associations. Beginning at the end of the fourth century B.C., associations of *neoi* appeared and gradually spread all over the Greek world, especially in the Near East, establishing an institution that would endure for seven centuries. Recognized by the Hellenistic rulers and the Roman emperors—even sponsored by them—these corporate associations of *neoi* (*neoteroi* or *neaniskoi*) accepted as members Greek youths who had passed the ephebic age, that is, young men from nineteen or twenty up. Though their membership and titles indicate generational consciousness, these youth associations existed largely as sports clubs for fostering gymnastic and athletic competitions.[109] Only in rare instances did the clubs engage in political activities. Such exception is to be found in the intense political struggles on the island of Crete in the early Hellenistic period, when organized youth groups obtained official recognition and some influence. For example, in the revolutionary situation in the city of Gortyn, which involved generational conflicts between young and old in the third century B.C., a council of youths (νεότας) was invested with official authority and judged cases concerning illegal currency.[110] Polybius tells us, tantalizingly, that in the Lyttian War of 221–219 B.C. Gortyn was in a state of civil war in which "the older generation was in a state of conflict with the younger generation, the elder siding with Cnossus, the youths with Lyttus."[111] The generational cleavage and civic disunity in Crete about this time—end of third century/early second century B.C.—led the elders to impose legal sanctions to strengthen their hold on the youth and keep the younger generation in line. At Drerus, the youth alone, as a separate group, were required to swear an oath, hedged around with powerful religious sanctions, that they would not aid the Lyttians in any way, that they would maintain loyalty to the city of Drerus and allied Cnossus, would not foment revolution, would oppose all who did so, and would denounce any who so conspired.[112] But this was a special, localized phenomenon, affecting a limited area of Crete under still unclear circumstances.

In general, our knowledge of the Hellenistic Age does not reveal generational friction, and we may assume that, whatever were the fateful vicissitudes the Hellenistic world experienced—frequent wars, economic disorders and stagnation, growing diminution of the dignity and worth of the individual—generational dissension was not one of them.

Farther to the east, in India, in a region that was socially, economically, and politically retarded as compared with the Greek world, great upheavals tore the social fabric apart during the early part of the third century B.C., creating instability and confusion in values. When Asoka (ca. 269–232 B.C.) succeeded to the royal power, he became a great conqueror and unifier. Grandson of Chandragupta, the founder of the Mauryan dynasty, Asoka Maurya united India with brutal violence (the Kalinga War) and tyranny. But suddenly he was converted to Buddhism, and, eschewing force, he sought to unify his vast empire of many classes, castes, sects, and religions by proclaiming the reign of moral law and advocating the spread of righteousness (dharma). It was a period in Indian history when the subcontinent was undergoing great social dislocation and instability attendant upon the transition from pastoral to agrarian village economy, and when the family as an institution was developing out of the kinship-based tribal castes. Because previous human relations had disintegrated, Asoka sought to cement them on a new level through centralization and authoritarian restrictions on individual liberty.[113] Accordingly, he presented himself as a "father figure," and stressed the importance of the harmonious family as the ideal nucleus for spreading dharma and thus achieving harmony throughout the empire. Hence in the edicts inscribed along the borders of his empire, through which he published his code of piety and morality in the form of advocacy of specific approved forms of human and social relations, Asoka propounds as one of the basic bonds of social unity the duty of obedience to father, mother, and elders. We may assume that the unrest of his times had involved generational frictions, for he tells us (in the Greek text of a recently discovered bilingual inscription set up at Kandahar [in Afghanistan] in the Indian province previously part of the Persian and Seleucid Empires) that ten years after his conversion and the promulgation of his code, "Whosoever were lacking in self-control, have ceased from such lack of control, each according to his ability, and they have become obedient to their fathers and mothers and elders, contrary to what had been the case previously. And in the future, by so acting, they will live better and more advantageously in every respect."[114] In other edicts addressed to all the people, written in Prakrit, Asoka constantly reiterated the obligations and advantages of obedience and respect to superiors, elders, and parents.[115] Though Asoka tells us that after "he made men more pious . . . he caused all to flourish throughout the entire country," we do not know how his program of social harmony in the rapidly changing society of India worked out in actual practice. Suffice it to say that after his death his experiment with dharma disappeared. Asoka's experiment is, however, instructive as another example of the possibilities of generational dislocations in antiquity in times of great crisis and of the efforts, usually successful, to control the younger generation through maintaining the unity of the family.

Turning our eyes westward to Italy, we find in the Roman experience an idiosyncratic pattern of self-renewing social and legal traditions and of stern controls that methodically channeled each new generation into the ways of the fathers. For more than a thousand years of their history, the Romans—except for a brief period at the end of the Republic—succeeded in preventing generational deviation. The extraordinary authority of the *mos maiorum*, the cult of the ancestors, whose worship held up to each new generation behavioral paradigms authenticated in the past, the systematic inculcation of such Roman virtues as *disciplina* and *pietas*—all these served to mold each generation in the image of the elders and forefathers. Above all loomed the total control over the younger generation inherent in the *patria potestas*. This unlimited power of the head of the family over the sons, which embodied the legal power of life and death and left the sons without economic and juridical personality, and which was not extinguished by adulthood as it was in the Greek city-states, represented the most extreme form of parental control in the ancient world. Despite the mitigation by custom of the absolute power of the *paterfamilias* over his household beginning with the second century B.C., the Roman government was disinclined to interfere with the *patria potestas*, and the total power it embodied remained as a legal right until the end of Roman civilization, indeed into the Christian period. "The legal authority of the power which we have over children," wrote the jurist Gaius, "is peculiar to Roman citizens; there are no other men who have such power as we have over our sons."[116]

Reverence and obedience to fathers were second nature to Roman youths; it was also "the duty of a young man to respect elders."[117] For Cicero the virtues peculiar to the younger generation—particularly modesty and self-control—were better cultivated if the younger generation did not segregate itself from the older generation even in its pleasures.[118] Extraordinary sanction was given to filial duties of the youth by associating the Roman concept of *pietas* both with parents and gods, thus giving identical religious content to correct relations with both authorities.[119] And just as among the Greeks, the Romans hedged around filial duty with the threat of the father's curse. An early Roman law read: "If a boy strike his father, and the father complains, let the boy be accursed."[120]

In consequence of the Roman high estimation of the fathers and devaluation of the legal and social personality of children, the term "youth" was associated with shallowness, foolishness, and ineptitude. In the second century B.C., when the Roman as an individual was emerging out of the rigid Roman family controls and the absolute subordination to the state, "youth" appears as a derogatory appellation. For example, Plautus, in reworking the Greek New Comedy for Roman ears, made the stock "Good Old Man" of Menander into a tedious moralizer, and the "Good Young Man" into a spineless, shallow, trivial, often roguish figure.[121] At about the same time, the Roman poet Naevius expressed his view as to how a powerful state might be destroyed in a line that Cicero admired: "New orators came forth, foolish young men."[122]

Motivated by the needs and traditions of Roman society, early Roman educational procedures and aims were directed not at intellectual achievements but principally at the inculcation into the young of discipline, duty, and filial submission. This was achieved mainly by the constant companionship of the son with the father, "the living representative of Roman authority," whom he imitated and served, as it were, as apprentice and understudy.[123] In this connection, Cato the Elder undertook personally to instruct his son even in the elements of learning, rather than allow a surrogate father in the form of a slave or freedman teacher to intervene.[124]

Any sense of generational consciousness or disaffection with the older generation was rendered negligible not only by Roman traditions and education, but also by the frequent wars and the safety valve of colonies sent out by the Roman government, first in Italy and later in the provinces. Harmony with the older generation was especially cultivated by the Roman upper-class youth, who were eager to assume their places on the ladder of the administrative and military organs of the world power.

But the world crisis during the hundred years from the Gracchi to Augustus eventually had the impact of a generational event that aroused massive disaffection from the Roman government and the ways of the fathers. Yet this deauthori-

tization of the Senatorial Order and the disillusionment with the older generation in Rome did not lead to strong generational consciousness among the youth
or generational conflict. It is characteristic of the Romans that many alienated
youth, such as Vergil and Horace, remained strongly devoted to their fathers
while seeking peace of mind from the insecurities, anxieties, and turmoil of the
times in the doctrines and living style of Epicureanism. Others expressed their
rejection of society through unrestrained dissipation of all sorts.[125] In the troubled
and chaotic times of the last decades of the Roman Republic, Cicero reiterated
the merits of inculcating the Roman virtues and of maintaining the traditional
father-son relationship, reaffirming the efficacy of self-restraint, filial duty to
parents, devotion to kin, the practice of attaching a young man as understudy
to a wise elder experienced in public affairs.[126] Cicero was, nevertheless, fully
aware of the disaffection and alienation of the youth of the ruling classes. Indeed, in 44 B.C. he expressed the conservative view that the history of other
societies showed that great states were undermined by the younger generation
and restored by the elders.[127]

Cicero's pessimistic valuation and fears of dissolute Roman youth were shared
by many. But in debates of the time, more forward-looking political theorists like
Sallust, while equally aware of the collapse among Roman youth of a sense of social
direction, sought basic reforms to overcome the moral crisis. The corruption of
the youth, asserted Sallust, was brought about by the riches that poured into Rome
from the second century B.C. "As the result of riches, luxury and greed united with
insolence took possession of our youth."[128] Those affected were not only the upper-
class youths, but also those among the common people in the country, who flocked
to the city of Rome preferring dissolute idleness on the dole there to poorly paid
manual labor in the fields.[129] All the youth, asserted Sallust, "were utterly thought-
less and reckless," indulging in all sorts of depravity—gluttony, sexual dissipation,
self-indulgence, illicit gain, and extravagances.[130]

Some of the youth—Sallust occasionally uses the term *homines adulescentuli*
in a derogatory sense—sought to achieve influence through political adventurism.
Sallust was critical of several young men, "whose age and disposition made them
aggressive," who obtained the tribuneship after 70 B.C. and used their political
authority to inflame the plebs against the Senate by doles and promises.[131] It was
especially the young men of the upper classes—greedy for gain, reckless, impressionable—who were attracted to the revolutionary program of Catiline in 64–63
B.C., and whom he particularly courted.[132] When Caesar held supreme power in
the early 40s, Sallust advised him that a basic reform in the spirit of the youth was
indispensable. "If our youth continue to have the same desires and habits as at
present, beyond doubt that eminent renown of yours will come to a speedy end,
along with the city of Rome."[133] Above all, advised Sallust, what was needed to
curb the license and lack of restraint of the Roman youth was a turning away from
materialism and a return to respect for and practice of the old Roman values of
discipline, industry, and integrity.[134] The analysis and recommendation of Sallust,
while motivated in part by partisan politics, are a valuable commentary on the

tendency of the Roman youth toward pleasure seeking and on their susceptibility to participation in violence.[135]

The advent of the principate of Augustus did not succeed in effectively controlling either materialism in the Roman world or the youth's disposition to and opportunities for pleasure seeking as a way of life. In this connection one of Augustus's mouthpieces, the poet Horace, commented in 28 B.C. on the degeneracy of both the young men and young women of Rome. "The age of our parents was worse than that of our grandparents; it made us even more worthless, and soon we shall produce a more corrupt generation."[136] But the imperial power did put brakes on the recourse to violence as a tool of change endemic in the last century of the Republic. It is characteristic of the Roman mind that Augustus (and the emperors after him) assumed the role of father figure for many Romans and the provincials, and that *pietas* was redirected for the Romans to a new level of submission and duty to the emperor. Henceforth we do not hear of generational disaffection in the Roman Empire. Both the authority of the emperor and that of the *paterfamilias* in each household imposed on the younger generation submission and obedience as the normal way of life.

Augustus's concern for the youth, particularly of the two upper classes (Senatorial and Equestrian Orders) led to the institution and spread of associations of youths in the Roman world, comparable with the *neoi* of the Greek East. *Collegia invenum*, each one approved by the Roman government, common at first in the cities of Italy and then in the western provinces, are known during the first three centuries of the Empire. These youth associations had high status in their communities and played a substantial role in their civic life as municipal youth clubs. But their functions were limited to participation in sports, athletic contests, and religious ceremonies, as were the Greek associations of *neoi*.[137]

Thus, after the turmoil and dislocations of the first century B.C., which produced the only generational friction in Roman history, we find generational balance and harmony restored under the imperial regime. This remained one of the foundations of social life in the Roman Empire to the end of the urban civilization of antiquity, when the rigidities of feudal society descended.

2

Usurpation of Status and Status Symbols in the Roman Empire

THE BASIC ORGANIZATIONAL PRINCIPLE OF THE SOCIAL SYSTEMS of the ancient world was hierarchic structure, but social mobility existed in varying degrees. Roman society evolved into one of the most hierarchic and status-conscious social orders in human history. In the imperial period, under the influence of the sociopolitical philosophy of Augustus, the Romans developed the highest degree and diversity of formal social stratification,[1] and at the same time the highest incidence of social mobility in antiquity. This social elasticity—conservative and limited though it was, but greater than in any other culture until modern times—is "the special characteristic of the Roman state that distinguished it from all other states of the ancient world . . . : its ability to renew itself with the changing realities of political and social conditions, thanks to its original freedom from the concept of a closed genetic aristocracy,"[2] and, in general, thanks also to its freedom from ethnic or racial prejudices. Thus, at the same time that an elaborate hierarchical order of social classes (often fragmented into subgroups), each invested with special privileges and extrinsic status symbols, was systematically defined and demarcated by statutes, the Roman world was always in some measure an "open society." Social mobility between various strata was always possible and, indeed, vigorously pursued, from the early Republic to the very end of urban civilization in antiquity about the sixth century A.D.

The removal of barriers to social advancement by legal means for the benefit of groups and individuals—from the status of *peregrinus* to *civis Romanis*, slave to freedman, plebeian to equestrian, equestrian to senator—is a well-known phenomenon in Roman political and social history. Less familiar is the extent and variety of illicit social mobility, through fraud and other surreptitious means, that afforded to many persons leaps across social lines within the established order. The Roman government, in its continuing efforts to preserve statutory social distinctions and maintain social distance[3] between classes and subclasses, legislated frequently against *usurpatio* of rank, privileges, and status insignia.[4] Penalties for such usurpation varied in different periods and in relation to the type of offense. The legal rule cited in Paul's *Sententiae*[5] is not a general one but involves essentially usurpation of military status and applies penalties adapted to specific conditions of the early third century A.D.: "Whoever uses the insignia of a higher class and impersonates the military in order to terrorize or oppress anyone, shall suffer capital punishment if he belongs to the *humiliores*, or deportation if he belongs to the *honestiores*." We have evidence of a multiplicity of means practiced to circumvent such restrictive legislation through fraud, bribery, collusion with officials, and open flouting of the law. Social legislation of this sort was essentially programmatic and was simply not enforced systematically. Nor could police and administrative authorities control illegalities in this area in the absence of the institution of official identification papers and because of the virtual nonexistence of police surveillance mechanisms in most parts of the empire. The police power (*coercitio*) of officials, periodic census registrations, other forms of official scrutiny, and occasional systematic purging of social ranks might curb abuses from time to time,[6] but when the pressure was relaxed the momentum of infractions was resumed. "Many modern historians . . . have too readily assumed that Roman citizens obeyed the law, and that everything was done as the imperial government directed."[7]

The intensity of such usurpation of rank and distinctive badges during the politically and economically unstable period beginning with the third century A.D. is well attested.[8] The incidence of such evasions in the early empire, when conditions were more stable, could not have been as great or as flagrant. Obviously, every period of acute crisis, when military, political, and economic conditions were in flux, tended to disrupt social relations and afforded greater opportunity for individuals to use fraud to move upward in the social scale through encroachment upon class distinctions.[9] Tacitus affords us a glimpse into the frustrations of the Roman government in the face of such illegalities in connection with a communication of Tiberius to the Senate regarding the flouting of laws restricting luxury spending.[10] It is well known that sumptuary laws have been very difficult to enforce in all societies that have adopted them. But, though directed at the problem of flouting of sumptuary laws, Tiberius's remarks also reflect the similar frustration of the Roman authorities in the face of widespread illegalities relating to status distinctions. "In this proposition," reflects Tiberius, "it was better that my eyes should be averted. Otherwise, with you (senators) betraying the fear on the faces of individuals who might be charged with shameful luxury spending, I might see them, and, so to speak, detect them. But if our diligent aediles had consulted me previously, I am not sure but that I should not have urged them to ignore prevalent and full-blown vices rather than bring it about that it become a matter of public knowledge with what abuses we are powerless to cope. . . . All the laws our ancestors devised, all those enacted by the deified Augustus are now buried, the former in oblivion, the latter—to our greater shame—in contempt."[11] Hundreds of years later we hear the Emperors Theodosius and Valentinian, in another connection, utter the same pessimistic frustration about widespread flouting of the law in the Roman Empire.[12]

The earliest known case of illegal assumption of status in Rome—and the most flagrant—is that of M. Perperna in the second century B.C. Bearing a name of Etruscan origin, the Perperna family, through association with patrician adventurers, especially the Valerii Flacci, had managed to insinuate itself into the ruling circles of Rome. M. Perperna had thus apparently usurped Roman citizenship, and, indeed, in 168 B.C. participated in military operations in Illyria in a relatively high post. His son, also M. Perperna, succeeded in winning election to the consulship in 130 B.C., the first person with a non-Roman *nomen* to rise to consular rank in Roman history, and the only such prior to the Social War. It was this Perperna who, as consul, defeated and captured Aristonicus in the new Province of Asia. For this he anticipated the celebration of a triumph, but he died of illness suddenly in 129 B.C. in Pergamum. In 126 B.C., his father was charged with illegal usurpation of Roman citizenship, expelled from Rome, and compelled to return to his original home, thus casting a shadow on the repute of his famous son, whose legal status and consulship were as a result patently tainted.[13] This scandal grew out of the enormous power wielded by senatorial families, under whose protective patronage many flagrant illegalities were perpetrated. This influence was later transformed into the legal powers and authority vested in Roman generals and emperors, who exercised great influence in molding social changes. In 95 B.C. the Lex Licinia Mucia defined usurpation of Roman citizenship as a crime; the lives of many Italians must have been affected by the *quaestio* established under this law.[14]

The political upheavals and civil wars of the last century of the Roman republic created a major dislocation of social relationships and a discernible blurring of traditional social lines. Aside from the deliberate radical social policies of some political leaders, public record keeping was rendered defective in the disorders, and the manumission of slaves was at an all-time high in Italy, thus catapulting into the Roman body politic a large new freedman class endowed with the Roman franchise. Indeed, large numbers, both in Italy and the provinces, entered the Roman citizenship in this period.[15] Shortages of soldiers had even led to the incorporation of slaves in the armies, a rare phenomenon in antiquity. Many new families had risen to prominence in the Senatorial Order in the social struggles of the dying Republic, partly because the proscriptions had denuded the old senatorial families, and partly because the political leaders reached out for the support of competent and influential men of wealth outside the ranks of the traditional nobility. The elevation of favored individuals to the Equestrian Order at the whim of Roman officials seems to have been a common practice. Cicero, for example, denounced Verres's grant of the golden ring, status symbol of the Equestrian Order, to his clerk Maevius, who had aided him in his extortion in the Province of Sicily in 73–71 B.C., as incredible and done with *singulari impudentia nova*.[16] A decade or so earlier the dictator Sulla had raised to equestrian rank the famous and wealthy actor Q. Roscius Gallus, by bestowing upon him the *anulus aureus*.[17] Similarly, Caesar in 46 B.C. honored D. Laberius, a composer of mimes, who had lost his equestrian rank, by giving him 500,000 sesterces and restoring to him his golden ring and the privilege of sitting in theater seats reserved for equestrians.[18] In imitation of Caesar, L. Cornelius Balbus, quaestor in Spain, though he did not possess *imperium* and hence lacked the authority to grant such honors, bestowed upon the actor Herennius Gallus, at public games in Gades, the golden ring and the privilege of sitting in special seats in the theater at Gades.[19]

The social tendencies of the age generated considerable leveling among the classes, and the radical policies of Julius Caesar, imbued with ecumenical perspectives and directed toward the destruction of the old nobility and its removal from the seats of power, appeared headed toward the institutionalization of such leveling. But it remained for Augustus to work out a viable compromise between the hereditary aristocratic-agricultural Senatorial Order and the large group of powerful men in the empire, particularly Italy, who possessed other forms of wealth and influence. Augustus not only halted the social leveling that was in process but reorganized the social structure of the empire, molding it more formally into an "estate" system of stratification with legal distinctions between statuses.[20] Underlying the Augustan system was not only a Roman-Italian bias, but the decision to establish an imperial hierarchy of social classes with an increased range of social stratification everywhere in the empire.[21] The Augustan social structure was patently plutocratic: everywhere the essential criterion of distinction was, with some exceptions, property ownership. The new social order was, in Gagé's apt phrase, "hiérarchique et censitaire."[22]

Though Augustus's purpose was to make the two upper orders into an aristocratic hierarchy of governmental aides of the emperor, kept markedly at a distance from a variety of lower classes, the system did not exclude, and was capable of, a moderate amount of social mobility. Pivotal in the new social order was the class of knights, a new "demi-noblesse" brought into the imperial service. Widespread ambition to enter this new class revealed itself at once. The title *eques* (somewhat like "esquire") embraced not only the elite nucleus, which received a grant of the *equus publicus* by the emperor and was the labor pool from which the emperor drew many of the lower functionaries of the imperial administration, but all those of free birth who possessed a property valuation of 400,000 sesterces. While explicit approval and grant by the emperor was necessary for admission to the first category, the term *eques Romanus* tended to be usurped informally by all free Roman citizens who had this property rating. Augustus's demographic policies also included retardation of manumission of slaves, restrictions on privileges of freedmen, the establishment of several inferior grades of freedmen (Junian Latins, *liberti dediticii*), stringent curbs on slaves, favoritism to Hellenes among the provincials, privileged status for the well-to-do all over the empire who constituted a local aristocracy (*ordo decurionum*) in Italian and provincial municipalities, a degraded status to certain peregrine peoples of the empire (*dediticii*), particularly to the Egyptians, and a sharp distinction between *ingenuus* and *libertinus*.[23]

Attempts to encroach upon the status of the Senatorial Order and its status insignia were unthinkable in the early period of the principate, not only because the size of the class was small (six hundred senators and their families), but also because Augustus exercised a close scrutiny of this class, purging the order of undesirable elements three times during his reign. A bizarre incident connected with the Senatorial Order in the reign of Augustus was the gesture of G. Thorianus, tribune of 25 B.C., the son of a freedman, who escorted his father into the theater and sat him down beside himself on seats reserved for tribunes.[24]

It was, however, in relation to the Equestrian Order that usurpation of status on a wide scale began very early. Straining for equestrian status mounted steadily, especially because individuals of the freedman class, grown wealthy in the prosperity of the times, often obtained the property qualification for admission to the order but were excluded by the requirement of free birth.[25] Apparently, the enforcement of the provisions of the Lex Roscia of 67 B.C., which reserved for equestrians the first fourteen rows in the theater behind the senators, was laxly handled during the civil wars. The prestige of occupying these special seats was so great that unauthorized persons frequently attempted to usurp this privilege. Horace, himself the son of a freedman, attacked an upstart freedman, a tribune of the soldiers who displayed his wealth ostentatiously and illegally usurped a place in the first rows of the theater.[26] A certain Sarmentus, a freedman of Maecenas, who was popular as an urbane wit during the 40s and early years of the empire, acquired wealth and openly conducted himself as an equestrian, assuming the privileges and insignia of the rank. Subsequently his status was challenged in a *causa usurpatae dignitatis*. When Sarmentus, whose first master had been M. Favonius (proscribed and executed after Philippi), proved that he was legally the freedman of Maecenas, the case was dismissed, and presumably no penalty was imposed.[27]

Despite the property requirement for admission to the order, bankrupt equestrians, in accordance with the Lex Roscia, were not automatically excluded from the privileged seats: a special area (*certus locus*) was set aside in the prestige rows for bankrupts whose economic difficulties were judged to be involuntary. Nevertheless, ineligible equestrian bankrupts sometimes usurped such seats during the civil war period.[28] Despite the personal nature of membership in the Equestrian Order, some people tended to regard equestrian status as hereditary, in imitation of the status of the Senatorial Order. It is noteworthy that even Augustus was ready to wink at the occupying of the special seats of the equestrians by improper persons, presumably because there were empty seats at times. For when equites whose property had declined because of the civil wars did not dare to sit in the fourteen rows through fear of the penalties of the law, Augustus lifted the ban for those who themselves or whose parents had ever possessed an equestrian rating.[29]

The provisions of the law regarding prestige seats for the equestrians could not, in general, have been strictly enforced. For example, it pleased the Emperor Caligula on occasion to stir up animosity between plebeians and equites by arranging for the former to occupy seats normally assigned to knights.[30] Apparently respect for this privilege of the knights deteriorated until the time of the Emperor Domitian, who, when he assumed censorial powers, "restrained the license of sitting promiscuously with the Knights in the theater."[31] From a number of epigrams written by Martial after Domitian's edict regarding this equestrian privilege, we learn the names of two special theater attendants, Leïtus and Oceanus, probably imperial freedmen, who policed the fourteen rows of the equestrians. It is obvious that, even after the emperor's reaffirmation of the privilege, some unauthorized persons, including freedmen and slaves, tried to usurp this privilege under the noses of the theater attendants, employing various evasions and sub-

terfuges to obtain the prestigious places and even arguing with them. Martial refers to the edict of Domitian *quo subsellia certiora fiunt / et puros eques ordines
recepit*, and describes the subterfuge of wearing expensive purple outer garments.
Nunc est reddita dignitas equestris declares the fraudulent equestrian named Phasis,
ensconcing himself in a reserved seat just prior to being expelled by Leïtus.[32]
Another bogus knight, Nanneius, previously accustomed with impunity to usurping
a seat in the first row, has been expelled by Leïtus; but he cannot bear to abandon
the distinction, and so he half sits, half stands in the last row.[33]

The institutionalization of distinctive modes of dress as status symbols of class
gradations, common in many cultures, did not characterize Roman society in the
first few centuries of the empire, despite the intensity of class consciousness. There
was never any serious intention of establishing a "hierarchy of clothing" during
the principate, not merely because of the force of tradition but also because of
fear of arousing class friction.[34] The toga, as insignia of Roman citizenship status,
was forbidden to those of peregrine and *dediticius* status, as well as to exiles.[35]
Since there was relative uniformity in outer clothing during the principate, and
the toga gradually went out of common use, the principal concern of the emperors was not the permissive wide range of personal preference for private use[36] but
rather the usurpation of official garb by unauthorized persons. In 36 B.C., Octavian,
acting as triumvir, forbade the use of purple outer garments by men except as
official garb of certain magistrates.[37] Despite this ban, during the reign of Tiberius
it was common practice for men to wear purple outer garb. It is noteworthy that
Tiberius tried to correct this widespread usurpation not by imposing the legal
penalties in existence but by his own example.[38] There ensued a centuries-long
tension between the emperors and the affluent classes over the use of the highest
grades of purple garments. Efforts to restrict this elite color as an imperial pre-
rogative in the early empire failed. The wearing of purple garments and insignia
by private persons was widespread throughout the Roman Empire,[39] despite efforts to control its use, made possible for even the middle and lower classes through
inexpensive imitation purples of inferior grade. In the third and fourth centuries
A.D., purple became increasingly associated with the emperors as special insignia. But imperial decrees restricted the use of only the highest qualities of Tyrian
purple, particularly garments of purple-dyed silk, which were reserved for the court
and declared "forbidden and unauthorized clothing."[40] The reiteration in the fourth
and fifth centuries A.D. of imperial directives forbidding the use of clothing of purple
silk and gold-embroidered cloth reveals rampant flouting of the imperial will in
this matter. In 424 A.D., Theodosius II issued a sweeping order concerning silk
garments dyed with highest qualities of Tyrian purple, ordering all persons possessing such garments to surrender them to the authorities: "There is no reason
why anyone should complain of having been deprived of the price, because it is
enough that he obtains impunity for having trampled on the law, nor is there occasion to be concerned about profits, since his life does not have to be placed at
stake. But let no one now by concealment of this sort incur the toils of the new

constitution; otherwise he will be subject to the danger of a crime similar to that of high treason."[41] Such was apparently the crime of a certain Maras, a deacon of the Christian church, and his accomplices, who in 354 A.D. were tortured and executed by Constantius Gallus for complicity in the illegal manufacture of a purple garment of silk for private use.[42] Manufacture and use of purple silk were, for a time, equated with high treason, *non sine laesae maiestatis crimine*.[43] But no efforts to control the use of purple were successful, and despite dire penalties for such use,[44] the law was without doubt frequently disobeyed. Eventually, by a typical imperial concession in the face of widespread violations, purple silk cloth of the highest quality was reaffirmed as reserved for imperial use as exclusive insignia, but manufacture and trade in purple cloth of inferior quality were permitted.

Such display was but one aspect of the high degree of luxury consumption and conspicuous spending indulged in by the upper social strata in Rome and the Roman Empire—unparalleled on a wide scale until modern times. This ostentation was a distinctive characteristic of the Roman social order from about the middle of the second century B.C., reaching its height in the first century of the empire.[45] Persons of limited means, in an effort to pass for members of higher social strata, also practiced extravagant display. Martial in his epigrams provides us with examples of such persons. In this connection the Roman craze for antiques and for parade of wealth produced a thriving market among less affluent Romans for forgeries, inexpensive copies, cheap substitutes, and imitation gems for display purposes as extrinsic symbols of wealth.[46] Pliny reports that even slaves and freedmen affected such display by wearing gold-plated iron rings in order to pass as members of the Equestrian Order.[47] A good example of such prestige display to exhibit status is the freedman in one of Martial's epigrams, probably of equestrian rank, seated in elegant display in the front rows of the theater, trying to conceal evidence of his servile origin.[48]

In a timocratic society it is natural that people should aspire to enter the next rank higher as soon as their property reaches the minimum requirement for such advancement. Official membership in the Equestrian Order required ceremonial granting by the emperor of the *ius anuli aurei* and, in some cases, the "public horse." Besides these, other status insignia of the class included the right to wear the *angustus clavus*, the narrow stripes on the tunic, the purple *trabea*, parade uniform of an *eques Romanus* on ceremonial occasions, and *proedria*, the privilege of occupying special places in theaters and other places of public spectacles in Rome, Italian and provincial cities.[49] But as we have seen, many wealthy persons usurped the title *eques* and acted as members of the order, adherence to which fluctuated widely. Martial describes the amusing case of a certain Calliodorus, of equestrian status, whose brother did not qualify financially but yearned for the privileges of the class. Martial suggests that they might solve the personal anguish by sitting in the section reserved for knights on alternate days (like Castor and Pollux sharing immortality): "*Uno credis equo posse sedere duos?*"[50] In the first century A.D. there was apparently such extensive usurpation and imitation of equestrian symbols and displays of wealth that Martial implies that it was not possible at times to tell the difference between a *iustus eques* and fraudulent imitators.[51] Such usurpation of Equestrian rank was especially practiced by the one group barred from membership, no matter how wealthy they became: freedmen. Augustus himself unleashed a torrent of problems in this regard by granting equestrian status and privileges to a number of freedmen, including Titus Vinius Philopoemen, the admiral Pompeius Menas, and the physician Antonius Musa. After Augustus's death, control over membership in this order was flagrantly neglected during the early years of Tiberius's reign. As a result no doubt of its promiscuous growth, the order was regularized in 23 A.D. A young senator, C. Sulpicius Galba, of old aristocratic family, complained that tradespeople, some even owners of eating houses, wore the gold ring and exercised the privileges of the Equestrian Order. Accordingly, a *senatus consultum* was promulgated restricting membership in the order not only to those who were freeborn (*ingenui*), but also whose fathers and grandfathers were freeborn. The census valuation of 400,000 sesterces remained the same, but membership was restricted to those who were authorized by the Julian Law on the theater to sit in the fourteen rows of seats designated for the knights.[52] One of the results of this decree was a massive flood of applications for admission to the rank.[53] Moreover, the decree had the effect of increasing irregularities. For the requirement of *ingenuus* status for three generations was a formidable barrier to many. Hence arose the efforts of rich freedmen to erase the stigma and obtain the privilege of fictive *ingenuitas* through imperial favor, or to usurp such status. Technically, when the emperor granted admission to the order to a freedman, he was, in effect, also thereby bestowing fictive *ingenuitas*. The ambition for admission to the rank of *eques* must have impelled others to pose as freeborn. Pliny the Elder tells us that during the Flavian period, "it was a widespread phenomenon for liberated slaves to make the leap across to these distinctions—a thing which had never occurred before. . . . As a result, an order intended to afford distance from other men of free birth was shared with slaves."[54]

But grants by the emperor of the *anulus aureus* of equestrian rank, implying fictive *ingenuitas*, or the illicit usurpation of equestrian status by freedmen, with *ingenuitas* implicit, raised legal problems concerning the obligations that freedmen owed their former masters in accordance with Roman law. It was therefore found necessary the very next year after the *senatus consultum* to plug some of the loopholes by legislation. The Lex Visellia de Libertinis of 24 A.D. prosecuted freedmen who usurped the offices and ranks of freeborn persons—for example, the office of decurion of a municipality—unless they had obtained the *ius anuli aurei* from the emperor. The legal penalty for the offense was *infamia* as well as a fine. Further, "when a freedman declares himself freeborn, he can be sued both in a civil action for his services [due to his patron], as well as in a criminal action, under the Visellian Law."[55] The confusion, however, was still such that in 48 A.D., during the censorship of the Emperor Claudius, an equestrian named Flavius Proculus arraigned four hundred persons on the charge of usurpation of equestrian rank. These were perhaps the fraudulent equestrians whose names Claudius published: *Libertinos qui se pro equitibus Romanis agerent publicavit.*[56] Since the granting of the gold ring not only deleted former servile status but also dissolved the rights of patrons over freedmen, the grant of separate fictive *ingenuitas* solved the contradiction between the existence of otherwise qualified or favored individuals who were not freeborn. This was probably intended, in part, to stem the incidence of fraudulent encroachment on this class distinction. Ultimately, the granting of *ingenuitas* to non-freeborn persons through the *anulus aureus* was separated from the granting of equestrian rank, probably beginning with Commodus,[57] and this grant of the *ius anuli aurei* became the general form of bestowing fictitious *ingenuitas*. The privileges inherent in the *ius anuli aurei* were further weakened when Septimius Severus granted the gold ring to all soldiers.[58] Nevertheless, admission to the Equestrian Order itself remained an object of high ambition, especially when the order was the official aristocracy of the empire in the third century A.D. Eventually the Equestrian Order faded and disappeared in the social and administrative transformations of the middle of the fourth century, when the Senatorial Order became the single aristocratic class of the empire.

One of the most characteristic devices of the Roman legal and administrative imagination was the institution of fictive offices and honors to satisfy the pressing ambition for such prestige. Beginning in the late Republican period and mounting in intensity throughout the empire to its decline, a host of such substitute privileges and grants was devised, including *ornamenta consularia, ornamenta praetoria, ornamenta quaestoria, ornamenta triumphalia*.[59] One of the principal emphases of Augustus's social legislation had been to put a brake on the flow of persons formerly of servile status into the Roman citizen body. In addition to legal restrictions that kept freedmen out of the Senate, Equestrian Order, priesthoods, and many governmental and military posts, there was the fanatical prejudice against *libertini* on the part of the aristocracy, which put an additional stigma upon this class and impeded their rise to high social rank.[60] In the municipalities of the empire freedmen were debarred from holding local magistracies and from membership in the local senates. But here too the Roman gift for adjustment to social pressures and realities prevailed—witness the institution of the fictive device of granting ornamenta *decurionalia*, the external badges and honors of municipal aristocracy, to otherwise ineligible freedmen.[61]

Upon becoming a freedman and receiving restricted Roman citizenship, the former slave adopted the Roman *tria nomina*, consisting of a Roman *praenomen*, the *nomen* of his patron, and as *cognomen* his original name. In his foreign-sounding name it was usually easy to detect the former servile status of the freedman. Therefore, to extinguish the social stigma involved, freedmen gave their children Roman *cognomina*. Some also sought to alter their own names for this purpose; L. Crassicius Pasicles, for example, changed his *cognomen* to Pansa, and the Cinnamus in one of Martial's epigrams sought to alter his name to Cinna.[62] Others altered their Greek names to the Latin equivalents: Philetos to Amatus, Eudaemon to Felix, Irenaeus to Pacatus. Measures were taken by the Roman government to control usurpation of Roman names by unauthorized persons.

Claudius, for example, forbade persons of peregrine status to usurp Roman names, particularly *gens* names, because use of these implied possession of Roman citizenship.[63] Use of false names and false descriptions of oneself incurred penalties under Roman law.[64] The close legal ties between freedmen and patrons were a constant reminder of servile origin. Opportunities for posing as *ingenuus* were therefore easier if the patron died, or if the freedman moved far from his patron.

The most notorious case of usurpation of status by a freedman is that of Marcius Agrippa. Though originally a slave serving as a beautician, after obtaining his freedom he somehow encroached illegally on equestrian status and was serving in the first stage of the equestrian career as *advocatus fisci*, during the reign of Septimius Severus, when his deception was discovered. Agrippa was discharged from his post by the emperor, and the penalty imposed on him was banishment to an island, presumably because he was considered *honestior*. Subsequently, he was recalled by Caracalla, and presumably given a grant of *ingenuitas*. He then served as *a cognitionibus* and *ab epistulis*, and was finally advanced to senator by Caracalla, reaching the consulship and provincial governorships under the Emperor Macrinus.[65]

A much more serious offense in Roman eyes was the usurpation of Roman citizenship. Claudius executed persons *civitatem Romanam usurpantes*,[66] despite his liberal policy with regard to the extension of Roman citizenship in the provinces. An interesting case of usurpation of Roman citizenship and of Roman flexibility in handling complex problems is revealed in the case of a group of Alpine tribes, the Anaunians, Tulliassians, and Sindunians. In the reign of Claudius it was discovered that they had been conducting themselves as Roman citizens, acting in good faith, but without ever having been granted such status *de jure*. As a result there was a blurring of lines among the statuses of Roman citizens, Latins, and allies in the region. To deny these peoples the right of citizenship, after such a long time, would have invalidated property rights, marriages, and similar legal relationships. Moreover, persons from this area were already in the Praetorian Guard (some of officer rank), and were serving on jury panels in Rome (therefore of equestrian rank). Accordingly, for these reasons and in line with the Roman principle of accommodation to situations of long usage, Claudius in an edict of 46 A.D. formally granted the tribes Roman citizenship, retroactively. "Although I am aware," he declared,

> that persons of this category do not have too strong a basis for Roman citizenship, nevertheless, since they are said to have been in possession of it by usurpation of long standing, and are so intermingled with the Tridentines that they cannot be separated from them without serious harm to the distinguished municipality, I permit them by my indulgence to remain in the legal status in which they believed themselves to be. . . . And I grant them this benefaction in such manner that I order all acts performed by them acting as if Roman citizens, whether among themselves or in relations with the Tridentines or others, shall be valid, and I permit them to keep the names which they previously used when acting as if Roman citizens.[67]

However innocent of wrongdoing the members of these Alpine tribes may in fact have been, there was indeed a sizable traffic in irregular acquisition of Roman citizenship, through fraudulent declarations, bribe taking on the part of officials, and the carelessness of legionary commanders in selection of recruits.[68] According to Cassius Dio (though we may discount some of his rhetoric), citizenship was liberally sold, at varying prices, by Claudius, Messalina, and members of the imperial household, including freedmen.[69] A remarkable case is that of Claudius Lysias of the Acts, an officer of the auxiliary forces of the Province of Syria who took St. Paul into custody. Lysias confided to Paul that he "obtained this [Roman] citizenship for a large sum," and Sherwin-White concludes that he also purchased equestrian status and the military tribunate through intermediaries in the imperial secretariat or the provincial administration.[70] Beginning with the social legislation of Augustus (Lex Aelia Sentia, 4 A.D., and Lex Papia Poppaea, 9 A.D.) registration of the birth of legitimate children (later extended by Marcus Aurelius to illegitimate births) was required in order to facilitate proof of citizen status. Such registrations, and the birth certificates obtainable from governmental bureaus, were assumed to be based on truthful declarations, subject to penalty for fraud, and were accepted as prima facie evidence of Roman citizenship *citra causarum cognitionem* (without investigation of the truth).[71] But there was in fact nothing, except fear of the penalty, to prevent the fraudulent registration of children as Roman citizens or the forging of birth certificates,[72] and we may assume that such fraud was practiced, even though the lists of Roman citizens were reviewed locally in the municipal censuses throughout the empire every five years and periodically elsewhere in the provinces. Collusion, moreover, may have been practiced between peregrines desiring Roman citizenship status and Roman citizens by arranging for fictitious enslavement of the peregrine followed by swift manumission.[73]

Bribery and collusion with officials to attain social advancement must have been fairly common in the early empire.[74] We are best informed concerning such practices in the Province of Egypt, from the papyri. Here we find vivid documentation of various fraudulent practices to obtain relief from oppressive burdens in the province: evasion of compulsory liturgic services by influential people through pressure and intimidation of local of officials, despite frequent governmental orders to the contrary; flight from fiscal oppression of Egyptian natives to the Hellenized cities of Egypt so as to merge with the urban population and thus attempt to pass themselves off as members of a higher class.[75]

The repressive policy of the Romans in Egypt, the economic and fiscal exploitation of the native Egyptians, and the rigid social hierarchy imposed on the population are well known. The nationalistic upsurge of the Egyptians in the time of the last Ptolemaic rulers was definitively curbed by Augustus. He thrust down the mass of Egyptian peasants into a degraded social and economic position, so that they were permanently treated as an inferior conquered people with little hope of the social advancement held forth by the Romans to other peoples of the empire. Augustus, in conformity with his policy of preferential treatment to Greeks, imposed on Egypt an elite of Hellenes to be forever rigidly separated from the native Egyptian population. This policy was, however, in conflict with the timocratic principle in the social hierarchies established in the Roman provinces: sentimental favoritism to the Hellenes, at variance with the usual policy of the Romans of placing power in the hands of the well-to-do irrespective of race or ethnic origin, was bound to generate social malaise. Augustus's policy, maintained for about two hundred years, was to grant special privileges to the Hellenes of Alexandria, particularly to an elite smaller body of Alexandrian citizens with hereditary rights to elect the local officials and to enter their sons in the system of ephebic training and gymnastic education that was prerequisite for admission to Alexandrian citizenship. The same policy of favoring Hellenes was in effect in the metropoleis of the Egyptian nomes, where they composed a similar privileged class of metropolites, subject there, however, to payment of the *laographia* (poll tax), though at a level lower than that paid by Egyptian natives.

Nevertheless, in Alexandria the upper strata of Greeks, members of the elite social clubs and the gymnasia, harbored a traditional anti-Roman sentiment. This was one of the reasons Augustus did not permit Alexandria, the second-largest city in the Roman Empire, to have a city council, the standard governing instrument of most municipalities of the empire. Membership in such a council and election to local magistracies in the municipalities of the empire afforded one of the normal avenues to admission to Roman citizenship for provincials. Probably because of the political unreliability of the Alexandrian Greeks and the frequency of infiltration of Hellenized Egyptians into Alexandrian society, the city of Alexandria was assigned an inferior political status by the Romans, and the social distance between Romans, Hellenes, and Egyptians was carefully policed. No inhabitant of the province of Egypt could become a Roman citizen unless he was first a citizen of Alexandria, and such Alexandrians, to acquire Roman franchise, required a personal grant from the emperor. The omnipresent mark of the personal degradation of members of the Egyptian masses was the poll tax, which was introduced into Egypt by Augustus, probably in 24 or 23 B.C., and imposed upon all but Roman citizens and the privileged Alexandrian elite.[76]

Despite the segregation of Egyptians from Greeks and Romans and the rigid class hierarchy the Romans sought to maintain in this province, the most thoroughly policed in the empire, efforts to break through class lines and attain higher privileged status were rampant—and were systematically penalized by the emperors. The *Gnomon of the Idiologus*, known from a papyrus summarizing the regulations of this "Department of Special Revenues" drafted in the reign of Antoninus Pius, embodies the accumulated experience of about two centuries of Roman rule in Egypt in its efforts to maintain status distances. In the *Gnomon* we find regulations penalizing various types of usurpation of status, including Roman citizenship. Cases involving the fraudulent registration of persons as Alexandrian citizens were regarded as so important that they were referred up to the jurisdiction of the prefect of Egypt himself. The most common practice of Egyptians seeking both to escape fiscal oppression and to achieve social advancement was to infiltrate the cities and seek to pass themselves off as Hellenes. Repeatedly, prefects of Egypt were constrained to order such people back to their places of origin. Another subterfuge to attain Roman franchise was for an Egyptian to declare in writing, after his father's death, that the deceased was a Roman citizen. The penalty for fraud in this connection was confiscation of one-fourth of the property of the offender. Egyptians who registered their sons as ephebes were also penalized by confiscation of one-fourth of their property. Intermarriage between Greek and Macedonian immigrants and local women had been so frequent in Ptolemaic Egypt (especially since the end of the third century B.C., with the revival of Egyptian nationalism), and so extensive had been the assimilation of Greeks and Macedonians in the villages and provincial towns of Egypt,[77] that it was often possible for persons of Egyptian status to pass as Greeks.[78] If a woman of Alexandrian citizenship status married an Egyptian, believing him, in good faith, to be an Alexandrian citizen, then the citizenship of their children was not jeopardized. Roman citizens could not legally marry Egyptian women, and children born of such unions, being illegitimate, took the status of the mother. But if Roman citizens married Egyptian women (presumably of mixed ancestry but Hellenic in appearance) in ignorance of their status, with no guile involved, the children followed the status of the father and were declared Roman citizens. This was a frank admission by the Roman government that it was often difficult to discriminate between those of Greek and Egyptian status. Moreover, Egyptian women who married Roman veterans were forbidden to describe themselves as Romans. If they so did, they were fined one-quarter of their property, in accordance with the law concerning improper designation. The same penalty was imposed on soldiers who though not properly discharged from the army described themselves as Roman citizens.[79]

It is noteworthy that even after the Constitutio Antoniniana of 213 A.D., which altered the status of numerous persons in the empire, Caracalla himself in 215 A.D. ordered Egyptian natives driven out of Alexandria and assailed them for seeking to pass themselves off in Alexandria as members of a higher class:

> All Egyptians who are in Alexandria, especially peasants, who have fled hither from other parts of Egypt and can easily be detected, are to be driven from the city in every possible way. . . . For genuine Egyptians can readily be recognized among the linen-weavers by their speech, while they have assumed the appearance and dress of the others. Moreover, by their mode of living and their less civilized customs they reveal themselves as Egyptian peasants.[80]

It is obvious, therefore, that people were not required to carry official identification papers describing their status, and that Egyptians whose speech, dress, and style of living were Hellenized could escape detection.

One of the lesser privileged groups in Roman Egypt was the Jews. In the Augustan reorganization of Egypt, they were ranked politically and juridically inferior to the Greeks, reduced to a status closer to the ranks of the Egyptians than

had been the case in the Ptolemaic system. Ever since the Ptolemaic period some
of the Alexandrian Jews—wealthy, thoroughly Hellenized and assimilated—had
sought to achieve a status of social and political equality with the Greeks. Beginning with the Augustan dispensation, more Jews than ever before sought to acquire Alexandrian citizenship. Not only was Alexandrian citizenship a prestige
symbol in the imperial system and a prerequisite for the Roman franchise, but it
also sufficed to separate holders from the stigma of the poll tax, which was associated in the public mind with the degraded status of the Egyptians. Only a minority of the inhabitants of the capital of Egypt possessed Alexandrian citizenship,
among them a few wealthy Jews. But more and more Jews sought this privilege,
especially since elsewhere in the empire Jews could possess local municipal citizenship on a par with the rest of the population. Jewish communities in all cities
of the Roman world, including Alexandria, enjoyed special privileges, mostly of a
religious nature, granted by the Roman government in continuation of the policies of most Hellenistic rulers. But in Alexandria all Jews who did not possess
Alexandrian citizenship, rich and poor alike, appeared in the census lists with
virtually the same status as Egyptians. Hence the pressure on the part of the upper
stratum among the Jews to enter Alexandrian citizenship and thus emancipate
themselves from inferior status. This they sought to acquire especially for their
sons by infiltrating them, by fraudulent means, into the citizen body through enrollment in the gymnasium education and the roster of the ephebes of the city, the
legal route for admission to Alexandrian citizenship. An Athenian institution of
the fourth century B.C., Ephebic training had spread rapidly all over the Greek
East. In Egypt this training—very expensive everywhere—was confined to the
hereditary class of members of the gymnasia, symbol of Hellenism, both in Alexandria and the metropoleis of the nomes. Fraudulent enrollment in the ephebate
by bribery or falsification appears to have been practiced both by Jews and Hellenized Egyptians. The tense relationship between Jews and Hellenes in Alexandria, an inheritance from the Ptolemaic period, was, as a result of the Augustan
system, exacerbated to the point of riots and massacres, in a bitter struggle against
the efforts of the Jews to secure equality with Alexandrian citizens. This flared
into intense communal strife at the end of the reign of Caligula.

At the beginning of Claudius's principate three embassies came to Rome from
Alexandria: one from the Alexandrian citizens group, one from the Jews desirous
of obtaining the Alexandrian citizenship, and the third representing the official
Jewish community seeking to have its traditional privileges reaffirmed by the new
emperor. Because of the dispute over usurpation of status by Jews who enrolled
their sons in the ephebate, Claudius ruled such enrollment to be fraudulent. In a
letter to the city of Alexandria in 41 A.D., he writes,

> For all who have become ephebes up to my rule, I maintain in confirmed
> possession of Alexandrian citizenship with the privileges and indulgences
> of the city, for all except those who fraudulently contrived to become ephebes

though born of slaves. . . . And the Jews I explicitly order not to agitate for
more privileges than they previously possessed, and in the future not to dis-
patch two embassies, as if they lived in two cities—something that has never
before been done—and not to force their way into gymnasiarchic and cos-
metic games, while enjoying their own privileges and sharing an abundance
of advantages in an alien city.[81]

Thus Claudius, declaring the Jews to be living, as it were, in a foreign city, curbed
the efforts of the Jews to penetrate the elite circle of Alexandrian citizens, denying them equal rights with Hellenes and ruling their encroachment into the
ephebate as fraudulent.[82] Such was the death blow given to the aspirations of
Egyptian Jewry for equality with the Hellenes.

In the tendentious anti-Roman, anti-Jewish propagandistic literature of Alexandria during this period, the so-called *Acts of the Pagan Martyrs*, there is recorded
in the "Boule Papyrus" a proposal for the establishment of a local city council in
Alexandria, a privilege which the Alexandrian citizens had always desired. The
document expresses concern with regard to the efforts on the part of non-
Alexandrians to penetrate the citizen body through fraudulent enrollment in the
ephebate: "The [local] Senate will take care that none of those liable to the
laographia reduce the revenue by being inscribed in the public records among
the ephebes for each year, and that the existing pure citizen body of the
Alexandrians is not corrupted by uncultured and uneducated men."[83] Of course,
when Septimius Severus established city councils in Alexandria and also the nome
capitals of Egypt in 199/200 A.D. as a measure of fiscal efficiency, and when
Caracalla in 213 A.D. granted Roman citizenship to all free men in the empire,
the anti-Roman faction in Egypt faded. These problems gave way to the more
turbulent ones of the crisis of the third century. In the Jewish Revolt of 115–117
A.D. the Jews of Egypt were reduced to a mere remnant by massacre, flight, and
expulsion, but a Jewish community survived, and Greek-Jewish tensions continued until the Jewish community was expelled in the years 412–415 A.D. by the
patriarch Cyril after seven centuries of continuous existence in Alexandria.

The vigilance of the Roman government in upholding the social stratification established in the Province of Egypt is nowhere more evident than in the *Gnomon
of the Idiologus*. Penalties ranging from confiscation of one-fourth to the whole of
one's property were imposed on persons who altered the description of house-
born slaves of Egyptian status with a view to exporting them from the province.
Just as Egyptians were not permitted to leave the province without official permit, so also they were debarred from serving in the Roman legions, since they could
not, generally, be Roman citizens. Accordingly, it was ruled that if an Egyptian
did succeed in being fraudulently enrolled in a Roman legion without being de-
tected, upon completion of his military service and official discharge, he might
not, nevertheless, act as a Roman citizen, but reverted to his Egyptian status. The

same rule applied to Egyptians who infiltrated the naval crews of the imperial fleet, with the exception of those who were permitted to serve in the fleets stationed at the naval base of Misenum (and perhaps also at Ravenna).[84]

Usurpation of military status was an especially serious offense. For example, such fraudulent usurpation for the purpose of terrifying or oppressing anyone was penalized by capital punishment in the third century A.D. in the case of *humiliores* and by deportation for others.[85] The prevailing practice of the Greeks against the use of slaves in war was strictly observed by the Romans, with few exceptions, and only during shortages of soldiers in times of crisis, such as after the battle of Cannae, in the war between Octavius and Sextus Pompey, in the civil war of 68–69 A.D., and in the early fourth century when slaves were called to arms against the Goths.[86] In general the death penalty was imposed for usurpation of military status, especially in the case of slaves.[87] An exception is the case of Claudius Pacatus, an ex-centurion, who was subsequently discovered to have been a fugitive slave and was ordered by the Emperor Domitian in 94 A.D., by virtue of his censorial power, to be restored to his servile status and returned to his former master.[88]

The letters of Pliny and the Emperor Trajan contain correspondence concerning two recruits in the Province of Bithynia, ca. 110 A.D., who were discovered to be slaves after they had taken the military oath. The emperor ruled that if they were drafted by recruiting officers (and presumably the slaves might have been too terrified to reveal their true status), then neglect was involved as to proper inquiry into their status; if they were offered for service as proxies, the blame rested with those who presented them as substitutes, assuming that these were not acting in good faith; but if the slaves volunteered for service, concealing the truth about their status, then the death penalty was to be imposed on them.[89]

Two centuries later, when military titles, insignia, uniforms and their privileges could be widely obtained by fraudulent means, such as bribery and collusion, as well as by official letters patent, Constantine merely declares of free persons of higher social rank who obtained military status: "It is intolerable that persons should insinuate themselves into titles of military distinction who have not seen a battle line, who have not looked upon the standards and who have not handled arms." Accordingly, those who received such honorary military titles by letters patent were to be denied the privileges accorded to persons who earned the ranks by actual military service.[90] At the end of the fourth century the usurpation of military status was so widespread and the prestige and influence of military uniforms so great that senators, as well as *apparitors*, were forbidden to wear military uniforms in Constantinople and Rome. Senators who usurped military garb in the capital cities were ordered stripped of their senatorial status; the punishment for others was exile. Collusion and acceptance of bribes by imperial bureaus to conceal such usurpation from public notice were punishable by a fine of twenty pounds of gold.[91] The privileges accorded to veterans in the later Roman Empire led to fraudulent usurpation of such status. An imperial statute of 400 A.D. ruled: "Very many persons who have never been soldiers are being made veterans by testimonial letters obtained by fraud, and some are deserting at the start of their military service. . . . Therefore, if anyone who is subject to draft, and who ought to be incorporated in our most excellent legions, obtains a testimonial letter conferring the rank of honorary imperial bodyguard or any rank whatsoever, or if he obtains the testimonial letters that are sometimes granted on the authority of counts, he shall be trained in the recruit camp, so that he may not hide away."[92]

It would be supererogatory to elaborate upon and document in detail the well-known massive increase in fraudulent practices and evasions, including widespread usurpation of titles, ranks, privileges, and insignia, that characterized the Roman Empire from the crisis of the third century to the breakup of the supranational Roman state. An unmistakable initial leveling process tended more and more to polarize society into the privileged *honestiores* (*potentiores*) and the mass of *humiliores* (*tenuiores*), and the class structure of the empire was altered in many ways. The generalizing of Roman citizenship by the Constitutio Antoniniana of 213 A.D., which extended the franchise to all free persons resident in municipalities of the Roman Empire, erased many status distinctions. Further, the gap between free men and slaves tended to close up gradually, both socioeconomically and juridically. In the third century the Senatorial Order receded and was replaced by the Equestrian Order as the official supreme nobility of the empire, and many persons strove to gain admittance to this status, often by corrupt means, including bribery and the use of influence. A third order of nobility, the *comites* (imperial "companions"), created by Constantine, soon became the object of similar social aspirations. Eventually, however, the Senatorial Order, restored to favor by Constantine and his successors, became again the premier social class, and the Equestrian Order faded and disappeared by the middle of the fourth century. Beginning with the fifth century the senatorial class was the sole aristocracy of the empire, and it was the consuming ambition of all influential people to enter this prestigious status by codicils of honorary rank, influence, collusion, and bribery.

It has been a cliché of historians to label the period beginning with Diocletian a caste system, characterized by closed social classes maintained in a rigid hierarchical society.[93] The evidence reveals, however, that social mobility was not at a standstill by any means, but that, in fact, it was greater than at any other time during the Roman Empire—even if such movement was frequently generated by numerous surreptitious practices.[94] Beginning with Constantine's reign, the passion for ranks and the proliferation of titles was at an all-time high. The overpowering ambition of powerful, wealthy, and influential people was to attain the coveted title of *clarissimus* of the imperial nobility for themselves and their families. Despite the expense of acquiring this rank, and the burdens and financial obligations of the Senatorial Order, this hereditary nobility enjoyed many coveted privileges and exemptions. The striving to enter this order is thus to be accounted for, in part, by "the common human desire to have a handle to one's name and to take precedence over one's neighbours."[95] Wealthy landed families throughout the empire, usually the richest strata of the provincial aristocracy, exerted unrelenting pressure to enter the imperial nobility. Often the rank was obtained by imperial letters patent, beginning with the age of Constantine, which granted honorary titles and titular offices; and generally the securing of such honorary codicils was illegal, nearly always involving bribery on a vast scale. Often they were obtained through collusion with officials, or merely assumed by powerful individuals without authority—and often with impunity.[96]

The social movement upward from the lowest strata of the population in the later empire was minimal. The masses remained passive before the government and the local aristocracies.[97] We hear of such sporadic instances as a slave of the Roman Church who usurped curial rank to escape servile status. There is the strange case of the Egyptian woman Martha, in the sixth century, who was apparently freeborn but assumed the legal status of a slave to gain some advantage.[98] But the principal arena of social flux all over the empire was in the upper strata of the municipal aristocracy who constituted the *ordo decurionum* (*curiales*), generally the top one hundred wealthiest men in each city. The efforts of the curiales to extricate themselves, by every means, fair or foul, from the crushing burdens of this class have been elaborately explored in the last fifty years. The various devices employed by curiales to escape from the order, known especially from the law codes and the letters and orations of Libanius, are quite familiar: entry into the Senatorial Order by valid or fraudulent codicils; admission into various exempt professions; escape into the clergy or monastic communities; employment in the civil service; acquisition of military status; even acceptance of the status of a *colonus* of a large landowner.[99]

The leakage from the curial class, especially into the Senatorial Order, was so great that the government strove repeatedly to stem the breaching of class barriers—but without success. The frequency with which the same laws restraining social movement were reiterated is indicative of how constantly the statutes were being violated. The constant preoccupation of the imperial administration with the problem of defection from the curial class is revealed, for instance, in the 192 constitutions of book 12.1 of the Theodosian Code. The emperors here constantly speak of usurpation of "undue honors and insignia," "undeserved honors," "empty titles," evasion of duties, illegalities of all sorts, corruption, collusion, bribery, and other fraudulent practices. These repeated imperial constitutions reveal how powerless the imperial government was to control abuses perpetrated by wealthy persons who pulled strings or used graft to obtain honorary codicils. Nor did periodic governmental purges and roundups succeed in stemming this powerful displacement of social forces: the incidence of mobility did not decrease. Enforcement of the laws was lax and unsystematic, sometimes indeed impossible. Often the laws were broken with impunity, for officials were easy to bribe, and the irregular political support of influential persons (*patrocinium, suffragium*) was very effective. The codes reveal how widespread and frequent was the flouting of the law and how frustrated the government was in the face of massive infractions. The imperial authority could only resort to periodic threats and reenactments of the same laws; or it accepted faits accompli, condoning past offenses and making frequent concessions.[100] "There was in effect a tacit conspiracy among all the parties concerned to evade the laws."[101] Quite flagrant is the case of a certain Valerian, decurion of Emesa in 444 A.D., who usurped admission to the Senatorial Order as well as illustrious status through fraudulent honorary codicils. Armed with this prestigious status, he surrounded himself with a band of barbarian retainers, burst into the governor's palace, sat on the governor's right, and virtually took over the administration. The penalty for this high-handed behavior of Valerian was extraordinarily mild: he was merely stripped of his senatorial rank and of the title *illustris*.[102]

A few characteristic imperial pronouncements concerning the illegalities and fraud in this period will serve as an illuminating commentary. Constantine, in 321/324 A.D., declared:

> If anyone should allege that he has obtained imperial letters patent by our judgment, and either the outer imprint or the inner writing of the letters patent should agree with this, still, if it is established that money was expected for this, nevertheless, he shall be put back into the plebeian class [*curiales*] out of which he attempted to extricate himself, and be repudiated.[103]

In 338 A.D., Constantius warned: "Trafficking in honors [honorary titles] through patronage or procuring them through any solicitation whatever has been forbidden under an established penalty."[104] Regarding the order of precedence of ranks, Gratian, Valentinian, and Theodosius ruled, in 383 A.D.:

> But if anyone should disregard the established order of precedence or should presume to usurp and obtain any higher position with regard to the aforesaid honorary ranks than the reasonable claim and the general rule of his own status allows, he must know that not only is he to be deprived of that rank which he obtained contrary to the law, but he is also to be fined twenty pounds of gold.[105]

Likewise, Gratian, Valentinian, and Theodosius declared:

> Nothing is so injurious to the preservation and protection of the grades of rank as the ambition for usurpation. For every prerogative of merit perishes if a status of honor that ought to be guarded is usurped rather than maintained, aside from any respect and consideration or from the nature of a promotion, even one deserved, with the result that either better men are robbed of what is due them, or that which appears undeserved is of advantage to inferiors.[106] In a law the next year, they added: Valentinian of celestial memory, the ancestor of our imperial name, prescribed a fixed status of merit for each and every rank. If anyone, therefore, should usurp a status not due him, he may not defend himself by a plea of ignorance, and he is clearly guilty of sacrilege in that he has ignored the divine imperial commands.[107]

The pessimism of Theodosius in respect to the continual fraud is noteworthy: "Almost nothing is devised for the welfare of the human race which is not converted by the clever plans of men into fraud and malice."[108]

Theodosius's frustration took the form of a generalized reflection on human nature, but it is at the same time an accurate commentary on a persistent phenomenon of the social history of the Roman Empire: an ever-present tension among the statutory hierarchical structure, the legal avenues of upward movement, and the usurpation by a variety of fraudulent practices of higher social status and status symbols.

3

Human Nature as Cause in Ancient Historiography

A NUMBER OF ANCIENT HISTORIANS CONSCIOUSLY AND EXPLIC-
itly isolated "human nature" as a specific causative factor, or subjected events to
analyses based on the presumed existence of such an operant force. This chapter
engages this delimited aspect of ancient historiography. A. W. H. Adkins, who
has illuminated many other aspects of human nature in Greek thought, acknowledges that "of the making of books on human nature there is no end, and will be
no end,"[1] and David Hume called the subject one of "unspeakable importance."[2]

The concept of human nature (φύσις ἀνθρωπίνη) was invented in the mid-
fifth century B.C. by the later pre-Socratic philosophers, and it has remained in
our intellectual baggage ever since. The nature of human nature was enunciated by
Greek *physikoi* aprioristically, in line with the fashionable tendency of the time to
propound one-key theories of phenomena based on speculative deductive generalizations. Thinkers such as Democritus of Abdera, Prodicus of Ceos, Diogenes of
Apollonia (all of whom wrote treatises on "the nature of man") strove in this sphere,
too, to reduce the complicated phenomenon of man to some primary essence, uniform human nature. Thus they employed here the same bold reductionism they
applied to the physical universe. As Werner Jaeger pointed out, this link between
the *physis* of the universe and the *physis* of man was "a most momentous departure"
in man's intellectual history. "The idea of human nature now formulated for the
first time . . . was a great and fundamental discovery of the Greek mind."[3]

But such philosophical monism tended to cast on human thought the strait-
jacket of a one-key explanation of human nature as an unchangeable universal substance. Even medical practitioners began speedily to be influenced by
such theories of human nature as a basic given, but they were just as speedily
challenged. About 420–400 B.C. there appeared a remarkable manifesto from
the Hippocratic school of medicine that sharply assailed philosophical abstractions in the field of medicine. In the treatise "On the Ancient Medicine," the
author warned that such monistic generalizations, while appropriate to philosophy and literature, do not belong to medicine. In the Hippocratic essay
"On the Nature of Man" (of the second half of the fifth century), the author
rejects all talk of human nature not based on rational empiricism and on the
accumulation of observed evidence. These were momentous words, for the

possibility of prognosis in illness was introduced through such empirical data
patiently accumulated by itinerant Greek doctors.[4]

In this intellectual milieu the Sophists formulated conceptions of a common nature of man from observed social behavior both in Greek cities and among non-
Hellenes. For example, in the 430s and 420s the Sophist Antiphon in his essay "On
Truth" expressed the view that all men are members of the human race and that,
based on observed behavior, human nature is an absolute fixed norm. "We are all,"
he wrote, "by nature alike in all respects, non-Hellenes as well as Hellenes. We can
observe those factors among the nature of things that are independent of the will of
men." Similarly, other Sophists tended to describe human nature as a static essence.
To the Sophists human nature in the raw exhibited proneness of all humans to self-
interest, sometimes enlightened, sometimes ruthless. Typical is the statement of
Hippias that "it is human nature for the stronger to rule the weaker and to lead, and
for the weaker to submit and follow." The most extreme formulation of human nature
in the raw is the famous dictum of the Sophist Thrasymachus, preserved by Plato,
that injustice is the fulfillment of man's true nature.[5]

It was in the midst of this ferment of ideas that the writing of history was invented, and the first to use the concept of human nature as motive force in history
was not Herodotus, but Thucydides.[6] His *History of the Peloponnesian War* reflects
an interpretation of historical events and movements that resembles the theory and
practice of the Hippocratic school as well as the thinking of some Sophists. The
communis opinio has long been that Thucydides derived his understanding of
human nature directly from the Hippocratic doctors. While his procedures and conclusions most closely resemble theirs, we cannot posit as certainty that Thucydides
was a disciple of Hippocrates or that they even met, though some scholars have maintained this. Nor should we conclude that Thucydides's conception of human nature as a constant was derived directly from the pre-Socratics or the Sophists. Such
speculation was common property at the end of the fifth century.[7]

Thucydides's terminology for "human nature" (whether to express his own view
or attributed to speakers in his many contrived speeches) is characteristically varied: ἡ ἀνθρωπεία φύσις (1.76.3, 2.50.1); ἡ φύσις ἀνθρώπων (3.82.2; cp. 5.105.2);
ὁ ἀνθρώπειος τρόπος (1.76.2); πέφυκε ἄνθρωπος (3.39.5); πεφύκασι πάντες
(3.45.3). (On τὸ ἀνθρώπινον see below.) The bedrock of human behavior for
Thucydides, the basic motivating factor in all history, is a constant, relatively
unchanging universal human nature, what Pouncey has aptly called the "archi-
tectonic concept" of his history.[8]

The root characteristics of raw human nature for Thucydides are self-aggrandizement, greed, naked aggression, lust for power, desire to dominate others, and
propensity to tyrannical behavior. This primitive core of human nature is always latent
in man as a fixed, ineluctable norm of behavior, the "real" nature of man lurking
beneath appearances. This dark side of man is ineradicable by law, religion, or any
other restraint, operating through a mix of expediency, fear, and pursuit of honor.[9]
Accordingly, it is "natural" for all to be ever on guard, for the weaker to submit to

the stronger, for the stronger to rule over those who submit, and to have contempt for those who yield and admiration for those who resist.[10] A special characteristic attributed by Thucydides to human nature is that all men are prone to make mistakes (ἁμαρτάνειν),[11] a commonplace of proverbial wisdom.[12]

For Thucydides the existence of such a constant human nature makes possible prognosis and therefore control in political affairs,[13] paralleling the practice of Hippocratic physicians. Having studied the Peloponnesian War as a sort of laboratory for diagnosing human behavior operating as a constant, he proclaimed his history to have universal validity, as a κτῆμα ἐς αἰεί that will be useful for all time to "whoever will wish to understand accurately what has happened and what will happen (or something close to that) in the future sometime again, in accordance with the human condition." The behavior patterns he observed during this particular war were then "such as will always happen so long as human nature remains the same."[14] Indeed, Thucydides thus claimed to make possible prognosis not only for the political illness of the Greek world of his own time but for all future times.

But as he knew that prediction never can be made with perfect confidence, Thucydides acknowledged that he was not an absolute determinist.[15] He admits other causative factors: chance (τύχη) and the diverse personalities of leaders, both of which are present in a great variety of mixes bearing on the shaping of individual events.[16] Thucydides's deviation from one-key determinism is also evidenced by the differentiation he appears to make between two separate formulations: ἡ ἀνθρωπεία φύσις and τὸ ἀνθρώπινον (1.22.4, 2.48.3, 3.50.1, 4.45.7, 5.68.2). The distinction between the two has recently been subjected to rigorous analysis: Müri defined τὸ ἀνθρώπινον as "the human condition."[17] Rivier further distinguished "the human condition" from ἡ ἀνθρωπεία φύσις, "human nature."[18] Edmunds, calling the latter the "psychology" of human behavior, differentiates it from τὸ ἀνθρώπινον, objective limitations on humans.[19] Cogan regards ἡ ἀνθρωπεία φύσις as individual nature and behavior, that is, "the biological content of human nature," while τὸ ἀνθρώπινον as causative principle is social behavior (class or state), public image, in short, "public human nature," or the "human nature of society."[20]

The latter was surely Thucydides's principal interest. Clearly the goal of Thucydides was prognosis in a new sphere: the political arena. His sights turned from the nature of the individual to the typology of group behavior, its norms, recurrent patterns, and the symptoms of political disease. Thucydides thus advanced the process of the transfer of *physis* begun by the pre-Socratics one daring step further: from *physis anthrōpinē* to *physis politikē* (though he did not actually use this formulation). For Thucydides the behavior of men in classes and states within the Greek city-state system could be predicted more confidently than that of the individual, and thus prognosis in the political realm was possible.[21]

Thucydides's analyses of collective behavior are obviously polis centered and ethnocentric (and thus war and human nature are for him indissolubly linked).[22] He reflects fundamental characteristics of polis culture, which was highly agonistic

and fragmented into many power bases. Further, Thucydides's observations did
not embrace the behavior of women, slaves, metics, and non-Hellenes, but were
restricted to the thinking and conduct of adult males on both sides of the
Peloponnesian War, the members of the dominant decision-making classes.[23]

There are other flaws in Thucydides's efforts to apply his conception of human
nature as cause in historical events. His usurpation of analogy to medical practice is faulty (an early example of the well-known fallacy of transfer of methods of
natural science to social science). Greek doctors sought to develop prognostic skills
through tentative generalizations based on slow empirical observation and accumulation of the symptoms of numerous patients.[24] Thucydides is more daring,
more definitive: he leaps confidently from limited information and randomly
empirical observation to generalizations presented as universal truths. Indeed, he
tends to give great importance to particular instances and to elevate these into
universals as laws of history. His generalizations thus resemble philosophical hy-
potheses and are reductionist conclusions.[25] But in reducing man's "real" nature
to innate aggression and self-interest—a consistently negative, pessimistic view
of states—he concentrated his attention on behavior that was dramatically visible during great crises, such as war, revolution, plague.[26] Moreover, in striving to
develop universal laws of human behavior, he selected events and methodically
arranged them artfully and purposefully, delineating especially behavior in times
of crisis, when discussions of human nature are more frequent and highly colored emotionally.[27] And, like all ancient historians, Thucydides structured events
so as to provide striking moral *exempla*. In so doing he manifests a prevailing pattern of Greek (and Roman) thought: the tendency to generalize individuals into
stereotypes, without adequate knowledge of the multifaceted dynamic personalities of individuals.[28] And, finally, in his effort to bolster such generalizations
Thucydides also tends to fall back on inference and likelihood ($\epsilon i\kappa\acute{o}\tau a$).[29]

It is supererogatory to complain that Thucydides's conception of human nature was not based on modern methods of field study.[30] In sum, what we have
from Thucydides is an idiosyncratic analysis of human nature formulated as a priori
inference, constituting abstract assumptions of a behavioral constant that present
a negative view of human group behavior. Yet in 3.82.2 he ventures the generali-
zation that man's inhumanity to man will repeat itself "so long as human nature is
the same." We will never know whether he glimpsed the possibility of changes in
the basic human drives he delineated in his *History*.[31]

Thucydides's view of human nature has its roots not only in the Greek polis
culture but also in his own oligarchic class connections. Indeed, Thomas Hobbes,
recognizing in Thucydides an ideological blood brother, enthusiastically acclaimed
Thucydides's conception of human nature and said of him that "he had in his veins
the blood of kings."[32]

After Thucydides, waning confidence in the city-state and its institutions, and
the growth of individualism and professionalism in the fourth century B.C. all
combined to shift the focus of interest from group behavior to individual psychology: the personalities of leaders, their peculiar mix of virtues and vices as opera-

tive forces in history. The actions of great men thus became the events of history, and the causation of events was treated largely as resulting from the personalities and behavior of the dominant figures, modified by the intervention of *tyche* (chance, contingency).[33] This is particularly true of Hellenistic historiography.

Regrettably, Polybius's own statement of his theory of historical causation has not survived. Discernible in the extant parts of his history, however, is an eclectic, inconsistent view, a virtual admission that knowledge of causation is limited. While acknowledging the force of *tyche*, Polybius posits a basic, unchanging nature of historical figures (τὴν ἰδίαν φύσιν), modified by external circumstances that compel them at times to act contrary to their natures.[34] Such shifts in behavior also result from the very multiform character of the nature of men.[35] A prime example is the transformation of the character of Philip V for the worse under force of circumstances.[36] It is noteworthy that Polybius does not consider generalized human nature as a given, as operative force in history. Thus even in his treatment of mass psychology, Polybius does not isolate human nature as cause of the excesses of the masses. He attributes such behavior rather to deficiencies in education, upbringing, and capacity to set goals.[37] Regarding the brutality of the mutinous mercenaries of Carthage his comment is moralizing: "No animal turns out to be more wicked or cruel than man."[38] In crises men become so brutalized that they "depart from humankind" (ἐξέστησαν τῆς ἀνθρωπίνης φύσεως).[39] Thus in Polybius's comments we discern a new shift: from Thucydidean generalized "human nature" to the term's becoming a virtual synonym for humanity and a subject for moralizing comment.[40]

With the shift of interest from collective behavior to the individual, biography came into being, thriving as a highly popular form of literature from the fourth century B.C. throughout the Hellenistic and Roman periods. Though a distinction is made, notably by Polybius and Plutarch, between biography and history,[41] and greater emphasis is placed on the unexpected (*tyche, fortuna*),[42] still the generalizing tendency survives in the presentation of paradigmatic models in both historical and biographical works based on a conception of similarities in human nature.[43]

In Roman historiography theoretical or systematic reflections on historical causation are rare. Following Hellenistic methods, Roman historians made the thoughts and acts of individuals the central feature, and were addicted to the delineating character types and to moralizing conclusions. But they often introduced fatalistic or religious forces through *fatum, fortuna*, and divine intervention. Pervasive among Roman historians was the influence of Stoicism, as well as patriotic nationalistic bias. Thus Roman historians were less concerned with generalized human nature than with the collective behavior of the Roman people and with conviction of the superiority of Romans over other peoples.[44]

Thucydidean generalized human nature reappears, however, in the works of Sallust. Reacting to the crises in his lifetime, he was moved to ponder on human nature as causative factor in history.[45] Sallust isolated in human nature an innate flaw that wrecked Roman society: Nobis primae dissensiones vitio humani ingenii evenere, quod inquies atque indomitum semper inter certamina libertatis aut gloriae aut dominationis agit ("Among us the origins of our disputes came about through a fault of human nature: restlessness and an irrepressible factor is always operative in our struggles for liberty, or glory, or domination").[46] Here is a direct influence of Thucydides, but Sallust channels Thucydides's stress on divisiveness, especially among states, into moral and biographical emphases. Thucydides's objective analysis of ἡ ἀνθρωπεία φύσις has become in Sallust's vitium humani ingenii a bleak view of the moral disease of the Roman ruling classes. The aspirations ascribed to "us" are clearly those of the dominant classes of the last decades of the Roman republic.[47] It is not clear whether this should be interpreted as basic pessimism of Sallust or rather historical realism applied specifically to a particular context.[48] For elsewhere he is more generous with humanity: sed nostra omnis vis in animo et corpore sita est; animi imperio, corporis servitio magis utimur; alterum nobis cum dis, alterum cum beluis commune est ("But all our power is situated in the mind and body. We submit to the rule of the mind, but more so to the slavery of the body. The former we have in common with the gods, the latter with animals").[49] In these analyses of the essence of human nature Sallust associates the highest potential of human nature with the divine.[50] Despite this more sympathetic view of human nature, it would appear that for Sallust vitium remains for him the primary trait of humanity.[51] Yet he comments that falso queritur de natura sua genus humanum ("people unjustly complain about human nature").[52] In other words, they complain that man is weak, has a short life, and is ruled by chance. Those who devote themselves to idleness and physical pleasures, he wrote, blame it on the innate weakness of human nature (naturae infirmitas), assigning their faults to something outside their control,[53] when in fact the weaknesses of human nature can be overcome only by the exercise of virtue.[54] There is indeed discernible in the Sallustian conception of human nature a mix of Thucydidean views, Platonism, Aristotelianism, and Stoicism. This eclecticism may account for the conspicuous divergences in his views about human nature, in particular his oscillation between determinism and indeterminism in history. The shift from a positive view in the Catiline to a pessimistic one in the Histories seems to represent a turn of thinking in his last work, in response to the growing final crisis of the Republic.[55] In sum, Sallust's conceptions of human nature, like those of Thucydides, are ethnocentric, and based on random empirical observations from the behavior especially of the Senatorial Order.

Livy's historiography is dominated by Neo-Stoicism's waffling between predestination in human affairs, through fatum and fortuna, and the incalculable element of contingency.[56] His occasional moralizing observations on human nature concern the behavior of crowds, greed, and disclaimers of personal guilt in mutinies.[57] Livy's thinking does not embrace a generalized conception of human nature but is rather based on patriotic bias that tends to create stereotypes—idealized heroes, evil villains, and the natural character of the Roman people as an eternal given outside history.[58]

Yet Stoic doctrine, which posited the existence of the intrinsic identity of all human experience, encouraged acceptance of a uniform human nature. Thus Diodorus Siculus in his *Universal History* (under influence of Posidonius and Neo-Stoicism) propounded as the basic element in humanity the concept of the universal powerlessness of human nature (τὴν τῆς φύσεως ἀσθένειαν: 1.2.3, 13.24.2–4, 17.59.5): most people live short lives in obscurity, the playthings of *tyche*. But some great men overcome this natural human impotence by heroic virtue and thus achieve an immortal fame that merits a place for them in history.[59]

We may pass over such historians as Dionysius of Halicarnassus, Quintus Curtius Rufus, Josephus, Arrian, and Appian, who treat causality variously as based on fate, personal *fortuna*, personal qualities, divine intervention, or contingency, in mixes of determinism and indeterminism. In the biographers of the Roman imperial period, Plutarch and Suetonius, the nature of individual figures is inborn and fixed, not amenable to change and development, though they are sometimes affected by the unexpected (*tyche, fortuna*).[60]

Thucydidean influence reappears in Tacitus's grim assessment of human nature.[61] The general terms he uses for human nature are *insita mortalibus natura*; *ingenium humanum; natura humana*.[62] The specific traits he associates with raw human nature are greed for power;[63] eagerness to follow a course initiated by someone else that one is reluctant to begin oneself;[64] watchful jealousy of the good fortune of others, especially of one's peers;[65] and readiness to believe the mysterious.[66] No doubt these pronouncements of Tacitus are for the most part rhetorical commonplaces, for example the famous judgment about hating those whom one has injured, which parallels Seneca's *quos laeserunt et oderunt* in *De Ira*.[67] Tacitus's conception of human nature is, like Thucydides's, based on random observations of the conduct of the Roman ruling class, intuitive reductionism, and shrewd character portrayal.[68] This is in keeping with both the deep pessimism of Roman historiography in general and with Tacitus's own gloomy view of Roman government and society.[69] Characteristic is his penchant for sharp polarization of good and evil, presentation of stereotypical *exempla* of behavior, distrustful analysis of the behavior of women as emotional and immodest (*Annals* 3.34.9: *sexum natura invalidum*), and similar treatment of mobs as being like women and revealing their inferiority to the intellectual elite, and his depiction of individuals as static in character.[70] Like Thucydides and Sallust, Tacitus considered his task as historian to provide *empla virtutis* for edification and imitation, and of vices to avoid. This concern resulted in the structuring of generalized static treatment of personalities, and encouraged the positing of an innate human nature.[71]

The "most comprehensive reflections on historiography since Polybius,"[72] were written not by a historian but by Lucian in his essay *How to Write History*. He reports that in his day (middle of the second century) it was the high fashion to try to imitate and rival Thucydides.[73] This emulation is especially true of Cassius

Dio in the third century, who was the ultimate heir in antiquity of efforts since Thucydides to read human nature into historical events. Dio not only refers to "human nature" more frequently than any other ancient historian, but his terminology is exceedingly varied: he employs Thucydides's terminology, and devises ten other ways of expressing "human nature."[74] This plethora of applications of human nature by Dio has elicited from Fergus Millar the passing judgment that most of his comments are pessimistic and "no more than commonplaces."[75] Some are indeed quite general: success motivates the pursuit of further aims (12.50.2); it is easier to give comfort to others than to endure suffering oneself (38.18.2), and so on. But most frequently, like Thucydides, Dio broods on the dark side of human behavior: men are selfish and resort to violence for self-aggrandizement (52.2.6); men are incapable of enduring excessive honors (76[77].5.1); men are greedy for acquiring more, especially when successful (4.17.7); ambition for sole power is not inconsistent with human nature (52.18.1); those who hold positions of authority for a long time tend to deviate from ancestral practices (36.31.4); men do wrong through fear, inexperience, audacity, rashness based on possession of power (8.36.1–2); it is human nature to plot against authority (55.14.4); men give their support to those moving up in status and seek to bring down those already in power (14.57.18); men are by nature tempted to violate the laws (52.34.6–8);[76] men are always engaged in wrongdoing (55.16.3); it is human nature for men in mortal danger to destroy those guilty of endangering them (78[79].15.3).

Dio makes two apparently contradictory statements on the essence of human nature. In connection with his treatment of the campaign against piracy in the Mediterranean in 67 B.C. under Pompey, he comments that piracy and brigandage have always existed and will probably never cease "so long as human nature is the same" (ἕως ἄν ἡ αὐτὴ φύσις ἀνθρώπων: 36.20.1).[77] But in recording Pompey's aid in the recall of Cicero from exile, though he had previously been instrumental in bringing about the exile, Dio was moved to write that "human nature sometimes changes" (39.6.1). It is obvious here that Dio was simply elevating a single change in political tactics into a deviation from a general principle in his thinking that human nature does not change.

Not only is there no consistency in Dio's view of human nature, but it is to be noted that all his comments, whether his own animadversions or those he puts into the contrived speeches of historical figures, concern (almost without exception) Roman senators and emperors. Though he uses commonplaces, his analyses of historical events by reference to "human nature" are in the tradition of Thucydides, Sallust, and Tacitus. At times he is clearly "bookish," relying on a catch phrase or idea borrowed from wide reading. Like those of his predecessors, Dio's judgments apply to upper-class males, and they are random extrapolations from single incidents often at moments of crisis.

Thus, in the use of the concept of "human nature" in ancient historiography there was no substantial advance for nearly 650 years in the classical view—from Thucydides to Cassius Dio. The introduction of human nature as efficient cause in historical events was simplistic, arbitrary, or traditional. Because we cannot carry out field study or conduct controlled experiments to understand human nature in past cultures we are compelled to employ other techniques. A. W. H. Adkins has admirably outlined the proper procedures. We must first establish objective determinants and seek approximate answers from a wide array of information and sources. We need a psychological model of human beings, a physiological model, and a sexual model. We need an understanding of the relationship of man to the animal kingdom; of societal relationships, both of the individual to society and of intergroup relations; and of the relationship of human to gods.[78]

Because of the failure to study human nature along these lines, from Thucydides to the end of the eighteenth century (and, indeed, beyond), even political philosophers have spoken confidently of human nature as a universal constant.[79] In popular formulation this appears commonly as "You can't change human nature." David Hume expressed it as follows: "Human nature remains the same. . . . Would you know the sentiments, inclinations, and course of life of the Greeks and Romans? Study well the temper and actions of the French and English. . . . Mankind are so much the same in all times and places, that history informs us nothing new or strange in this particular. Its chief use is to discover the constant and universal principles of human nature."[80] It is only in the last few decades that in place of such traditional, simplistic, often emotionally loaded generalizations, there have emerged new perceptions of human nature based on scientific, empirical study, such as B. F. Skinner's operant behaviorism, which rejects consideration of human nature as an innate, autonomous, substantive reality, and holds that people are shaped exclusively by the environment, and the competing theory of Edward O. Wilson (under the label of sociobiology), which states that there are fixities in all human behavior controlled by genes, with man's innate aggressiveness and altruism genetically passed on to perpetuate the species. Or is the best guide for historians the view of Ortega y Gasset that "Man . . . has no nature; what he has is . . . history"?[81]

4

The Declaration of War
against Cleopatra

PARAMOUNT IN THE POLITICAL TACTICS OF OCTAVIAN IN 32 B.C.
was the conversion of the de facto civil conflict with Antony and his adherents
into a *bellum externum* with Cleopatra as queen of Egypt. The surviving sources
dramatize the maneuver by featuring antithetically the datum that declaration of
war, at the end of October 32, was issued against Cleopatra, not Antony.[1] They
do not, however, specify the formal charges against Cleopatra detailed in justifi-
cation of a *iustum piumque bellum* in accordance with Roman public law. The
savage propaganda campaign unleashed against Cleopatra poured out a flood of
extravagant indictments and recriminations (lust, whoring, incest, use of magic
and drugs, drunkenness, animal worship, rampant luxury) that have echoed down
through the ages in history, literature, and the popular image of her.[2] A formal
declaration of war, however, required a diplomatically formulated bill of particu-
lars. Can we recover the actual charges against her?

Before the promulgation of the formal declaration of war, with its ritual legiti-
mation through the spear rite of the fetials, steps were taken to reduce Antony's
status to that of a *privatus*: he was stripped of whatever remnants of residual power
he retained as triumvir, and his impending term as consul, to which post he had
been designated for 31 B.C., was abrogated.[3] While it was in the Roman tradition
for a *privatus* as a dedicated citizen to intervene in the public interest to preserve
the state when existing institutions and management of the state proved inadequate,[4] Antony no longer possessed constitutional authority to summon assistance
from client states. Thus, even though Cleopatra's military resources were small,
Antony was condemned in the public eye in the west for acting "against his own
country" by supporting a *hostis* in a war against Rome.[5]

It was "for her acts" that Cleopatra was declared a *hostis*.[6] Neither widespread
Roman fear of the Orient[7] nor Cleopatra's reported habit of saying "as one day
I shall dispense justice on the Capitoline,"[8] however offensive to Roman sensibilities, could be elevated into formal charges so as to serve as documentation
of overt acts.

In order to recover the "acts" that warranted a declaration of war, we need to
consider her status and obligations as client ruler of a country *in fide populi Romani*.
Since the time of Ptolemy VI Philometor, from the middle of the second century
B.C., Egypt had been a Roman client state, and no doubt each successor to the

Ptolemaic throne renewed, in some fashion, the monarch's official status as *amicus et socius populi Romani*.[9] And so it must have been with Cleopatra. Indeed, from the beginning of her reign in 57 B.C. she had maintained a correct role in fulfilling her obligations as Roman vassal. Together with many other client rulers she had responded, for example, to Pompey's orders in 49 B.C., supplying ships, men, and money to him; and in 42 B.C. she had tried to make her resources available to Octavian and Antony against the "liberators" before the battle of Philippi.[10] She was also correct in her obedient response to the *evocatio* of holders of *imperium* when she reported to Caesar in Alexandria in 48 B.C. at his summons, and later to Antony in Tarsus in Cilicia in 42 B.C., and again at Antioch in 37 B.C.[11] Client rulers were accountable to Rome in many ways: they especially had the obligation to aid Rome on request, to obey a summons (*evocatio*) by a Roman imperator, and, whether explicitly in a formal treaty at the time of investiture, or implicitly by tradition, to preserve the *maiestas* of the Roman people. Thus Cleopatra's aid to Antony at his request was eminently proper, indeed obligatory, as it was for numerous other client kings and dynasts under Antony's jurisdiction in the East.[12] But when he became officially *a privatus* by action in Rome, response to his orders in the East was rendered ambiguous and perilous. It was not to be expected that in the eastern part of the empire, which Antony had dominated for ten years, there would be absolute certainty where responsible power was located, given the shifting political alignments and the frequent constitutional maneuvers. But it is clear that numerous client rulers besides Cleopatra, and many cities in the East, honored Antony's call for aid, and indeed participated in the Battle of Actium at his side.[13] Despite this, most of these client rulers were retained by Octavian in his settlement of the East after the death of Antony.

The dangerous dilemmas confronted by Roman client rulers in the last decades of the Republic are exemplified by the hazards of King Deiotarus of Armenia Minor, loyal Roman client from Sulla's time, whom Cicero defended in Rome before Caesar in 45 B.C. (in his *Pro Deiotaro*; he was charged with plotting to murder Caesar). Pursuant to Pompey's request, he had sent aid to him in 48 B.C. against Caesar, and was present at Pharsalus with Pompey.[14] In 47 B.C. he appeared before Caesar as suppliant, and *depositis regiis insignibus* ("laying down his royal insignia," i.e., his crown and scepter) he solicited pardon on the grounds that he was compelled by Pompey's orders (and the threat of military force) to aid Pompey. His vindication was forthright: neque se debuisse iudicem esse controversiarum populi Romani, sed parere praesentibus imperiis ("It was not his obligation to be a judge of the controversies of the Roman people but to obey the commanders at hand").[15] Cicero defended Deiotarus's rendering of assistance to Pompey as incumbent upon him, arguing that he came at the request not only of a friend, but *arcessitus ut socius, vel evocatus ut is qui senatui parere didicisset* ("called upon as ally, or summoned as one who had learned to obey the Senate").[16] Moreover, the situation in 48 B.C. was confused, making it uncertain whose authority prevailed; the consuls of the year and the former consuls had left Italy, and the Senate was scattered. Caesar's response was brusque: a man of such political skill and experience *scire potuisset quis urbem Italiamque teneret, ubi senatus populusque Romanus, ubi res publica esset, quis denique . . . consul esset* ("ought to have known who controlled Rome and Italy, where the Senate and the Roman people were, where the government was, who, in short, . . . was consul").[17] The obligation of client rulers, Caesar here lays down, was to obey the orders of the central government. Thus when Deiotarus responded to Pompey's call for aid he was effectively in rebellion against the legal authority in Rome, for new consuls for 48 B.C. had been elected (i.e., Caesar himself and P. Servilius Vagia Isauricus). The position of Caesar was that there was only one Senate and one duly elected college of consuls, and that the senators who went over to Pompey had in effect resigned from the Senate.[18] In the end, however, Caesar restored Deiotarus's royal insignia because of his former loyal services.[19] Whether Caesar also considered as a mitigating factor the uncertainty confronting Deiotarus, even if we concede self-serving decisions of Deiotarus, the king's dilemma was a common one. The status of all Roman client rulers, including Cleopatra, in the turbulent years between 48 and 30 B.C. was constantly in jeopardy. Indeed, during the preceding fifty years Roman vassal rulers, drawn into the civil conflicts of Rome, were likely to give precedence to personal attachments to Roman leaders rather than loyalty to the Roman state.[20]

Treaties with Roman client rulers varied in specifics,[21] but all were expected, explicitly or implicitly, to do everything in their power to uphold, and nothing to diminish, the *maiestas populi Romani*.[22] Military capability did not figure in this expectation; it was acknowledged, for example, that Deiotarus did not possess military power sufficient to threaten the Roman state,[23] and this was the case with Cleopatra as well.

But Roman law and practice regarding *maiestas populi Romani* allowed for great latitude in interpretation. Inherent was Rome's peculiar claim of priority (*maiestas*, literally "greatness") over all the rest of the lands in her orbit. The basic formula in treaties was *maiestatem populi Romani conservanto*. In practice the concept could be interpreted (and was applied) elastically[24] to embrace not only charges of weakening the empire in any way but offenses to magistrats and injury to the good name of Rome.[25] Of the trial of Deiotarus, Cicero says that it was unparalleled for a king to be on trial for his life.[26] Later, though, under Augustus and Tiberius, charges of *maiestas imminuta* were brought against four client kings—Archelaus of Cappadocia, Archelaus of Judea, Antiochus of Commagene, and Rhescoporis of Thrace—with penalties ranging from banishment or confiscation of property to execution.[27]

Similarly, Cleopatra as client ruler was exposed not only to the hazards of the political shifts but also to the dangers inherent in the concept of *maiestas imminuta*. After Antony was relegated to the status of *privatus*, so that she could no longer claim obligations to obey *praesens imperium*, Octavian might have summoned her to Rome (by *evocatio*), but he did not. It would have been a trivial charge to declare that Roman soldiers were in her bodyguard and that her name was inscribed on the shields of Roman legionaries,[28] for this was done at Antony's orders when he was invested with supreme authority in the East. More solid grounds for a charge of *maiestas imminuta* lay in the territorial grants made by Antony to Cleopatra and her children. But here, too, while Roman sensibilities might be outraged by the alienation of Roman territory, the situation was anomalous, and the extent of the alienation limited.

In the rhetorical set speech that Cassius Dio put into the mouth of Octavian before the battle of Actium, he is made to speak of Antony's gifts to Cleopatra and her children as giving away "just about all your possessions," and to charge that Cleopatra had designs "on all your possessions."[29] It was, however, normal practice for Roman imperators, especially since the 60s, to make territorial adjustments in Roman vassal states, and Antony was acting properly in this regard. Octavian's propaganda magnified the territorial assignments to Cleopatra and her children (Ptolemy Caesarion, Alexander Helios, Cleopatra Selene, and Ptolemy Philadelphus) in order to highlight Antony's bewitchment by and enslavement to Cleopatra. Indeed, at first Antony was reluctant, cautious, and pragmatic in making grants (he needed supplies, money, ships). In the donations of 36 B.C. very little Roman provincial land was transferred to Cleopatra: her possession of Cyprus was confirmed (Caesar had assigned the island to her in 47 B.C.), and Antony added to her realm Phoenicia, parts of Coele-Syria, Cilicia, Crete, Judea, and Arabia Nabataea, and perhaps Cyrenaica as well. Antony did not do this only out of sentiment but because he had need of her assistance in the building of ships and supplying of funds for his military operations in the East.[30] In the "Donations of Alexandria" in 34 B.C., Alexander Helios was proclaimed overlord of all rulers east of the Euphrates. This grant included Media Atropatene (the land of King Artavasdes, to whose daughter Iotape Antony had just engaged Alexander), the entire Parthian Empire(!), and Armenia. The latter had only just been organized by Antony as a Roman province. It was, in fact, the only province Antony added to the empire, and as such it lasted for under two years, for Antony soon dismembered it, assigning parts to Kings Artavasdes and Polemo of Pontus. Cyrenaica, together probably with Crete, was transferred to Cleopatra Selene. Ptolemy Philadelphus received parts of the Roman provinces of Syria and Cilicia, and was named overlord of all client rulers west of the Euphrates. Cleopatra herself, together with Ptolemy Caesarion, retained Coele-Syria and Cyprus. In October 32 B.C. Caesarion was fifteen years old; Alexander Helios, eight; Cleopatra Selene, eight; Ptolemy Philadelphus, four. It is noteworthy that Antony's eldest son, Antyllus, by Fulvia, who was with him in Alexandria, received neither title nor grant.[31]

Despite the propaganda broadcast by Octavian, these lands contained much territory that was still unconquered or still under Roman rule as lands previously held by other client rulers. True, the title Antony bestowed on Cleopatra, "Queen of Kings and her Sons who are Kings," and that bestowed on Ptolemy Caesarion, "King of Kings," were unparalleled in the management of Roman client-king relationships. These were, of course, flamboyant titles, not declarative of territorial possessions, but they could easily be interpreted as threatening the "greatness" of the Roman people. Rome did not countenance easily such indirect relationships among client rulers not directly accountable to her. Here, then, were two possible grounds for a charge of *maiestas imminuta*. Though Antony had possessed the authority to regulate relations with client rulers in the East before the end of October 32 B.C., Cleopatra's continuation in this novel arrangement could now be isolated and defined as a threat to Roman *maiestas*.

For a *iustum piumque bellum* to be waged, traditionally a demand for restitution was first required (*res repetuntur*).[32] A *locus classicus* for this is Cicero, *De Off.* 1.11.36: neque ullum bellum iustum esse existimaverunt [Romani] nisi quod aut rebus repetitis gereretur, aut denuntiatum ante esset et indictum ("The Romans considered no war to be just unless it was waged after restitution was demanded, or warning was first given, and it was formally declared").[33] To dramatize and validate the legitimacy of a declaration of war against Cleopatra in 32 B.C., and to proclaim, as it were, a national crusade in defense of *Romanitas* and the West, Octavian revived the long-obsolete fetial rite by which wars were declared with archaic religious solemnity.[34] It was a ritual ceremony, Livy tells us, *quo res repetuntur*. It is not likely, however, that satisfaction was sought through diplomatic channels, or that Cleopatra was summoned to Rome.

The most demonstrable charges against Cleopatra would then have been offenses against the state through betrayal of her *fides* and of her obligations to Rome as client ruler. Aside from charges that the integrity of Roman territory was jeopardized through Antony's grants to her and her children, the specific acts that could be cited were her contributions to Antony, from the time he was stripped of his powers, for a war against Italy, and, in general, the *crimen maiestatis populi Romani imminutae*.[35] True, just as in the conflict between Caesar and Pompey in 48 B.C., there were three hundred to four hundred senators in the east with Antony. Yet Octavian could charge against Cleopatra, as Caesar had said of Deiotarus, that she ought to have known *quis urbem Italiamque teneret, ubi res publica esset, quis denique consul esset*.[36]

5

Augustus's Conception of Himself

Ciel, à qui voulez-vous désmormais que je fie
Les secrets de mon âme et le soin da ma vie!
(Lord, to whom is it now your will that I entrust
The secrets of my soul and the cares of my life?)

—Augustus, in Corneille, *Cinna*, act 4, scene 1

IT IS A RECEIVED COMMONPLACE THAT THE PERSONALITY OF Augustus, the founder of the Roman Empire and its sole ruler for almost fifty years, is an enigma, "puzzling," "elusive," "baffling," "inscrutable."[1] Though his acts and times are among the most extensively documented in antiquity, no written record captures the psychic texture, inner life, and motives of the first *princeps*. Whatever light Augustus himself would have shed in his autobiography was lost with that document; one may regret, too, the loss of Plutarch's life of Augustus.[2] True, we have the *ipsissima verba* of Augustus preserved in scattered quotations and in letters, and in the "queen of Latin inscriptions," the *Res Gestae Divi Augusti* (Achievements of the deified Augustus),[3] that extraordinary summation of his career. But this "obituary notice" of himself compels caution because of its selectivity and calculated aim to bequeath at the end of his life a posthumous image of his place in history.

Augustus's longevity, the dynamically transitional character of his times, his consummate skill as mythmaker for his age and posterity, his artful use of propaganda and symbols, and the numerous crises and blows of fortune he encountered all make it difficult to grasp the man.[4] It is now possible, however, to reexamine the evidence and elicit insights into his inner world, his conception of himself and his role. We can do this thanks, in part, to the tools at hand from the avalanche of fundamental studies in the past half century in humanistic psychology, the nature of power and leadership, the personality of power seekers and power wielders, and the typology of political personalities.[5] Equally important, we may in conjunction bring to bear on Augustus's words and deeds our increasingly refined knowledge of the Roman ethos, of the motives of Romans of his social stratum, and of Roman political, social, and economic institutions.

The information we possess about Augustus's earliest years, before he emerged in the political arena at the age of eighteen as Caesar's heir, are sparse but telling. They afford us glimpses into events and circumstances that affected the emotional life of the intensely ambitious young man he was: his birth to the heiress Atia, niece of Julius Caesar, in 63 B.C. in the small Italian town of Velitrae (modern Velletri) in Latium and into the family of the Octavii, of plebeian but equestrian stock; the sudden death of his father, Gaius Octavius, when the boy was only four years old; the *ignobilitas* of the family—his father was a *novus homo*, who had risen as far as the rank of praetor and provincial governor; his upbringing at Rome in the house of his grandmother Julia (Caesar's sister) until she died in 50 B.C. when he was twelve; finally his transfer to the home of his mother and his stepfather, Lucius Marcius Philippus.[6]

It is speculative, of course, to try to assess the degree of psychic damage caused by this series of personal dislocations at such an impressionable age, but we may confidently record that he was ashamed of his father's famiy background and of the relatively humble rank of the Octavii within the highly stratified, status-conscious Roman social and political hierarchy.[7] Stories were allowed to circulate later—not without his own connivance—that he was sired on Atia by the god Apollo, and there was even attributed to him the statement, "Some think I was the son of Octavius; some suspect that I was born from someone else."[8] It was therefore balm to his ego when at the age of fourteen he received marks of favor from his patrician great-uncle, the glamorous Julius Caesar (who lacked a legitimate male heir), and when he was adopted by Caesar's will at the age of eighteen. Shortly after the death of Caesar, when the comet known as *sidus Julium* ("Caesar's star") was seen, the young Caesar Octavian, as he was now called, declared its coming a personal annunciation for himself, and interpreted it to signify that he was "born in it."[9] Other compensatory mitigations of his low social self-esteem were his elevation to patrician status by Caesar when he was eighteen; his assumption of Caesar's name in 44 B.C.; his alliance a few years later (in 38 B.C.) with a very distinguished patrician family through marriage to his second wife, Livia.[10]

Roman youths of the higher classes grew up in an atmosphere of aspirations for political and military careers. Octavian's ambitions at the age of eighteen, however, were inordinately high-flown and precocious when he plunged into the maelstrom of Roman politics as Caesar's heir. His alarmed stepfather counseled him not to accept Caesar's inheritance and not to run the risks of the stormy political arena, but he rejected the advice, for he already had his "mind on great things."[11] It was on such a high crest of the political wave that Octavian began his extraordinary career. And at the outset he already conforms to one of the classic patterns of the power seeker, one who has experienced psychic damage in childhood and youth: determination to overcome doubts about his own worth by winning power and prestige to compensate for deprivation of self-esteem; relentless pursuit of the means to impose his will on others; the need to prove himself superior in leadership ability; compensation for damaged self-esteem by inner conviction of uniqueness and of unparalleled qualifications to succeed in great achievements.[12]

Contributing strongly to Augustus's self-doubts was his chronic sickly nature. His illnesses and disabilities are extensively documented from age seventeen to seventy-six.[13] Hypochondriacal and a lifelong valetudinarian, he was constantly solicitious about his health, with a strong will to overcome his weaknesses: he exercised great care in his living habits, disciplining his eating, drinking, sleep, and rest periods.[14] We are reminded that the sickly Woodrow Wilson said of himself as a young law student: "How can a man with a weak body ever arrive anywhere?"[15] Augustus's physical appearance, moreover, was unprepossessing. He was short (under five feet, seven inches tall, according to his freedman secretary, Julius Marathus), and as a result wore somewhat thick-soled shoes to make him appear taller. His teeth were wide apart and poorly kept, and his body had numerous calluses from chronic itching and use of the strigil.[16] Eschewing the traditional Roman preference for realistic portraits, Augustus wished always to be depicted in idealized form; the approximately 150 known portraits of him in sculpture, based on authorized official prototypes, consistently show him as a handsome person, and this style was maintained even in portraits made in his old age.[17]

Yet there is little doubt that Augustus fully recognized his own limitations, not only in health but in spheres that brought fame and glory to many other Romans: He was neither a great general, nor orator, nor intellectual, nor political theorist, nor writer. No wonder that his attitude toward his adoptive father Julius Caesar as role model was ambiguous. Though he owed the launching of his career to Caesar's adoption of him (Cicero mocked "O puer . . . , qui omnia nomini debes" [O boy . . . , who owes all to a name]),[18] diligently performed his duty as ultor Caesaris (avenger of Caesar), and eagerly inherited his wealth, clientela, and veterans, he studiously maintained a conscious distance from the memory of Caesar himself.

This negative reaction to his famous adoptive father was a consequence not merely of personality differences but of compelling ideological and tactical considerations: he wanted to separate himself from Caesar's liaison with Cleopatra and his monarchical aspirations, supranational cosmopolitanism, and notorious trampling on due process. True, the name "Caesar" and the patronymic divi filius ("son of a deified person") were both used by Augustus in his official titulature as glamorous, potent, authoritative, but little was said in the Augustan Age of the acts and memory of Caesar himself.[19]

It was rather with Alexander the Great that Augustus consciously and calculatedly associated himself, both as universal conqueror and ruler, and champion of Western civilization over the East. After the deaths of Cleopatra and Antony in 30 B.C., Augustus visited the tomb of Alexander in Alexandria, touched his mummy (presumably to absorb its "power"), placed a crown on it, and strewed it with flowers.[20] Indeed, Augustus's seal ring from 30–23 B.C. bore a portrait of Alexander.[21] Moreover, in the high enthusiasm created by his victories in the East, Augustus's imitatio Alexandri spawned ambitious, romantic plans for massive expansion on all frontiers to achieve a dream of universal empire, *imperium sine fine*, in Vergil's classic formulation.[22]

It is characteristic of Augustus's ego needs that he was determined to surpass Alexander. When he soon abandoned his grandiose dreams of world conquest, he faulted Alexander for not deeming the administration of the existing empire of greater import than winning it.[23] Moreover, he was younger than Alexander when he entered public affairs. When Alexander's father Philip II was assassinated, Alexander was twenty; on Caesar's murder, Augustus was only eighteen.[24] (It also did not escape Augustus that he attained high political power earlier than Pompey, Scipio Africanus, even Romulus—in his nineteenth year, *undeviginti natus*, he proudly tells us in the first two words of the *Res Gestae*.)[25]

Augustus's need to present himself as exceeding Alexander stems from his conception of himself as an extraordinary and unique person, a man of paramount virtues and achievements, a leader unparalleled in the annals of Rome, indeed in world history. He resented being called *puer* in his younger upward-striving days,[26] but in later years he boasted that he was the youngest in world history to rise to power. It is true that it was through Caesar's favor that he was early brought into the entourage of the great dictator, and even elected pontifex at the age of fifteen. But after Caesar's death he mounted his own drive for power: at nineteen he mobilized an army (of Caesar's veterans, of course), was co-opted into the Senate, and unprecedentedly elected consul;[27] at twenty he was one of the triumvirs for reorganizing the state (with Antony and Lepidus).[28] Unprecedented as these early conquests were, Augustus took pains throughout the *Res Gestae* to parade the many unparalleled "firsts" and "mosts" in his career, including honors, victories, offices, in his private expenditures for public purposes, in census statistics, in his building program, shows, and spectacles provided for Rome, and in expansion of Roman territory.[29] Typical are such boasts as "an honor which hitherto had been decreed to no one besides myself" (ch. 12); "I was the first and only one to have done [this] . . . in the memory of my generation" (ch. 16); [Envoys from India came to him] "previously not seen in the presence of any Roman general" (ch. 31); [At his election to *pontifex maximus*] "a great multitude flocked from all of Italy such as never before had been recorded at Rome" (ch. 10). The most self-revealing phrase is *prius quam nascerer* ("before I was born"), in reference to the fact that in all Roman history only twice before was the Temple of Janus closed—to signify peace in the entire empire—but in his principate it was closed three times (ch. 13).

One may readily grant him his pride in his achievements and his awareness of the mark he made in history. But Augustus's need to demonstrate his uniqueness with such overkill is, one may posit, a reflection of deep-rooted incapability to abide competition with his contemporaries. Indeed, not once in his long political career did he subject himself to the normal competitive electoral chance, neither as consul (thirteen times), nor when he became a triumvir (for ten years), nor even as *pontifex maximus*. The extraordinary powers he obtained from 23 B.C. to the end of his life—the *imperium proconsulare maius* (superior proconsular power) and the *tribunicia potestas* (tribunician power)—were overriding supramagisterial innovations that removed him from the indignity of the electoral process and assured him unique superiority and priority in decision making without competition in both the military and civil spheres. Accordingly, until very near the end of his rule he could even tolerate verbal attacks, lampoons, and insults to him and his kin. He counseled the touchy Tiberius not to take it to heart when anyone spoke evil of him: "It is sufficient," he said, "if we can prevent anyone from doing evil to us."[30]

In this light we may understand Augustus's longing for consensus and unanimity with regard to himself and his acts, as expressed in the *Res Gestae* by *universi cives* (the entire citizen body); *consensus universorum* (unanimous consent); *senatus et equester ordo populusque Romanus universus* (the Senate, the Equestrian Order, and the Roman people unanimously).[31] Under the Roman republic *consensus senatus* was a procedural decision-making expression signifying "sense of the senate." Augustus's extension of *consensus* to "unanimous consent" (of all the Roman people) was an extraconstitutional statement, merely his own personal interpretation of the presumed will of the entire citizen body. In the name of such declared *consensus universorum*, implying the total absence of opposition, he could interpret at will the high honors to himself and his family, and justify any of his decisions and acts.[32] In 2 B.C., when he was accorded the title *Pater Patriae* in an outpouring of sentiment by the people and the Senate ("Father of His Country" was, however, an appellation not without many precedents during the Republic, given as thanksgiving gesture to eminent Romans), Augustus interpreted this honor as vouchsafing him universal consensus and approval to the end of his life.[33]

Augustus designated his unique role as focal point of all authority, as "top man" in the Roman state, by the preferred term he adopted for himself, *princeps*.[34] Not an official title but an extraconstitutional complimentary appellation, it marked him out as possessor of the highest rank in the Roman social and political order, signifying priority and superiority in prestige and esteem, capacity to take initiative and command respect. As in the Republic, such a "first man" among the citizens was influential not as magistrate but as *privatus*.[35] Such a "private citizen" was characteristically a man of extraordinary qualifications, resources, and proven accomplishments, who, without being subject to electoral process and debate, intervened disinterestedly in the public interest when governmental and social institutions proved inadequate. There were, indeed, not a few classic exemplars during the Republic as precedents, with Lucius Brutus as prototype at the very founding of the Republic.[36] Augustus's conception of himself was so in line with this tradition that he was acting out of a sense of duty and high civic mission to preserve and enlarge the state as a dedicated citizen.[37]

A similar supraconstitutional overriding personal preeminence was afforded by Augustus's *auctoritas*. After 27 B.C., he tells us, "I excelled all in *auctoritas*."[38] This "authority" did not, in the Roman sense, connote legitimated power, the right to command, but rather esteem for preeminent status and soundness of judgment, and recognized priority in consultation. It signified a unique ethical-political relationship between himself and all others that was nontransferable. Since this quality was not constitutionally defined, its scope was unlimited; it was a fuzzy concept that enabled Augustus to act as author-initiator and to take unrestricted action in a wide range of matters.[39]

Eager to enhance his capacity to make independent decisions, Augustus embraced the enormous increase in his authoritative status that came to him when the name "Augustus" was bestowed on him in 27 B.C. An alternative proposal to name him "Second Romulus" was rejected by him because of the royal status of the founder of Rome and the well-known competition and strife between him and his brother, Remus.[40] An unprecedented name, "Augustus" was pregnant with potent polyvalent implications: sanctity; heroization; divine election; mediation between gods and the Roman people; relationship with Romulus, who had founded Rome *augusto augurio*, in the famous phrase of the Roman poet Ennius; association with *auctoritas* and with the sense of "increase" in the root *aug-*, as well as with augury, originally associated with rites of fertility.[41] Contemporaries among sophisticated Romans might see in the name "Augustus," he could anticipate, the divinely chosen and favored leader, preserver and increaser of the Roman state, who augmented the greatness (*maiestas*) of Rome in its territory, population, public buildings, public works, prosperity, stable order, and who mediated with the gods as augur to assure such increase for the country.[42]

At about the same time (27–26 B.C.) Augustus assisted in formulating a constellation of virtues to serve as the moral foundation of himself and his regime. The four cardinal virtues—which launched the myth of the "virtues of the Roman emperor" that endured to the end of the empire—were endorsed by him in all earnestness as model of the good ruler and as manifesto of the policies of his administration: *virtus* (military power); *clementia* (reconciliation and internal peace, replacing force); *justitia* (law and order, due process, sanctity of property); and *pietas* (dedicated service to gods and country). It is self-revelatory that Augustus associated himself with the cardinal virtues previously established (e.g., by Cicero in the *Republic*) as those of the good ruler in Stoic doctrine. Note also that Greek and Roman virtues were intermingled; that some of the traditional Roman virtues, such as *gravitas* and *fides*, were passed over; and that he did not claim for himself *sapientia* (wisdom, a high Greek virtue), nor the gentler virtues, such as *humanitas*.[43]

Thus Augustus's need for and love of unrestricted personal power are unmistakable. Yet it would be simplistic to apply to Augustus without qualification Harold Lasswell's classic formulation that the power holder displaces private "affects onto public objects,"[44] that is, that he rationalizes his private ego needs in terms of public interest. Augustus's long career witnessed many inner conflicts and a fluid mix of motives, embracing demonstrations of superiority, the need to excel, a fear of displacement, the sheer momentum of decision making, and sincere civic duty. As an adolescent Augustus was under the instruction of a number of philosopher-teachers, all of whom were Stoics: Athenodorus of Tarsus, Areius of Alexandria, Didymus, and Zenarchus. The Stoic influence followed him throughout his life, and in Stoicism he found a doctrine compatible with his ego needs: that each person has a given role to play in life, and that it is the moral obligation of the individual—even as a private person—to intervene in the public interest to restore and maintain the natural order.[45]

For about sixty years Augustus was indeed "the first servant of the State," to which he rendered "constant unwavering laborious service."[46] He rarely took a vacation from matters of state; he was one of the master toilers in world history. From Stoic teaching of the "assigned post" and Roman military language he formulated the political concept of his mission as *statio principis* (the ruler's post),[47] his legacy to all future emperors. Whether we view him as fulfilling strong ego needs or as proceeding out of a principled sense of public duty, Augustus was a devoted, untiring public servant with an enormous capacity for work. Painstaking, meticulous, omnipresent, he was constantly involved in decision making, legislation, and administration, even in the smallest details, in all spheres: military, political, religious, economic, social, cultural. Cassius Dio put the following words into Augustus's mouth: "I have devoted myself unstintingly to you in all circumstances. . . . From all this I have derived no gain for myself."[48] In the dedication of his work on architecture, composed early in Augustus's principate, Vitruvius wrote: "I observe that you are concerned not only for the common life of all but also for the constitution of the state."[49] In 22 B.C., in the treason trial of Marcus Primus, Augustus attended the trial though he was not summoned to testify. When asked bluntly by Primus's attorney why he was present, Augustus replied, "In the public interest."[50] Augustus's claim of the public interest (*rei publicae causa*) is thus recorded by the jurist Paulus:

> The deified Augustus preferred that this [specific matter] be arranged through himself. . . . For he believed that the protection of the safety of the state devolved on no one more than the emperor, and that no one else was adequate for this matter.[51]

In 4 B.C., at the age of sixty, when he communicated a decree of the Senate to the Province of Crete-Cyrene, he added:

> Since it affects the welfare of the allies of the Roman people, and so that it may be known to all for whom I have a care, I decided to send it into all the provinces. From this it will be evident to all the inhabitants of the provinces how much I and the Senate are concerned that none of our subjects should suffer any impropriety.[52]

Augustus made gestures of refusal of power, but it is clear that he never seriously contemplated resigning power and retiring to private life. In the *Res Gestae* (ch. 6), he asserts that he "accepted no office contrary to the ancestral tradition." In 22 B.C., after he stepped down from the consulship (his eleventh, held nine years in a row), the urban plebs in a season of great distress in Rome took to the streets to urge the Senate to appoint him dictator for life. He thereupon made a dramatic appearance before the people: he went down on his knees before them,

and bared his breast, in token of readiness to die rather than accept such an office. Augustus acted here in all sincerity regarding the dictatorship, which had
been fatal to Caesar, even though we know that the gesture of refusal of power
was a traditional *topos* associated with the *vir bonus*.[53] The year before, in 23 B.C.,
when he was almost fatally ill, he is said to have contemplated resigning his authority. "But reconsidering that as a private person he would not be without danger, and that the State would thus be entrusted rashly to the judgment of the
masses, he continued to maintain his hold on power."[54] Seneca writes that
Augustus constantly prayed for a rest and vacation from affairs of state, and for
the enjoyment of leisure, and he cites a letter sent by Augustus to the Senate in
which he expressed his expectation that if he retired he would not be diminished
in high status and his fame would remain unimpaired. Then he added,

> But these matters turn on actual deeds rather than promises that one can
> make. However, the yearning for that most hoped for time for me had so
> transported me that, since the actual joy is still delayed, I get some pleasure
> just out of the charm of the words.[55]

The whimsy is obvious, for Augustus never seriously contemplated stepping
down from his supreme status to a lower one. In 2 B.C., when he was hailed *Pater
Patriae*, he said, "Having achieved my highest hopes, Senators, what more do I
have to pray for to the immortal gods but that I may retain this consensus of yours
to the very end of my life."[56] In his old age, when he suffered a number of severe
setbacks (about A.D. 6), he did not offer to resign but, in a fit of depression, re-
solved on suicide by starvation.[57]

Augustus's inability to dissociate himself from his hold on power, originating
in his ego needs, was in time rationalized as society's need for himself as indispensable agent of the stability of the exemplary state he had created. In an edict,
he once proclaimed in memorable words:

> May it be granted to me to set the state firm in its place, safe and sound,
> and to reap the reward I aspire to from this, namely, that I be known as the
> author of the best type of government, and that when I die I may take with
> me the hope that the foundations of the government I have laid will remain
> in their original form.[58]

Augustus's conception of himself as "first servant of the state," as wholly dedicated to society's needs, is reflected in his enormous expenditures for public purposes out of his own vast private fortune, especially on distributions of food, on
games and spectacles, public buildings and public works, largesses to the people
of Rome, and donations and bonuses to the soldiers.[59] Moreover, since considerable sums of money tended to concentrate in his hands through legacies,[60] he
served as a sort of economic conduit for channeling the private wealth of others
into public uses. In his will he declared that he had little of his own wealth left at
the end of his life, having spent most of it *in rem publicam*. There is no reason to
doubt this. "In private life poor, in public life rich," wrote Cassius Dio of him.[61]

In keeeping with his dedication to public interests, throughout his regime Augustus maintained a relatively frugal lifestyle: his pleasures, food, and dress were simple and without ostentation, and he muted ceremonial gestures and did not give in to the pageantry of power. His personal home on the Palatine was not a "palace," though hardly as small as conventionally described; we now know that his property on the Palatine was indeed vast in extent. In contrast with the luxurious estates of many of his contemporaries, his villas were modest retreats.[62]

Despite his need for uninhibited power and constant approbation throughout his life, Augustus conceived of himself as cautious and low-key. His aversion to eccentricity and flamboyance in himself and others, and his calculating nature are revealed by his obsession with the Greek topos σπεῦδε βραδέως (in Latin *festina lente*, "Make haste slowly"), which he used over and over again; and he was prone also to quote Euripides (*Phoenissae* 599) that "A cautious general is better than a rash one."[63] Caution and prudence were also Augustus's guidelines as a speaker: he never spoke extemporaneously. It was his practice to read everything from a carefully prepared speech, whether before the Senate or the people or soldiers. In important private conversations (even, it is said, with his wife Livia) he spoke with a written text before him, "so that he might not say more or less."[64]

Similarly, in confronting the possibility of death, Augustus betrayed his characteristic caution and calculation. Whereas Caesar's rhythm was fast and intense, and he faced the danger of death with equanimity, Augustus, a sickly person, lived cautiously, avoiding dangers and undue strains.[65] At the age of about thirty-five he completed his mausoleum, in 28 B.C., Rome's largest monument of the time, erected in the very heart of the city. It is true that he had hastened to erect a grand Roman tomb for himself and his family as counterimage to the resplendent tomb of Antony and Cleopatra in Alexandria. But having made this political gesture that was valuable at the time, he was compelled to live within sight of his own tomb for more than forty years.[66]

Augustus lived to the age of seventy-six. He always hoped for a nonviolent, swift, and painless death (*euthanasia* was the term he used).[67] On his deathbed, having attained his wish, he asked his friends whether he had passed through the *mimus vitae* ("comedy of life") well, as if it were the proper time for them to applaud. His last words were to Livia: "Live mindful of our marriage, Livia, and farewell."[68] This was despite the fact that he must have endured emotional stress from the fact that their union had not produced a single child.

Augustus's characteristic restraint and moderation are also revealed by his response to the outpouring of divine honors to him throughout the empire, especially in the eastern provinces. Augustus studiously adhered to the Roman tradition that forbade public worship of a living person. Private worship of him as a god burgeoned, and formal cults of Augustus were established in many places. But, in a policy set down in 30–29 B.C., first in the Province of Asia, official authorization was granted only to temples jointly of the goddess Roma and Augustus as a mortal;[69] and as an instrument of policy he permitted, even encouraged, worship of his *genius* (protecting spirit of a Roman *paterfamilias*) in the West. In Augustus's own conception of himself, there was never any question that distance between himself and the gods should be maintained, and that his proper role was that of mortal mediator between the divine and human spheres.[70] It is noteworthy that in the *Res Gestae* he makes no claim to divine honors. Tiberius followed consciously the model of Augustus in rejecting divine honors. The words Tacitus gives to Tiberius in A.D. 25 might well have been spoken by Augustus:

> You are my witnesses, members of the Senate, that I am a mortal and per-form human functions, and am content to fill the role of *princeps*. And I desire posterity to remember me thus. They will pay tribute to my memory enough, and more than enough, if they deem me worthy of my ancestors, provident for your interests, firm in dangers, not timid in the face of attacks I encounter in the public interest. These will be my temples in your hearts, these my fairest and most enduring images.[71]

"Fame is the spur" that drove Augustus in his passion to leave his mark on history, so that he might win the immortality of glory in the memory of future generations. While there were doubtless not a few among his contemporaries who in fantasy condemned him to *damnatio memoriae*, Augustus himself was serenely confident that posterity would accord him fame and long-lasting *laudatio memoriae*. He was explicitly aware that he was handing down many memorials of himself[72] in his constitutional arrangements, institutional reforms, public works. Vitruvius, early in the principate, put it thus:

> I have observed that you have built many structures and are now building, and that in the future you will make provision for public and private build-ings conformable to the grandeur of your achievements, so that they may be a legacy to the memory of posterity.[73]

In the great national "Hall of Fame" that he dedicated in 2 B.C. in the new Forum Augustum, Augustus unveiled a massive portrait gallery of the most famous Roman *triumphatores* (each with inscription detailing his achievements). Pride of place was given, however, to the Julian family: to Caesar, Romulus, and Aeneas, all *divi* (deified persons). But the grandest figure in the Forum Augustum was Augustus himself, resplendent as *triumphator* on a four-horse chariot. There could be no doubt that the intention was to demonstrate that the Julian family surpassed all others, and that Augustus himself eclipsed all of his predecessors.[74] "Compare," the panorama suggested, "let posterity judge." In an edict he issued simultaneously, he proclaimed: "I have devised this so that by their lives as role models, both I, so long as I live, and the leaders of later times may be exactingly judged by the citizens."[75] While this grandiose display of Roman achievement honored only the great military leaders (documenting, as it were, the great Temple of Mars in the Forum), the *Res Gestae*, set up on bronze tablets before his mausoleum in A.D. 14, after his death, gave a more comprehensive statement of his conception of his unparal-leled contributions to Rome.

Indeed, Augustus recognized that his temperament was preeminently civilian, despite his quest for military éclat. His forte was that of mediator, between gods and men, past and future, Rome and Italy with the rest of the empire. We should concede to him that, for all his passion for power and yearning for fame and glory, Augustus was not cunningly dishonest, deceitful, or hypocritical, as some have depicted him, but rather basically sincere in his aims and methods.[76] It is doubtful that he distinguished between the young, ruthless, power-hungry Octavian and the benevolent statesman Augustus. His personal ego needs were inextricably fused with the work he did in tidying up the Mediterranean world, and moderating and holding in balance the great tensions of the times.

Augustus would have conceded that without the favor of Julius Caesar and the legacy of his name, his own ambitions would have come to naught. He surely understood that *fortuna*, his many loyal helpers, and his control over vast wealth all contributed greatly to his success. Though "the assemblage of qualities and capacities that made up his personality are not such as to strike the imagination of the world,"[77] he remains one of the *grands hommes politiques* in world history. Yet we may still applaud Mommsen's verdict that "Augustus habe mit Geschick den grosser Mann gespielt, ohne selbst gross zu sein"[78] (Augustus adroitly played the role of the great man without himself being great).

6

Cassius Dio's *History of Rome*: From Republic to Principate

IN A BUOYANT ASIDE AS HE APPROACHED THE END OF HIS LABORS, Cassius Dio expressed the hope that in his work he was leaving a legacy for the future, and that his *History*, the magnum opus to which he had devoted twenty-two years of his life, would "survive and never lose its lustre" (72.23.4). No one will deny that Dio stands in the shade of his illustrious predecessors—Herodotus, Thucydides, Polybius, Livy, Tacitus—but for many periods and aspects of the history of Rome he remains an indispensable resource, a veritable quarry for historians. This is especially true for the years he treated in books 49–52, that is, 36–29 B.C. One of the early moderns who appreciated Dio's value for the history of the times of Augustus was East Apthorp: "Dio Cassius connects the history of the republic with that of the empire. He has the merit and utility . . . of combining the interrupted narrations of Velleius, Tacitus, Herodian, and the Augustan history, in one copious detail. No other historian has given us so ample and methodical a recital of that celebrated era, the Augustan age."[1]

To appreciate the importance of Dio's account of the transition from republic to principate and of the Age of Augustus, consider how lacking our understanding would be if we did not have his *History*, how random and discontinuous would be our knowledge of the political, constitutional, and military history of this epochal period in the long annals of Rome, indeed of world history. Beset though Dio's work is with problems of fact, chronology, and interpretation, his account is "le plus prodigue en renseignements, vulnérable aux critiques"[2]—and remains indispensable.

Dio's shortcomings and limitations are patent: bookishness, rhetorical extravagances, penchant for patterned antitheses, lack of expertise in military strategy and tactics, proneness to stereotypical descriptions of battles and sieges, studied imitation of predecessors, especially Thucydides, simplistic economics, chronological displacements, anachronisms retrojected for the structuring of paradigms and parallels as edification for his own perilous times. Despite his experience and stature in Roman administration, he could even suffer from lapses of knowledge of law.[3]

The modern historian of Rome, dependent as he often is on Dio, must constantly be wary of his selection of events, his ordering of them, and his judgments on them. These patterns were, in varying degree, the outcome of his historiographical methods and literary style, the techniques and conceptions of the Greco-Roman historiographic tradition that he inherited, and his relationship to the sources he drew upon and compressed.[4] If one must always tread warily in relying on the ancient historians, this is surely true of Dio's work. For strewn throughout the vast fields of useful information there are many traps for the incautious.

But Dio was not, it needs to be emphasized, a mere excerptor, epitomist, or scissors-and-paste historian: he imposed upon the Roman past his own ideological perspectives. It is indeed indispensable to understand both his ideological commitments and his utilitarian purposes. As Gabba has cautioned, while Dio's work "is fundamental to an understanding of the Augustan Principate," for Dio "the past is important insofar as it survives in the present"—for its enrichment of the understanding of his own times.[5]

In order to discern the extent to which Dio was a creative thinker and writer, we must first scrutinize the sources he depended upon and the way he used them for his own purposes in the *History*.

DIO'S SOURCES FOR BOOKS 49–52

Millar had little confidence that it would be possible to discover the range and pattern of Dio's pool of sources and his selection, use, and manipulation of them for the enlightenment of his own times.[6] His sources, as Millar says, were surely very varied, and there can be little doubt that the purposes, partisan positions, tone, and style of his sources for books 49–52 filtered through to his own history. Unfortunately, however, Dio has left us largely in the dark regarding the precise sources he used. Only once in this section does he cite a source by name: ὡς μὲν αὐτὸς ὁ Ὀκτάουιος γράφει.[7] With the lost works of the leading contemporary historical writers for the period from 36 to the end of 29 B.C.—for example, the autobiographies of Augustus and Agrippa (and perhaps Maecenas), the history of Aufidius Bassus (though we cannot be certain that he reached back to the early years of Augustus's reign), and Livy's books 129–133 (the text of which in the *Periochae* is exiguous)—we are reduced to tenuous conjectures that do not convince. Moreover, Dio did not leave us a theoretical statement of principles to guide us to his preferences among specific authorities.[8] Nevertheless, Dio tells us (frag. 1.2) that, while he read almost everything written about his subject, he has set down in his *History* only selected matters: < Ἀνέγνων μὲν> πάντα ὡς εἰπεῖν τὰ περὶ αὐτῶν τισι γεγραμμένα, συνέγραψα δὲ οὐ πάντα ἀλλ' ὅσα ἐξέκρινα.

While he was writing for Greek readers in the East, in Dio's *History* Roman sources appear to predominate. This caused Dio problems in terminology, dating, and communication of Roman value patterns. All these factors in transmission from his sources constantly demand from the reader caution in the use of his *History*.[9]

While it is generally recognized that it is fruitless to determine the source or sources Dio used for books 49–50 (see the introduction to book 49), the *communis opinio* is that for books 51–52 Dio relied principally on Livy.[10] Implicit in this view that Livy was Dio's principal source for the early principate is the corollary that Livy was a pro-Augustan writer. Such a conception of Livy, however, is over-stated and requires considerable qualification.[11] More important here, the view that Dio followed Livy has also tended to be overstated (especially by Levi), and is indeed vulnerable for lack of conclusive probative support.[12] In fact, it is Manuwald's definitive conclusion, based on his superbly detailed comparative analysis of Livy's *Periochae* and Dio for books 45–56, that Livy was *not* one of Dio's sources at all.[13] Moreover, Manuwald makes a strong case for his conviction that, while Livy, Florus, Eutropius, and Orosius put Octavian in the right in his struggles with his fellow triumvirs, Dio does not follow a source or sources favorable to Octavian. For in keeping with his view that a contest for sole power was inevi-table, Dio portrays all three triumvirs as equally driven by *cupido dominandi* (see the introduction to book 50).

At the beginning of the principate there is an obvious shift in Dio's tone to one more favorable to Octavian. This has led to the theory, first proposed by Schwartz,[14] that beginning with book 51 Dio abandoned Livy and went over to some annalis-tic writer of the early principate sympathetic to Augustus.[15] This theory, it cannot be emphasized strongly enough, is pure conjecture.[16]

Millar considers that Dio used "various and complex" sources,[17] thus reverting to a view antedating the unity theory of Schwartz and Levi, namely that Dio in his note taking plundered multiple sources randomly.[18] Parallels between Dio and Plutarch can be demonstrated (especially in the life of Antony), but it is not likely that Dio used Plutarch directly.[19] Similarly, the parallels between Dio's treatment of Augustus and Suetonius's life of him do not justify a commonly held earlier position that Dio used Suetonius directly as a source—a view now generally re-jected. Dio may have drawn on Suetonius indirectly, or it is possible that Dio and Suetonius used the same source.[20] Finally, we cannot prove that Dio used either Cremutius Cordus or Aufidius Bassus as a source.[21]

The suggestion has been made, by Andersen,[22] that Dio had access to a col-lection that gathered together the various honors and powers granted to both Julius Caesar and Augustus. Also not to be excluded is the possibility that Dio had at hand a collection of rhetorical topoi and *florilegia* readily available to the reading public in the Roman Empire.

However speculative the matter of Dio's actual sources is, there is no doubt that Dio, like Livy, was a "book historian." He did not have recourse to inscrip-tions; above all, he appears to have had no knowledge of Augustus's *Res Gestae*, for he is, in some details, patently at variance with the testimony in "the queen of Latin inscriptions."[23]

DIO'S METHODS AND STYLE

It is manifest that, in form and content, Dio's *History* is a selective pastiche, a blend of the information, tones, and prejudices of his sources, his own marshaling of events and judgments, and his personal interests as a political partisan in the early third century. It is, indeed, in books 51–56, more than anywhere else in his work, that Dio's personal imprint is most marked.[24] It is clear that Dio was not a slavish imitator of his sources. Independence of judgment both in the sources he chose to resort to and in his manipulation of them can be demonstrated.[25] He imposed his own persona and was motivated by his own general conception of events.[26] In fact, Dio occasionally provides evidence of this: he states, for example (53.21.1), that he will limit his account of Augustus's legislation to whatever has a bearing on his history: ὅσα τῇ συγγραφῇ πρόσφορά ἐστι; and that, in general, οὐδὲν δὲ δέομαι καθ᾽ ἕκαστον ἀκριβῶς ἐπεξιέναι ("I do not need to go into precise details"). And elsewhere he says that he will give his own opinion (τῆς ἐμῆς δοξασίας), whenever he is able, from the abundant evidence he has gathered from his reading, from hearsay, and from personal observation, with judgments that "do not follow the common report" (53.19.6: ἄλλο τι μᾶλλον ἢ τὸ θρυλούμενον). And he is especially cautious about the contents of official sources under the principate (53.19.4: "nearly everything is reported somewhat differently from what actually occurs," πάντα δέ ὡς εἰπεῖν ἄλλως πως ἢ ὡς πράττεται διαθροεῖται). It is instructive to read that Dio realized that it was difficult to know much about so extensive an empire or to attain accuracy on such a large number of events.[27] We need to recognize that, as in much of imperial historiography, for Dio the capital was the focal point, especially the tensions between *princeps* and Senate, and that caution is wise when Dio relates events as an "eyewitness."[28]

Dio's rationale for his purposeful selection from his sources was his consuming concern with the general tendencies and momentous events of the early third century. His aim was, in general, a paraenetic one for his own age. Though he is formally an annalist in method, Dio often violates strict chronological order when it suits some particular purpose. He has no compunction about such chronological misplacements, shifting events out of sequence, even from one year to another, either to gain a special emphasis thereby, or for convenience in gathering together related events and data.[29] For his purpose was not historical truth but political and moral instruction.

Thus one of Dio's principles of selection and emphasis is consciously (though not expressly) analogical. He is constantly seeking for and structuring models from the end of the Republic and the early principate (e.g., 49.4.1–4n, 16.1n; 51.2.1n) to support his own views of contemporary institutions and individuals, especially regarding the character of the monarchy of the third century and the status and power of his own social class. It is, accordingly, necessary to be on guard against Dio's many anachronisms. Further, beginning with books 51–52 Dio narrows his focus, thus conforming to the tendencies of imperial historiography: he shifts to a biographical emphasis, with the emperor at the center of events, as more appropriate to the reality of the concentration of power in the empire.[30] His eyes are rarely turned away from Octavian in these books.

In style and structure, moreover, Dio exhibits a distinctively characteristic antithetical manner in books 49–52, as elsewhere also (e.g., see the introduction to 49.2.1–8.4 and the introduction to 49.19.1–22.3; 51.7.2–7n), both for dramatic effect and to give trenchant emphasis to some personal viewpoint. For this purpose he sometimes elevates to undue prominence insignificant events of the Augustan Age, or wrenches them from their proper chronological order.

In Cassius Dio we find the victory of the Thucydidean-Polybian model advocated by Lucian in "How to Write History," as reaction to the Herodotean model followed by the historiographers of the second century (e.g., Appian and Arrian).[31] Dio's well-known predilection for Thucydides as a model goes far beyond the archaizing tendencies of his own times. As an imitator of Thucydides, he not only frequently extracts Thucydidean language, but at times stylizes events on Thucydidean models. More important, Dio's own conception of human nature—that self-interest and pragmatic purposes, not altruism and idealism, prevail—is similar to that of Thucydides. Dio seeks to imitate Thucydidean realism in dealing with events and personalities, and, like his great predecessor, emphasizes the contrast between appearance and reality.[32]

Though a bicultural native of Bithynia, Dio was, as Gibbon noted, not a Greek but a Roman. But he was the product of the Second Sophistic movement that flourished in his native land, and his history, in the dominant language of the eastern provinces of the empire, was directed to the educated elite there.[33]

ON THE DATE OF COMPOSITION OF BOOKS 49–52

Efforts to date the composition of Dio's *History* from internal evidence have yielded a variety of views. T. D. Barnes has conveniently recorded the documentation for the major scholarly theories to date.[34] Gabba and Millar argued for an early date of composition, before Severus Alexander, with the work completed no later than 218 or 219; Vrind for a period not before 201–223, with the final form at the beginning of the reign of Severus Alexander. Later dates, 212–234, have recently been proposed by Letta, with books 38–55 composed in 229–230. Barnes's reassessment of the evidence has yielded a late date also. His conclusion is that the composition took definite shape in the reign of Severus Alexander, with dates (at the earliest) of 211–220 for the ten years of collecting materials, and 220–231 for the twelve years of composition. Barnes holds that the early books of Dio were written not before 220, book 49 in its final form no earlier than ca. 225, and book 52 after 223.[35]

It seems doubtful that we can determine the dates of composition. From Dio's statement that he devoted ten years to collecting the material and twelve years to composition, we cannot proceed with the understanding that he meant twenty-two consecutive years. Eisman's proposal that Dio's *History* was published posthumously has merit.[36] It may not have seen the light of day until after the death of Severus Alexander.

DIO AND AUGUSTUS

With book 51 Dio enters an epoch of Roman history that he treats with increased scale. Books 49–50 cover a bit more than five years, books 51–52 about two years (from the battle of Actium to the autumn of 29), and the four books devoted to the rest of the reign of Augustus (books 53–56) span more than forty years. Beginning with book 51 he proceeds with heightened certainty and sympathy, for Dio is a "loyaler Anhänger der Monarchie."[37]

The shift to a favorable evaluation of Octavian has been variously placed: at the beginning of book 51 (after the victory at Actium), at the beginning of book 53 (the abolition of the residues of the triumvirate), and at 53.17–19 (the settlement of 27 B.C.). Some surmise that Dio then turned to a new, pro-Augustan source. There is greater merit in the view that the shift in tone resulted from his own fervent reaction to the inception of the monarchy, a system to which he was ideologically committed but which he saw was in process of substantive transformation in the third century.

The Augustan system represented for Dio the model of Roman monarchy, in the person of Augustus as *princeps* and in the constitutional and social modalities created by Augustus as the normative form. In his eyes the principate attained more or less completed form under the first *princeps*.[38] Deeply troubled about his own times, Dio feared that the very existence of the constitutionally legitimized monarchy was threatened. Moreover, he studied the newly founded monarchy from the viewpoint of a defender of the imperial aristocracy of the third century, which was apprehensive about its status and feared displacement from below.[39] Dio thus strives to mold his account of the principate of Augustus so as to emphasize its continuity into his own times.[40] Assessing the Severan monarchy and contemporary issues by the yardsticks of the "basic" Augustan monarchy and the principate of Marcus Aurelius as a sort of golden-age acme, and viewing them from his own partisan position, he imports anachronisms into the early principate and at the same time understates the historical evolutionary character of both the Augustan system and later imperial developments. Thus unhistorical information, ambiguities, and contradictions that do not have their origins in the varying views of his sources, appear time and time again in books 51–52.[41] Accordingly, in the absence of works that, by revealing how contemporaries viewed the early principate, would have served as a corrective, we must constantly read Dio with one eye on the third century.

Equally significant, Dio's treatment of Octavian himself in books 51–52, though favorable, does not conform to an official version of the new regime vigorously publicized in Augustus's time. In previous books (see the ntroduction to book 50) Dio had depicted the rising heir of Julius Caesar as ambitious, driven by power, never faltering in his aspirations for monarchy, unscrupulous and cruel in his march to sole power. But with the turning point of the battle of Actium, Dio's image of Octavian takes on a solemn and princely form. True, he does not entirely suppress unfavorable aspects of Octavian's actions, which he found in his sources (some of which were antagonistic toward Octavian, some indeed intensely hostile). But adverse statements and innuendoes are now sharply reduced in Dio's account. We find an ambivalent acceptance of Octavian, criticism together with acknowledgment of his constitutionalism, moderation, superb management, and great achievements.[42]

This double-edged treatment of the first *princeps*[43] has been masterfully elucidated by Manuwald's acute analysis of Dio's conception of Augustus. Dio presents *Augustus* in general in a favorable light, as imperial role model. Yet he does not, either in his selection of sources or in his presentation, adhere to an official version of events, but rather at times follows some pro-republican tradition critical of *Octavian*. Dio does not exculpate Octavian for his revolutionary ruthlessness. This negative view of Octavian in his march to power stems from Dio's understanding of Realpolitik in high human affairs. His model in this regard was Thucydides, and he found the Thucydidean view of human nature and political behavior confirmed by observation of events and historical figures in his own time. Dio distrusts official propaganda (more rampant under the principate, as he notes at 53.19.3), and he seeks through his *History* to unmask the mighty, as a lesson for his own times and the future.[44]

DIO AND THE THIRD CENTURY

Dio brought to his task as historian the education and experience of a well-informed, sophisticated senator with a long career in diversified posts in the imperial administration. He moved in the highest circles of Roman government and society under seven emperors, from Commodus to Severus Alexander. In his *History* he assumed the role of self-appointed spokesman of the senatorial order of the third century, a time when, he lamented, the principate had taken an ominous turn "from a monarchy of gold to one of iron and rust" (71.36.4). While Livy looked back nostalgically to the earlier glories of the Roman republic, Dio's feet were solidly planted in his own times, and his mind was saturated with the political and intellectual predicaments of the third century. In the forefront were his concerns not only for the empire, but also for the Senatorial Order.

Dio was motivated by an intense awareness of the great crisis of the Roman Empire, and of a general transformation in process. To Dio history was a usable past that offered guidance to an understanding of the present.[45] And he strove to set forth his own predilections, in both explicit and implicit form, formulated with a strong ideological base.[46] An analysis of Dio's portrayal of the events of his own time shows that the major concerns in his thinking were the self-serving emperors contrasted with the ideal *princeps* in the shape of Marcus Aurelius; the corruption of the armies with money, and the indispensability of discipline in the army and loyalty to *princeps* and state; an aggressive foreign policy, military adventurism, and new annexations; the search for military glory and self-aggrandizement by the emperors (particularly by Septimius Severus), who cast in the dark the superior accomplishments of subordinates in the imperial service; fiscal irresponsibility; threats to the preeminence of the ruling class in the social and economic life of the state, and to the institutions that provided for their participation in the governance of the empire.[47]

In the parallels from the past that he both discerned and contrived, Dio doubtless had in mind well-known contemporaries, though it is difficult for us now to venture to identify the figures.[48] It is fair to say that Dio's *History* was a sort of *histoire à clef*.

7

In Praise of Cassius Dio

IN USING CASSIUS DIO'S *HISTORY OF ROME* TO HELP US RECON-struct the course of events, we are so much on the *qui vive* to single out defects, and to point the finger at him when he nods, misinterprets, or distorts that we tend to slight or pass by the solid contributions he often makes to our knowledge. Greater alertness to his virtues as an historian, to the valuable, sometimes unique interpretations and information he provides, is needed to achieve a more balanced perception of Dio's work.

Particularly gratifying is the fact that we possess so much of the massive achieve-ment of the twenty-two-year labors of a member of the highest elite class of the Roman Empire, a senator with long, varied experience in the imperial adminis-tration. He has left us continuous and connected narrative (with chronological flow) for many periods from the end of the Republic to the middle of the third century A.D. And for the half century after Marcus Aurelius's reign we are fortu-nate to have an eyewitness account based on personal participation in many of the events. Dio's *History* is indeed our principal source for the Severan Age, how-ever filtered and prejudiced it may be.

In books 49 to 52, covering the years 36 through 29 B.C., more than a few de-tails and sections merit our appreciative attention. A loyal supporter of monar-chy, he had to deal credibly with numerous Roman leaders in the last decades of the Republic competing for glory and power under republican constitutional and legal institutions. Moreover, because he judged the Augustan monarchy as the normative form of the principate, he did not perceive the tentative and experi-mental nature of Augustus's constitutional arrangements, nor the evolutionary process through which the structure and modalities of the principate passed in the two centuries before his time.[1]

In his narrative of the transition from republic to monarchy in books 49 to 51, Dio's view is that Octavian triumphed not because of political, economic, and moral decay but through a decisive military victory, at Actium and in Egypt, which brought to a final end the long, disastrous conflict among the Roman dynasts. In essence, Dio also viewed the death of the Republic as brought about not by foreign problems and provincial unrest—both of which were formidable—but by the leading Roman antagonists themselves. No other extant source sought to distinguish the "real" from the professed motives of Octavian and Antony so relentlessly.[2] In threading his way through the maze of fierce, unsavory propaganda on both sides, whose motifs have left their mark indelibly on the literature of the times and of subsequent centuries, Dio staked out his personal interpretation: he sketched out unfavorable images of both Octavian and Antony in the struggle for power.[3]

In book 49 one of the dominant themes is the working of "human nature" on the relationship between those in high power and their subordinates. Dio attributes to Agrippa the view (49.4. 2–4) that the men who expect to survive should reserve the successes for the ones superior to them. They themselves should undertake the more difficult tasks, stopping short of complete success, for those in positions of power do not want anyone to be superior to them.[4] As if to illustrate this, Dio highlights, with implicit irony, the exploits of Marcus Agrippa and Publius Ventidius, both of whom achieved greater military successes than the triumvirs Octavian and Antony. Official policy later was to present Agrippa's subordinate role consistently as ideal *adiutor imperil*; Dio, however, documents extensively Agrippa's brilliant victories in the Sicilian War and at the battle of Actium.[5] In working out this theme of the role and fate of subordinates, Dio has given us an extremely valuable account of the spectacular exploits of the phenomenal Publius Ventidius, the first to celebrate a triumph over the Parthians, the climax of the brilliant career of this *novus homo*. By contrast with the more reserved Agrippa, Ventidius was relieved of his command in the East by Antony after his dazzling military successes—just before the debacle of Antony's own campaign against the Parthians.[6]

Further, Ventidius's career, like Agrippa's, served Dio as an historic paradigm of social mobility for his own shifting times that were bringing to the fore men of equestrian and plebeian rank.[7] Thus it would appear that, while Dio was anxiously protective of the privileges and status of the Senatorial Order, he recognized the claims of merit everywhere for the protection and administration of the empire. Finally, to underscore the valuable role of subordinates (like himself under the Severan dynasty), Dio put together an account of the failure of Antony's Parthian campaign in 36 B.C. that is highly prejudiced. Tainted by Octavian's propaganda, which falsified Antony's policies, strategy, and operational tactics, Dio's portrayal of Antony (unlike Plutarch's) is openly hostile to Antony and oversimplifies situations to magnify his incompetence.[8]

With regard to the battle of Actium in book 50, the dramatic "flight" of Antony and Cleopatra (50.15.1–4) handed the propagandists of Octavian a field day.[9] Despite this spate of anti-Cleopatra and anti-Antony literature, Dio's account of the event is the soundest interpretation we have of what happened at Actium. Antony was battle-ready in April of 31 B.C. But months passed in an apparent stalemate, and of these months we know nothing—until late August. Now Dio's conception of Antony's strategy is as follows: realizing finally that he was entrapped in the Ambracian Gulf, Antony skillfully planned to break out of the blockade, salvage the bulk of his forces, and reorganize in Egypt. The alternative view (held by Ferrabino and T. Rice Holmes) is that the flight was not prearranged, but that Antony planned fight, not flight, and that when he perceived himself betrayed by Cleopatra and her squadron of sixty ships, he followed her out of weakness. The facts are as follows: 1) Antony was very early successfully besieged by Octavian's fleet; 2) serious illness (dysentery, malaria) had afflicted his troops; 3) his lines of communication with his supply bases had been effectively cut by Agrippa; 4) numerous officers and troops had deserted. Accordingly, as Dio reports, a high council in Antony's headquarters decided to break out of the blockade—at an acceptable cost. It is to Dio's credit to have thus reported the battle, for the "flight" interpretation is deeply imbedded in most of sources as a result of anti-Cleopatra propaganda.[10]

With regard to the decree of *damnatio memoriae* enacted against Antony (51.19.3–5), Dio dates its promulgation before Antony's death, which took place on 1 August 30 B.C. In recording this order of events Dio is more credible than Plutarch, who dates the decree in the suffect consulship of Cicero's son Marcus— that is, to between 13 September and 30 November. Plutarch was tempted to displace it here by the value of the dramatic effect, so as to highlight the ironic justice played out against the great orator's mortal enemy.[11] Not that Dio himself was not prone to such chronological displacements. For example, he could not resist the temptation to give a specific date for the death of Sextus Pompey (49.18.6)—toward the end of 35 B.C.—because of the irony that one of the consuls then was a certain (unrelated) Sextus Pompey.[12]

In 51.23.2–27.2, Dio narrates in great detail the masterful operations of M. Licinius Crassus (the triumvir's grandson) against the Thracians and Getae. In his treatment of the campaign by Crassus in this region north of Macedonia as far as the Danube River, he provides information that is precious and unique, though it is true that we lack any controls because the events are not related in other sources. His motive in letting himself go in such detail about this area resulted from his special interest in the region, for he had been governor of Upper Pannonia, and had detailed personal knowledge of the terrain and the peoples.[13]

With regard to the vexing problem of the tribunician power of Octavian/ Augustus, Dio's treatment (51.21.19.6–7; 53.32.5) is more credible than the other principal source, Appian. The latter states that he received full tribunician power for life in 36 B.C.—clearly wrong. Augustus himself wrote (*RGDA* 10.1) that there were two stages involved: 1) *sacrosanctitas* and 2) full tribunician power. Dio had difficulty dating Octavian's acquisition of tribunician power. Because he conceived of the principate/monarchy as beginning sometime between 31 and 29 B.C. he opted for 30 B.C. for full tribunician power. Still, Dio was closer *to* the truth in his own "stage" presentation. He recorded *sacrosanctitas* and *ius subselli* (right to a seat on the tribunician bench in the Senate) in 36 B.C., then *ius auxilii* in 30 B.C., and finally regularization on annual basis of tribunician power in 23 B.C.[14]

In book 52 Dio departed from his general annalistic scheme to spread over almost the entire book the speeches of Agrippa and Maecenas before Octavian in 29 B.C. on the theme of "Whither Rome." Though the topic of the antithetical speeches—republic and tyranny versus monarchy—was a perennial theme in the rhetorical schools and in ancient historians from Herodotus on, Maecenas's speech takes its place as a prime document in Roman history. It is invaluable not only because it throws light on Dio's own political thinking and methods, but because it is the only theoretical analysis of Roman government and society from the third century. And it gives us profound insights into the mind and hopes of a distinguished senator of the time of the Severi.[15]

Maecenas's speech does not provide a clear definition of the principate at its inception and is not sensitive to the institutional gradualism and experimentation of Augustus. But it is the authentic voice of Dio himself, and embodies the essence of his thinking about the empire. He thus brings us in close touch with the views of a member of the highest elite of the empire, the expertise of a Roman senator with decades of experience, and an overview of his troubled concerns for the empire and his social class, threatened as they were by the upheavals of the time and by the stresses and changes under the Severi. It represents, moreover, the thought of a thoroughly Romanized Greek whose thinking was not merely bicultural but truly "ecumenical" as a result of the interplay between the Greek and Roman languages and cultures that had been going on for centuries, especially since Augustus's time.

Now the speech of Maecenas contains, in part, a summation of the political and social bases of the principate, mingling, in an undifferentiated manner, leading aspects of the evolution of the principate in the first two centuries. More important, it contains a program for reform in a series of vigorous proposals that addressed the needs of the empire in his own time. In general, they appear to be not mere visionary proposals, but formulations of tendencies in Dio's own time that were being discussed by thoughtful people. It is especially striking that his reform proposals take the form of a general plea for universalism: reform of finance and taxation of all forms of property, and the renewed concept of installment payments of the amount of the tax bill; uniformity in administration, including the concept—ahead of its time—of dividing the empire, including Italy, into smaller districts; and uniformity in the structure and hierarchy of the imperial bureaucracy.[16]

"Whence the money?" is Dio's cry. Where might money for running the Empire come from? The massive expenditures on the soldiers motivated Dio's extraordinary proposal here (never implemented, of course) that all imperial properties (especially the vast landed estates of the crown) be sold off to private owners, and that the capital generated be lent out at interest—a revolutionary concept. Dio was partly influenced by the crisis in agriculture in the time of the Severi. Under Dio's plan, public lands would be sold to small and medium cultivators, with the state acting as a sort of agrarian credit bank providing large agricultural credits at low interest.[17]

The fiscal irresponsibility and capital confiscations of Commodus and Caracalla had undermined the economic stability and confidence of the upper classes. Dio here (52.28.3–30.8) next proposes new ways to spread the burdens of taxation so as to ease the drain on the wealth of the large landed proprietors. His solution is again revolutionary: universal, uniform taxation on all forms of property, and plugging of the loopholes. To curb the vast unproductive expenditures of the empire, he suggested reducing or eliminating benefactions to towns and individuals, festivals, and unnecessary public construction, all of which contributed to the great economic burdens of the cities; halting the proliferation of public games; and abolishing chariot races in all cities except Rome (on economic grounds, though, he adds as a sweetener that there was a great need to reserve the best horses for the military).[18]

His plea for monetary uniformity (52.30.9–10) is especially interesting. He proposed the abolition of separate coinage by cities of the empire (i.e., the so-called Greek imperials—bronze small coins—which were issued by about 530 separate mints). While no immediate action was taken, it is interesting to note that monetary pluralism did, in fact, come to an end shortly after Dio's death, because the economic chaos of the empire demanded it.[19]

There is also in the speech of Maecenas a remarkable section on emperor worship (52.35.1–6), in which Dio boldly expresses the long unspoken view of earlier Greek intellectuals who did not believe in the divinity of the living emperor and were opposed to such a formal cult. "True immortality," he writes here, "is won through virtue and good works. No one has ever become a god by a show of hands."[20]

In conclusion, I endorse Fergus Millar's verdict that, despite all our caviling about Dio's lapses, "neither the magnitude of the achievement nor Dio's personal contribution to the work should be underestimated."[21] Indeed, precisely because Dio is so vulnerable to criticism, we need to be especially alert to recognizing and documenting his sound contributions to our knowledge.[22]

8

Historian of the Classic World:
A Critique of Rostovtzeff

A SYSTEMATIC ANALYSIS AND CRITICAL APPRAISAL OF THE HIS-torical methodology of Michael Rostovtzeff, the foremost ancient historian of the past generation, has long been wanting.[1] For the range of "the most prolific career in the study of ancient history since Mommsen's"[2] has been so vast that few serious scholars in the field of ancient studies have not been influenced by Rostovtzeff's writings; and many future authors and students are likely to absorb his views and to solicit credence for them under warrant of his authority, even as V. Gordon Childe and Bertrand Russell have done.[3] Archeologist, papyrologist, preeminently the historian of social and economic evolution, whose scholarly labors bestride the past half century of classical research, Rostovtzeff made one of the most momentous contributions of modern times toward a scientific understanding of ancient Mediterranean civilization.

While professing an "innate dislike" for a theoretical analysis of the writing of history,[4] Rostovtzeff had, nevertheless, already undertaken to formulate some basic principles of his own philosophy of history: "history tends to become more and more a science, whose end is to define the laws under which the life of man develops, and the regular process by which one type of communal life is displaced by another."[5] Thus it is the historian's task to discover the laws of motion, the "kinetics," of human society. But, he maintains, the historian can never attain the detachment of the "pure" scientist because "history still remains a branch of literature . . . a task of a purely literary and artistic nature. . . . While becoming more and more a department of exact science, history cannot and must not lose its literary, and therefore individual, character."[6] This categorical reservation, which seems to grant the historian his personal preconceptions and prejudices, provides a clue to Rostovtzeff's method. For his historiography evinces an ever-present contradiction between the objective, critical, scientific approach and the subjective, a priori method. The latter strand in his thinking explains why the central theory of his *Social and Economic History of the Roman Empire* was characterized by Frank as "philosophized history," and by Turner as "present politics."[7]

The fundamental doctrine of Rostovtzeff's historical "intuition" is the view that "the ancient world experienced, on a smaller scale, the same process of development which we are experiencing now. . . . The modern development . . . differs from the ancient only in quantity and not in quality."[8] This basic axiom

of the absence of qualitative differences between the structure of ancient civilization and that of modern capitalist society permits a transposition to antiquity of the pattern and categories of the capitalist mode of production and
exchange, its class structure, ideological configurations, and special terminology. All of Rostovtzeff's major efforts in the field of social and economic history
are "modernized" with such concepts as capitalists, bourgeoisis, proletariat, factories, and mass production.[9]

True, under pressure of criticism and of the objective facts themselves, he re-
treated to a more moderate position. He conceded that the similarities between
ancient and modern economy are superficial, that "the general trend is utterly
different." Nevertheless, he continued to believe in a "peculiar" form of capitalism, an "infant capitalistic system," "more or less similar to modern capitalism,"
whose most highly developed state "may be compared, to a certain extent, with
the development of modern Europe in the seventeenth, eighteenth, and early
nineteenth centuries. And yet it is so utterly different."[10] His latest formulation
was that "the innovations in the organization of economic life . . . tended towards
what, with all reserve, we may call 'capitalism' (I hesitate to use a term whose
meaning is so much disputed)."[11]

To meet criticism of his use of the term capitalism to describe certain epochs
of classical society, he eventually gave precise definition to his basic conception:

> The term "capitalism," as applied to the economic evolution of the Ancient
> world, means, to my mind, a form of economic life which was based on
> economic freedom and individual economic activity and which was directed
> toward the free accumulation of capital in the hands of individuals and
> groups of individuals. It was founded on rationally organized agriculture and
> industry, functioning not to satisfy the needs of the producers of a local
> and restricted market, but for an indefinite market, and tending toward mass
> production of specialized goods.[12]

That some attributes of the capitalist system of production were present with
varying degrees of intensity in certain periods of antiquity is not to be denied.
Rostovtzeff's definition of ancient capitalism confounds the part with the whole.
It is certain that some of the factors detailed by him were either not to be found
in or were peripheral to the economic order of the ancient world, and that he ignores some of the decisive characteristics of capitalism, for example, the primacy
of the wage system and the profit motive, long-term planning and a scientific system of capital accounting, and an expanding market. Finally, the earliest form of
capitalism emerging at the twilight of the feudal epoch can be shown to be quali-
tatively different from all analogous manifestations in antiquity.[13]

It is apparent that Rostovtzeff often used the term "capitalism" in a much looser
fashion. Mere bigness, abstractly conceived without reference to the mode of
production, is at times associated in his thinking with the nature of capitalism.[14]
Equating capital with precious metals, money, and wealth, in an economically naive
fashion, he regards such magnates as the wealthy Roman senators of the first

century B.C., in whose hands were concentrated large amounts of landed property, as "great capitalists."[15] Further, he regards "capitalistic agriculture" both in Greece and in Italy as developing from the absorption of small peasant holdings into large landed estates. Moreover, since he is aware that the primacy of commerce and industry over agriculture is a precondition for the proper functioning of capitalism, the mere existence of relatively intense commercial and industrial enterprise in a society (as, for example, Athens, the Hellenistic world, and the early Roman Empire) is sufficient ground for classifying its economy as capitalistic, even though, as he is well aware, these activities were not the prevailing and decisive ones in the economic life but secondary and peripheral to agriculture.

Here the economic prejudices of Rostovtzeff run counter to the objective facts, scientifically established by himself, which reveal unmistakably that the foundation of economic life in all periods of antiquity for all classes was agriculture,[16] upon which rested the ancillary superstructure of commerce and industry. Yet, under the sway of his original preconception, he is convinced, intuitively, that the main source of wealth in the Hellenistic world and in the early Roman Empire was commercial enterprise, which, together with a flourishing industry, pumped capital into the land and introduced the methods of "scientific agriculture."[17] The well-known facts that agriculture was the predominant form of economic life, that only a small fraction of the wealth of the ancient world was invested in commerce and industry, and that the major part of income derived by the wealthy from all sources was expended by them upon luxury consumption, enlargement of landed holdings, unproductive private and public building construction, and warfare—facts which Rostovtzeff not only recognizes but demonstrates—preclude the possibility that ancient society was at any period of its development capitalistic in nature. For under capitalism the relationship between productive reinvestment of profits and unproductive expenditure is reversed. The unproductive consumption of wealth, characteristic of societies in which landed wealth is primary, acts as a fetter arresting the development of productive forces.

Rostovtzeff admits that handicraft production in the home or by individual artisans in small workshops for a restricted local market, at the order of the consumer, was the predominant form of industry. He is, moreover, convinced that commercial capitalism "which started at many times and in many places, and prevailed in large portions of the ancient world for comparatively long periods . . . never reached the economic stage in which we live, the stage of industrial capitalism,"[18] but he professes to see in the industrial evolution of antiquity the earliest known tendency toward mass production of standardized goods for an indefinite market. That this is a subjective view that does not accord with the known evidence is, in fact, finally conceded by Rostovtzeff.[19] Yet, he describes Greek industry in the fifth and fourth centuries B.C. as "modernized" and developing along "capitalistic" lines. And though he has modified earlier views about the existence of "large factories" and "great industrial firms," he still clings to the belief, unsupported by the sources, that antiquity developed "specialized shops, approaching in character to small factories," "factories," "larger factory-like undertakings," "establishments resembling factories."[20] This despite his full realization that mechanization was almost completely absent, that technological progress in industry was not radical and dynamic but actually of negligible importance (except in military engineering and building construction), that, in fact, during the Roman Empire there was a noticeable decline in technology. And he is fully aware of the fact that "The fabric of Roman industry rested . . . on very weak foundations, and on such foundations no capitalist industry could be built up," because the purchasing power of the great masses of the population throughout antiquity was too low "to acquire anything whatever outside the limits of their most urgent needs."[21] "Hence industry is carried on to supply the needs of a comparatively small number."[22]

The primitive methods, costliness, insecurity, and slowness of all types of transport in antiquity are abundantly clear to Rostovtzeff. But he proceeds from a preconceived notion of a "natural" centralized system of production, and accordingly views the predominantly local character of ancient manufacture, imposed by the fetters of transportation limitations, as a calculated deviation from such a natural centralization. For the restricted range of industrial output and the absence of great industrial centers are attributed by Rostovtzeff, in one of his pet theories, to political or economic policies (in both the Hellenistic states and in the Roman Empire) of local self-sufficiency and emancipation from foreign markets. Trade in the prime necessities of life (especially grain) to supply the requirements of the military and of administrative and urban centers, and traffic in slaves and luxury articles for the few, admittedly constituted the main lines of commercial enterprise. This trade barely touched the surface of the basic structure of ancient economy: it did not penetrate every phase of economic life nor transform large areas into economically interdependent complexes. Such a development is not possible without modern techniques of transportation and communication.[23] Yet Rostovtzeff projected into antiquity the essentially modern concept of "economic unity" of extensive areas, even of entire civilizations.[24]

The same objections must be raised against the concepts of scientific agriculture and capitalistic farming employed by Rostovtzeff. It is clear that he understands by these terms merely large-scale agriculture. To his thinking, peasant economy and tenant farming by small holders preclude scientific management and advanced agricultural technique, which require abundant capital. Here again he is projecting modern conditions into antiquity. For it has been demonstrated by Mickwitz that scientific, rationalized agriculture is a product of modern times, very different from the empirical farm management and agricultural technique of the ancient world.[25]

It is not surprising, therefore, that, glossing over the impoverishment of the masses by an economic system that enriched a small, propertied minority, Rostovtzeff should define "prosperity" subjectively in terms of the well-being of a commercial and business class. "I use the term 'prosperity,'" he says, "to describe the general conditions of a period: progress in production, brisk trade, accumulation of capital. General

prosperity did not necessarily mean that the working classes enjoyed tolerably satisfactory conditions. They were the last to profit by it."[26] The image conjured in his
mind by the word "prosperity" is the existence of a strong urban bourgeoisie, a
moderately well-to-do middle class, possessing sizable sums of money. The subjec-
tivity of this formulation is evidenced by the fact that the wealth of kings, extensive
building operations both public and private, and idle accumulations of hoarded
wealth are often regarded by him as signs of prosperity.[27] It is clear that the standard of living and purchasing power of the masses of the population of a society do
not figure in Rostovtzeff's conception of prosperity—even though the working masses
should constitute for him the "economic backbone" of that society. The term "proletariat," employed by him without clear reference to the prevalent mode of production as a loose label for all but the propertied minority, is a catchall for "free
wage earners and slaves," "paupers," "the mob," "rabble of the citizens," "working
class," "have-nots," "poor peasants," "lower classes," "unemployed men in the cities,
tenants and hired laborers in the country."[28]

These judgments and values of Rostovtzeff reveal a pattern of social ideology
that probably took form during the turbulent transition from tsarism to the Soviet
regime in the land of his birth. His understanding of the term "bourgeoisie" must
also be placed in the context of pre-Soviet Russian society, predominantly agricultural, under the sway of a decaying feudal landed aristocracy, emerging into
the dawn of industrial capitalism, and generating an enterprising bourgeoisie
and a growing industrial proletariat. Situated socially and economically in an
intermediate position between the declining but politically dominant ruling
nobility and the increasingly class-conscious peasants and industrial workers,
the Russian bourgeoisie was truly a *middle* class, drawing its income both from
commercial and industrial enterprise and from rationalized agriculture.[29] But it
never succeeded, as did its counterparts in the more advanced capitalist countries, in becoming a ruling class. In the developed capitalist countries the polarization of classes into a big bourgeoisie and a proletariat left a heterogeneous
"aggregation of functional groups wavering between the proletariat and the
bourgeoisie,[30] often called the petite bourgeoisie or middle class. It is method-
ologically important to distinguish between the bourgeois middle class of early
capitalism and the petite bourgeois middle class of developed capitalism, which
is not a true economic class.[31]

This confusion of a bourgeoisie as a ruling class and as a middle class is evident in Rostovtzeff's economic and social writings. He attempts to give precise
definition to the concept bourgeoisie in economic terms:

> I understand by it . . . a class of men who had achieved by their efforts or
> inherited from their parents a certain degree of prosperity, and lived not on
> the income derived by manual labour but from the investment of their ac-
> cumulated capital in some branch of economic activity. . . . The main and
> most characteristic feature of the bourgeoisie from an economic standpoint
> was . . . the fact that they were not professionals, craftsmen of one kind or

another, salaried employees, or the like, but investors of accumulated capital and employers of labour.[32]

The bourgeois is the "average citizen," "not an aristocrat by birth and wealth. . . . He is a middle-class landowner, a business man, or a *rentier*, well-to-do but not extremely rich."[33] A careful study of his application interchangeably of the terms "bourgeoisie" and "middle class" to ancient times reveals that they serve to distinguish in his mind a moderately well-to-do propertied urban class from a fabulously wealthy minority and from the less prosperous or propertyless masses.

The income of this class may be derived from investments in agriculture, trade, or industry. At times the people of this class may be very rich or may be shopowners, moneychangers, artisans, or members of the liberal professions. It is even possible for members of this middle class to be poor. But Rostovtzeff's scientific reading of the evidence also forces him to the conclusion that the class which he has molded into a "bourgeois middle class" is actually the ruling class of the Hellenistic states and of the Roman Empire, whose economic interests were centered exclusively or predominantly in landowning. His "bourgeois middle class" is a myth.[34]

An important source of these confusions in Rostovtzeff's thinking is his failure to clarify the relation of his bourgeoisie to the machinery of state power both in Hellenistic and Roman imperial times. In general this class is treated as separated from the state and its policies. Thus it is not regarded as responsible for economic disasters. On the contrary, it is viewed as the principal sufferer from such catastrophes, and the responsibility for them is sought outside this class, which is pictured as squeezed between the pressure of the state from above and the masses from below. These pressures take the form of a threat of proletarianization by the big bourgeoisie and of expropriation by the proletariat: opposition "downward against the political and social demands of the laboring classes . . . and upward against monopoly capital"—leading traits of the modern petite bourgeois ideology.[35] Idealizing a capitalist society that nourishes a large and prosperous urban middle class, and yearning for stability in the social and economic order, Rostovtzeff views with apprehension economic bigness, concentration of wealth in the hands of a few, which brings in its train large masses of poor. Economic crises and social disorders are then inevitable, and since he regards the masses as incapable of ruling, tyranny and economic enslavement may follow. Hence, wherever in the history of mankind there is prosperity as he understands it, Rostovtzeff assumes a priori the existence of a bourgeois class.

This class is idealized by Rostovtzeff, in his social studies of the ancient world, as peaceful, thrifty, industrious—"the most civilized and best educated classes of the urbanized parts of the [Roman] Empire."[36] While admitting grave faults in the Hellenistic "bourgeoisie," he emphasizes its sturdy character and its preservation for posterity of the leading traits of Greek city life. "In my opinion it was the city bourgeoisie that was chiefly responsible for the great struggle for liberty carried on by the cities [of the Hellenistic world]," he writes, though he acknowledges that "the bourgeoisie was often prepared to make far-reaching concessions to the kings, especially when faced with social revolution from within."[37] It constitutes for him the leading force of the Hellenistic world and the Roman Empire, the "economic backbone" of both societies. Yet he also states—which is the true picture—that the natives of Hellenistic Egypt and Syria were "the economic backbone of the two countries"; that the "slaves were the backbone of the economic life of the [Roman] Empire"; that the "tenants and farmers formed its backbone"; and that the peasants of Roman Africa "formed the vast majority of the population and were the economic backbone of the country."[38]

In keeping with his idealization of ancient capitalism and its bourgeoisie, Rostovtzeff has transferred to antiquity the "typical modern bourgeois glorification of competitive capitalism as opposed to . . . bureaucratic . . . so-called socialistic national economy."[39] His personal predilection for a capitalist economy based on the open market, free enterprise, and unrestricted private ownership and management of the means of production leads him to assign to governmental interference (in antiquity) with this ideal situation the terms "planned economy," "etatization," "state capitalism," "state socialism," "socialism," "New Deal."[40] Greek democracy is condemned because of its "levelling tendency" which was inimical to the free development of "capitalism," for "capitalistic enterprise was interfered with by the state . . . [and] within each state capital had to fight the socialistic tendencies of the government and its inveterate jealousy of all, who either by wealth or intellectual and moral superiority, rose above the general level. Thus capitalism and individualism, growing irresistibly, came into conflict with democratic institutions."[41]

Rostovtzeff devoted a great deal of attention to what he calls the "planned economy" of Ptolemaic Egypt.[42] Documenting the crushing demands of the Ptolemaic system upon the masses of Egyptian natives, he concludes that "the Ptolemaic reform almost entirely ignored the essence of the Greek economic system: private property recognized and protected by the State as the basis of society, and the free play of economic forces and economic initiative."[43] Yet he admits that this control was not rigid and strict, that there was considerable freedom of private contract, extensive tracts of private land, a prosperous bourgeoisie in the cities and in the country, a considerable amount of private initiative in commerce—in fact it is "certain that, despite all restrictions, the use of money as the basis of private business was fairly well developed under Philadelphus. There were savings in the country which looked for safe investment and the business spirit was awake."[44] It is also certain that Rostovtzeff does not claim that the Ptolemaic system was the result of the inner compulsion of the economic order or that it involved a plan of consumption as well as an overall plan of production, all of which are fundamental to a planned economy.[45]

There being no such modern mechanism as public credit or a national debt, the government of Egypt endeavored to intensify the exploitation of the native population with the ultimate goal of increasing the royal revenues, of accumulating and hoarding precious metals which could be employed rapidly for administrative, diplomatic, and especially military outlays. The first concern of the Ptolemies was fiscal, the measuring rod of the efficiency of their rule the limitless dimensions of the royal purse: the laboring classes "existed primarily for the purpose of increasing the royal revenues by their toil." "The economic system . . . was inspired by one motive, the organization of production with the main purpose of making the State, in other words the king, rich and powerful."[46] Yet, since the system under the early Ptolemies "produced wonderful results"—it converted Egypt into a "flourishing center of developed agriculture, industry, and trade" with a prosperous, privileged, and relatively unhampered bourgeoisie—it is transformed, in his thinking, into a "benevolent domination," a "personal, paternal, benevolent rule" of kings "whose interests were identical with those of the country."[47]

In carrying out their exploitation of the masses of Egyptian natives the early Ptolemies relied on the support of a foreign bourgeoisie, essentially Greco-Macedonian, a ruling class imposed and maintained, as Rostovtzeff recognizes, by a conscious social policy as a privileged superstructure upon the conquered inhabitants. That the masses were antagonistic to the Ptolemaic system from the outset is admitted by Rostovtzeff. "But we must probably not seek the cause of these conflicts in any impoverishment brought about by the new economic system,"[48]—perforce, since in Rostovtzeff's view the Ptolemaic system under Philadelphus worked wonderfully, even creating tolerable conditions for the native peasantry. In his opinion, the unrest of the Egyptians under the early Ptolemies stemmed from administrative defects of the "planned economy" in its early experimental stage and from nationalist and religious opposition to foreign overlords. In stressing the nationalist-religious content of the native opposition of the third century B.C. Rostovtzeff does not come to grips with the crucial fact that the Ptolemaic system contained the seeds of decay from the very start because its early specious "prosperity" was based on economic oppression. He is unaware, for example, that the Ptolemies' imposition of a money economy on a predominantly natural economy created increased inequality of the distribution of wealth and ever sharper differentiation between rich and poor.

But he brilliantly demonstrates that the struggle of the exploited natives against the ruling class in the second and first centuries B.C., in the form of passive resistance, sabotage, and open revolt, stemmed not from nationalistic aspirations and religious fanaticism, but from intensification of the economic oppression of the laboring classes. The emergency measures taken by the Ptolemies to mitigate these revolts, protect themselves, and protect the revenues of the crown—enlargement of the ruling class by siphoning off into it the wealthy natives, partial concessions to the Egyptian peasants, some relaxations of the rigors of "planned economy," extension of private property, spreading of state control to the bourgeoisie, "the new oppressed class"—impress Rostovtzeff as evidences of a well-meaning attempt to eliminate oppression. He maintains that "the Ptolemies never pursued a class policy favorable to the *bourgeoisie* and bearing oppressively on the laboring class. They were impartial and just, and were inclined rather to protect the weak and the poor against the officials and the *bourgeoisie* than to give a free hand to the latter."[49] Further, aware that the condition of the natives steadily deteriorated and that discontent grew, he attributes this situation to the inability of the "reformist" kings to abolish the entire economic and fiscal system, thus tacitly admitting that the system per se, not merely when abused, was an intolerable burden to the Egyptian masses; to the growth of an all-pervading, deeply entrenched impersonal bureaucracy that ultimately superseded the royal power; or to "the country's general evolution under the system of planned economy built up by the Ptolemies."[50]

Since Rostovtzeff separates the ruling class from the state, and does not recognize that this bureaucracy constitutes one sector of his idealized bourgeois middle class, he subjectively transforms the administration of the Hellenistic kings into a benevolent, paternalistic rule. Yet he is fully aware that the "good intentions" of the Hellenistic kings are mythical; that, for instance, Ptolemy Euergetes's "practice was probably very different from his words, which as a matter of fact were not even invented by him but assumed at a very early time the form of conventional expressions for amnesty decrees, just like the decrees of the priests and similar Egyptian documents of the earlier period."[51] Unreconciled with this position is the view that the "documents show that all the Ptolemies were constantly repeating, in accordance with the immemorial tradition of Oriental kingship in general, that they wished everyone to be happy in their kingdom; nor have we any reason to disbelieve them."[52] He thus absolves the kings and the bourgeoisie of Egypt from any responsibility for the increased tempo of exploitation and attributes this to the "natural" evolution of a growing inhuman and impersonal bureaucratic machine. In doing so, he ignores the most important factor in the situation—the increased demands of the crown on the population caused by the loss of the Egyptian empire in the early second century B.C.[53] The only effective results of the class struggle carried on by the natives of Egypt, in Rostovtzeff's view, was the ruin of the entire country, for it was detrimental both to the interests of the king and the working classes, and resulted in the "proletarianization of the bourgeoisie."

Rostovtzeff's idealization of the "reformist" Ptolemies stems from his abhorrence of "revolution with all its horrors," and from a preference for harmony and compromise between hostile classes. Thus for him the unsolved problem of the later Ptolemies was a social one: "to find a satisfactory solution of the main problem that confronted them—how to develop friendly relations between the Greeks and the natives and secure their harmonious cooperation in the economic life of the country."[54] Hence the mitigation of class antagonism by the ruling class of Rhodes during the Hellenistic period through public provision for the poor is commended as "sound social policy," and a judicious and satisfactory solution of the class strife that ravaged the rest of the contemporary Greek world. The Gracchi are criticized because "they should have taken into account the power and influence of the highest classes. . . . The right course was to soften, not to exasperate the feelings of classes."[55] But the successful Roman revolution of the first century B.C., represented politically by the establishment of the Augustan principate, meets with Rostovtzeff's approbation precisely because it "represented a compromise between the opposing forces."[56]

One of the salient concepts of Rostovtzeff's historiography is his sustained and vigorous emphasis upon the struggle of antagonistic social classes in antiquity. Ascribing the origins of class differentiation to the institution of private property, he regards the conflict of classes as "primeval" and "eternal,"[57] generated by an inevitable polarization of society into rich and poor. It is clear that Rostovtzeff does not conceive of the friction of classes (which he generalizes as "the eternal social and economic antagonism between labor and the *bourgeoisie*")[58] as emanating, under concrete historically conditioned circumstances, from the dynamics of a given society, that is, from any maladjustments between the actual state of the productive forces in existence at a given historical moment and the prevailing relations of men in the productive process. Consciously divorcing the struggle of classes from the flux of the economic order, he regards this phenomenon as stemming largely from social and psychological causes, and from traits of human nature statically conceived: exclusiveness of the dominant classes and elemental hatred of the poor for their exploiters and oppressors in the upper strata of society.

In general the onslaughts of the lower classes against the ruling groups are conceived by him as destructive movements based on "negative" programs leading to social and economic disaster. Revolution from below in fact achieved no lasting results in Hellenistic society. This failure is analyzed by Rostovtzeff, with due appreciation for the most important factors involved, as owing to disorganization and lack of effective leadership of the masses, the intransigent resistance of the ruling class, the efforts of the kings, and the final military intervention of the Romans on the side of property. But he emphasizes as the final result of the class struggle in the Hellenistic world the mutual ruin of the contending classes, the "proletarianization of the bourgeoisie," and the concentration of wealth in the hands of a few magnates who formed a new ruling class.

Thus Rostovtzeff recognizes and methodically documents one of the fundamental laws of ancient economy—the gradual, sometimes retarded or temporarily reversed, concentration of wealth, especially landed property, in the hands of the few. This tendency, in his view, when it reaches moderate proportions, generates an ideal "bourgeois middle class," and periods of considerable "prosperity," notably in the early period of Hellenistic society and the first two centuries of the Roman Empire. But this is generally followed by the "proletarianization of the bourgeoisie," broadening of the base of the poor and sharp narrowing of the apex of the social pyramid into a small minority of extremely wealthy grandees.

The causes of the concentration of wealth in the ancient world are never thoroughly explored in economic terms by Rostovtzeff. Not subscribing to the principle that "the community as a whole may be impoverished through the very same means by which a portion of its number may be enriched,"[59] he formulates the problem in social terms as the decline of a mythical "bourgeoisie," and seeks the answer in social and political causes. In Hellenistic Egypt, in his view, it was both the hatred of the natives for the privileged classes and the compulsion of the state that "proletarianized" its "middle class." In Hellenistic Greece the fierce class antagonisms and Roman intervention, with its onslaughts on the "capital" of the "bourgeoisie," are regarded as the causative agents of the ultimate ruin of this class. For the Roman Empire his theory is that the masses of the peasants in the third century A.D., wanting to level and equalize the social classes, accomplished its ruin, with the support of a peasant army and the terror of the state. Thus, in the final analysis, Rostovtzeff seeks to explain the decline of a moderately well-to-do "back-bone of society," and the cause of bigness in economic life and a concomitant regression of "prosperity," by ascribing these phenomena to the destructive social program of the class-conscious masses or the political policy of an autocratic state, or both.

This is especially true of his interpretation of the revolution of the third century A.D., which affected the entire Roman Empire. The political structure of the Roman Empire in the first two centuries A.D. rested on the support of a ruling class that he terms the "urban bourgeoisie," which had a "system of economic exploitation [that] prevented the lower classes from raising themselves to a higher level and improving their material welfare."[60] To mitigate the mounting unrest among the peasant masses of the empire, palliative measures were adopted by the Flavian and Antonine emperors of the so-called enlightened monarchy in the first and second centuries A.D. Here too, as in his treatment of Hellenistic Egypt, Rostovtzeff, divorcing the state from the ruling class, transforms these emperors into protectors of the weak against the strong. Though he admits that the "tendency towards a strict maintenance of the privileges of the upper classes of the population . . . remained throughout the leading principle of the policy of the enlightened monarchy,"[61] the economic and social palliatives of the "enlightened" emperors are propounded as a social policy designed "to establish justice in economic relations and to make it possible for the lower classes gradually to reach the standards which would allow of their assimilation by the higher, privileged inhabitants of the Roman Empire."[62] Thus, transforming concessions granted to the laboring classes to allay discontent into a paternalistic policy, Rostovtzeff attributes to these emperors a conscious social policy of "levelling up" of the masses "to a working and active middle class."[63] In his view, this benevolent imperial policy of elevating as large as possible a section of the lower classes to the rank of the privileged strata failed because the "bourgeoisie" resisted it and closed its ranks against enlargement.

This social phenomenon, then, resulted in the revolution of the *humiliores* against the *potentiores* in the third century A.D. The resentment of the masses crystallized into a class-conscious alliance between the peasantry and the army against the "urban bourgeoisie," and eventually burst forth in the form of a sharp antagonism between the rural districts and the cities.[64] Thus, in Rostovtzeff's interpretation, this revolution was fundamentally a social upheaval, resulting from the conscious exclusiveness of the ruling classes. This generated in the working masses an equally conscious revengeful policy of leveling the upper classes downward to their own economic, social, and cultural standards. In carrying out this destructive policy they were aided by the terror and compulsion of the state power in the hands of the "military emperors" who seized the imperial authority with their support.[65]

Thus Rostovtzeff divorces the revolution of the third century from the dynamics of the economic order established and maintained by the ruling classes—a system that, he admits, prevented the material welfare of the lower classes from improving. That the struggle was a revolution participated in by a majority of the inhabitants of the Roman Empire is seriously open to question. The prime movers were the army and its leaders, and the masses maintained a passive attitude or in places gave support sporadically to the movement.[66] But in Rostovtzeff's view, the peasantry as a class dealt the death blow to the "urban bourgeoisie" of antiquity, which it ruined and destroyed—but in the process it gained nothing but slavery and financial ruin for itself, for "violent attempts at levelling have never helped to uplift the masses."[67] "The real point of the Rostovtzeff theory," as Turner puts it, "is that a movement of the masses against the ruling classes is certain to result in disaster."[68] This Rostovtzeff regards as one of the immutable "laws" of history.

It is fundamental, then, to Rostovtzeff's method and philosophy of history to seek the basic causes for catastrophic crises and for the general decline of societies in extraeconomic factors—in social disharmony, political evolution, mass psychological transformations, in any case in factors external to the development of the productive forces of a given society. "In Ancient times these institutions [i.e., beginnings of mass production and initial stage of capitalist development] were checked in their operation and growth by factors which had nothing to do with economic life."[69] His thinking thus is in accord with the Ricardian school, which regarded crises as fortuitous deviations from a predetermined equilibrium, as "due to external interference with the free working of economic forces . . . rather than as effects of any chronic malady internal to capitalist society."[70] In the final analysis, inevitable and insoluble contradictions between social classes are for him the ultimate cause of decline. His thinking is thus dominated by a sociological abstraction subjectively adapted to historical phenomena and not concretely anchored in the material causes of social friction.

Assuming the primacy of commercial and industrial activity in the economy of classical Greece, and the existence of an equilibrium between production and demand in the fifth century B.C., Rostovtzeff attributes the acute economic crisis in Greece in the fourth century to internal political developments, and especially to the alienation from Greece of her foreign markets through the development of local industries and the resultant shrinkage of the market for Greek agricultural and industrial products. Since Rostovtzeff regards this economic crisis as having causes external to any inherent maladjustments of the economic system, he concludes that Greece enjoyed renewed, though temporary, prosperity through a removal of the external hindrance by Alexander's conquest of the Persian Empire and the wars of the Successors, which put into circulation vast sums of money and opened up new markets and opportunities for the Greek homeland. The result was, in his view, a rapid increase in the demand for Greek commodities, and a new type of disequilibrium—inability of supply to keep pace with demand. Hence, he holds, eventually Greece again lost its prosperity because local industries in the East were forced into competition with her to make up the deficiencies. That Greece, during the period of "renewed prosperity" depicted by Rostovtzeff, was in reality suffering from ever-growing economic maladjustment seems more in accord with the evidence.[71]

The succeeding chronic depression and steady impoverishment of Greece, alleviated by temporary revivals of some levels of prosperity, were accompanied by growth in the number of the poor, increasing mass unemployment, and progressive concentration of wealth in the hands of the few. But it was "the *bourgeoisie* or the middle class in the Greek cities that chiefly suffered in the turmoil."[72] The causes of this steady decline are detailed by Rostovtzeff as chronic social disorder and warfare, mounting piracy, competition with slave labor, steady emancipation of the East from dependence on Greek products, and the assaults upon the capital of the bourgeoisie by the Roman intervention and domination. But the chief source of the economic distress was "the declining prosperity of the citizens and especially of the well-to-do *bourgeoisie*."[73] At times he views the basic difficulty as the reduced purchasing power of the population as a whole; at times he regards the real trouble, in terms of modern classical economic theory, as shortage of capital in the hands of a declining and increasingly "proletarianized bourgeoisie."

The gradual decline and decay of Ptolemaic Egypt are attributed, in the final analysis, not to inefficient rulers, or to nationalistic and religious opposition, or to the effects of Roman policy, but to "the mood of the population . . . especially the mood of the lower classes." "No doubt, it was the masses who were ultimately responsible for the decay. They refused actively or passively to respond to the call of the kings."[74] The primary cause of the undermining of the royal economy of Egypt is, in Rostovtzeff's view, the shrinking of the labor supply caused by the revolutionary mood of the masses, and general lack of initiative and apathy on the part of the native masses. Yet he admits, at times, that this "mood" was a product of economic oppression.[75]

Rostovtzeff rightly rejects the view that the fundamental cause of the atrophy and decay of Hellenistic society was the blow delivered to it from without by Roman intervention, which, however disastrous, merely accelerated and made catastrophic the internal process of disintegration. One of the underlying causes of this internal decay, he maintains, was political rivalry: the failure to establish political unity or peaceful political cooperation and a durable balance of power involved an incessant struggle for political hegemony and constant warfare. Another basic cause is regarded as economic, viewed in terms of an insoluble contradiction between two antagonistic economic systems, "the Greek economic system, based on freedom and private initiative, and the State economy of the East."[76] But unquestionably the decisive cause in his view is the inability of the

Hellenistic world to find a solution for the problem of social disharmony, "the great eternal problem of human society, as acute in the ancient world as it is in the modern: the antinomy between the rulers and the ruled, the 'haves' and the 'have-nots,' the *bourgeoisie* and the working classes, the city and the country."[77] Yet in his final summation of the achievements and defects of Hellenistic society, he maintains: "The Hellenistic genius might have created more than in effect it did. . . . It was handicapped in its natural development by external causes. After a century of intensive creation, the peculiar evolution of its political life and certain political ideas inherent in the Greek mind put an early end to progress."[78] Thus it is clear that he himself has not decided whether the essential cause was social or political.

It is also evident that he does not consider as the basic cause an economic order based on the intensive exploitation of the majority by a small, privileged ruling class that was uninterested in—nay, hostile to—solving the problem of mass impoverishment by elevating the standard of living of the masses, that despised manual labor, and that drained the wealth of the Hellenistic world in unproductive luxury expenditures and constant warfare.[79]

Paralleling his analysis of the crisis in Greece in the fourth century B.C., Rostovtzeff attributes the economic crisis in Italy in the first century A.D. to the emancipation of the provinces from dependence on Italian products, which led to a decay of industry and commerce, the concentration of land in the hands of the imperial aristocracy and other Italian magnates, and the consequent ruin of scientific agriculture. "In the crisis at the end of the first century the middle class was the first to suffer."[80]

The steady concentration of land in fewer and fewer hands, with the gradual disappearance of small independent peasant landowners in the provinces as well as in Italy, is the leading economic development in the Roman Empire from the reign of Augustus on. "The tendency towards concentration of landed property in the hands of capitalists and city residents could not be stopped."[81] From the very outset, and increasingly as time went on, the urban bourgeoisie attempted to solve the problem of the labor supply required to cultivate their landed estates by the institution of tenant smallholders. In Rostovtzeff's view, the developing scientific capitalistic agriculture of the early Roman Empire was ruined by this practice. The urban bourgeoisie withdrew their capital and management from their large-scale agricultural undertakings and became absentee landlords, living off income derived from less productive tenant farms. Since he holds the view that an energetic and enterprising middle class developed a thriving capitalism, that the primary source of the prosperity of his urban bourgeoisie of the early Roman Empire was commerce and industry, and that this class introduced the methods of progressive and scientific farming into agriculture as a supplementary field of investment, Rostovtzeff is compelled to attribute the growth of absentee landownership (actually the dominant form of Roman economy) to a psychological transformation in the urban bourgeoisie:

> This city-capitalism . . . gradually degenerated. The prevailing outlook of the municipal *bourgeoisie* was that of the *rentier*: the chief object of economic activity was to secure for the individual or for the family a placid and inactive life on a safe, if moderate, income. . . . The activity of the urban middle class degenerated into a systematic exploitation of the toiling lower classes. Its accumulated wealth was mostly invested in land. Commerce and industry became decentralized, and then they came to be pursued as a means of adding to an income derived mainly from agriculture.[82]

The predominance of agriculture is thus for Rostovtzeff not the actual foundation of economic life, existing independently of the will, but a moral deviation of the ruling class, which, commencing with the end of the first century A.D., was affected by apathy, indolent contentment, and paralysis of energy. "Thus the impotence and idleness of the directing classes brought about a new social and economic crisis in the empire."[83] "The result was the collapse of city-capitalism and the acute crisis of the third century, which brought about the rapid decline of business activity in general, the resuscitation of primitive forms of economy, and the growth of State-capitalism."[84]

The urban bourgeoisie, transformed by a changed attitude of mind from entrepreneurs into *rentiers*, became an exclusive minority:

> The existence of two castes, one ever more oppressed, the other ever more idle and indulging in the easy life of men of means, lay like an incubus on the Empire and arrested economic progress. All the efforts of the emperors to raise the lower classes to a working and active middle class were futile. The imperial power rested on the privileged classes, and the privileged classes were bound in a very short time to sink into sloth.[85]

The stubborn opposition of the ruling class to the imperial policy of reviving a class of independent peasant smallholders resulted in a psychological change in the rural masses, who renounced their century-old submissiveness in the social revolution of the third century against the "urban bourgeoisie." "It was this [social] antagonism which was the ultimate cause of the crisis of the third century."[86]

Equally disastrous to sound (for Rostovtzeff, "capitalistic") economic development, and in part engendered by the selfish policy of the ruling class (for, as has been pointed out, he separates the state power from the ruling class), was the steadily mounting supremacy of the interests of the state over those of the entire population. To solve economic problems and meet its own needs, the imperial government interfered with "free enterprise" through progressively more burdensome taxation, frequent requisitions, compulsory work and other forms of coercion, and eventually even assaults on the "capital" of the "bourgeoisie" in order to meet the administrative and military requirements of the state. These actions, and the apathy they led to among the ruling bourgeoisie as well as the masses, are at times regarded as the cause of the crisis of the third century A.D. and of the decay of the empire.

Rostovtzeff is cognizant of other fundamental factors, but he regards them as secondary. The "weakest feature" of the Roman Empire, he writes, "was the frailty of the foundations, especially the economic foundation, on which the whole fabric of the Empire rested." He sees clearly that the economic system could support in comfort only a small minority, whose prosperity rested on intensive exploitation of the masses living at a bare subsistence level; and that the wealth of the Empire was progressively drained by unproductive squandering of income and by exhausting military and administrative expenditures. But he insists on the psychological and social aspects as basic and primary: exclusiveness of the ruling "urban bourgeoisie" and consequent destructive hostility of the masses of peasants. The result of the overthrow of the bourgeoisie by civil war and direct assaults on their capital was a general social, economic, and intellectual leveling, the mutual ruin of both classes, universal impoverishment and decline of productivity, and the establishment of a bureaucratic state and an étatized economy. "This was the fatal blow to the aristocratic and urban civilization of the ancient world."[87]

The pattern of Rostovtzeff's thinking is thus abundantly clear. The ancient world experienced two periods of unprecedented expansion in the centuries after Alexander and Augustus. This achievement was accomplished, in his view, by an urban bourgeois middle class which created the earliest form of capitalism. Why did this development atrophy and decay? What is the fundamental cause of the process of decline, of the gradual "barbarization" of the Roman Empire—the reversion to the more primitive economic forms of "house economy," the disappearance of cities, the assimilation of the upper classes to the cultural and intellectual standards of the lower classes? The main problem for him is this:

> Why was the city civilization of Greece and Italy unable to assimilate the masses, why did it remain a civilization of the *élite*, why was it incapable of creating conditions which should secure for the ancient world a continuous, uninterrupted movement along the same path which our modern world is traversing again?[88]

Having formulated the problem in terms of a subjectively conceived "capitalism" not revealed by the evidence, and approaching it from a predominantly social viewpoint, Rostovtzeff finally acknowledges his inability to solve the problem at all. Or he has recourse to the gloomy abstraction that every society is doomed to inevitable decay because of irreconcilable aspirations of an exclusive ruling minority which is the bearer of the culture of that society and of the masses which destroy that culture by leveling it to their own inferior standards. Or he reduces the explanation to psychological changes in the ruling class:

> Thus here again, in the case of the Roman Empire, a steady decline in civilization is not to be traced to physical degeneration, or to any debasement of blood in the higher races due to slavery, or to political and economic conditions, but rather to a changed attitude of men's minds. That change

was due to the chain of circumstances which produced the specific conditions of life in the Roman Empire, and the process was the same in Greece. One of these conditions, and very important among them, was the aristocratic and exclusive nature of ancient civilization. The mental reaction and the social division, taken together, deprived the ancient world of power to maintain its civilization, or to defend it against internal dissolution and barbarian invasion from without.[89]

But he insists that the "economic explanation of the decay of the ancient world must be rejected completely."[90] His vigorous assault on the economic interpretation of the decline of ancient civilization is directed against those economic theoreticians and historians who view ancient society as one stage in a continuous upward development of economic evolution, notably Bücher, Weber, Salvioli, and the Marxists, because their conception of Greco-Roman economy affords no explanation of the collapse of what is to Rostovtzeff its highest and most fruitful economic achievement.[91] Taking his stand against the "evolutionists" with Eduard Meyer, Julius Beloch, and the other "modernizers," he holds that ancient economy possessed its own inner unity and underwent a complete cycle of development culminating in capitalism, which became the prevailing form in certain periods, before its decline to earlier, more primitive forms. Assailing especially Bücher's outmoded, because historically unfounded, *Oikenwirtschaft* theory (the most influential of the "economic stage" theories of the German Historical School of economists), which regards the closed autarcic slave-owning household as the dominant economic form throughout all antiquity, Rostovtzeff overemphasizes the intensity of commercial activity and production for an indefinite market. But it is equally true that the "household economy" school underestimated precapitalistic commodity production and the importance of free labor in ancient times. This controversy, which began in the 1890s, has its historical roots in conflicting currents of nineteenth-century thought—the idea of progress, Darwinism, liberal-bourgeois political movements, antislavery agitation, and the neo-humanistic idealization of classical antiquity. There were thereby created, in extreme outlines, two equally idealized and unhistorical pictures of ancient economic life, a primitivized oversimplification on the one hand, and a caricature of the modern capitalist world on the other.[92]

Because of the denial by Marxist dialectical materialism of the existence of capitalism in antiquity and its espousal of the view of a continuous spiral of progress in economic life, Rostovtzeff superficially lumps it together with the "household economy" school and summarily rejects "the Marxian philosophy of history, the so-called economic materialism or 'determinism.'"[93] But it is noteworthy that Rostovtzeff has been classed by some admirers and critics as a Marxist.[94] While he has taken pains to abjure Marxian tendencies,[95] the impress of Marxist thought upon him is indisputable. For he has methodically adopted certain fundamental Marxist concepts: class struggle, gradual proletarianization of the "middle class," the historical role of the bourgeoisie, the clash of interests between town and country, and the mutual ruin of antagonistic social classes—which is regarded, in the Marxian view, as inevitable unless a revolutionary reconstitution of society occurs.[96]

Rostovtzeff's rejection of an economic interpretation as the basic explanation of the decline of ancient civilization is in keeping with his vigorously avowed, though inconsistently applied, pluralistic interpretation of history.

> I cannot confidently speak of social and economic conditions as a background for the evolution of other manifestations of human life at any time or in any place. Social and economic conditions are as much aspects of human life as art, or any other field of human endeavor and human creative power. We may speak of inter-relations between these various manifestations, but not of dependence of one on the other. None of them may properly be spoken of as background for the others.[97]

Rejecting a monistic interpretation of history, Rostovtzeff dismembers the development of society into the abstractions of independent historical factors. No one of the various spheres of historical phenomena—political, constitutional, artistic, social, economic, cultural, religious—is to be regarded as basic and decisive. All are equally important threads in the complex web of society, "indivisible from and closely correlated" with each other. Each branch of history, however, somehow retains its separate individuality, steering a relatively independent course, but developing along the same general lines as the others.[98] Hence Rostovtzeff gives prominence now to one factor, now to another, with intuitive and deliberate arbitrariness, rarely attempting to examine the totality of all the opposing tendencies within a given historical phenomenon as a single, unified, mutually affecting process of evolution.

But it is only in part his pluralistic historical methodology that accounts for the glaring contradictions and inconsistencies in Rostovtzeff's judgments and conclusions. Equally responsible are his ambivalent petite bourgeois ideological position, which beguiles him into viewing the same historical phenomenon from conflicting social aspects, an eclecticism that reflects the divergent and often irreconcilable evidence both in the primary sources and in the secondary works upon which he relies, and his projection into antiquity of modern social and economic forms, which runs counter to the objective evidence well known to him.

Two of the historical "factors," the economic and social, are conceived as forming a uniquely integrated group. And "political and economic considerations are so closely connected that [it is] difficult to discriminate between them."[99] While he is especially careful to deny that the economic "factor" is the ultimate cause of historical phenomena, at times he treats it as primary and fundamental, determining the aspects of social and political life.[100]

In general, however, social and economic conditions are separated in Rostovtzeff's method, and greater weight is assigned to the social factor. This is seen even in his proposed order of treatment. The political aspect of any historical period is expounded first, then the social, and last the economic.[101] This divorce of social forces from economic development and the deliberate treatment of social conditions before economic[102] make it possible for Rostovtzeff, above all, to absolve the ruling classes of the Hellenistic world and the early Roman Empire, his idealized "bourgeoisie," of responsibility for economic crises and catastrophes.[103] But it also explains his failure to achieve a consistent understanding of the dynamics of historical evolution, undistorted by subjective intrusions. Walbank concludes: "His society is thus, fundamentally, without direction, the product of contingency, and not a developing organism, for which 'social,' 'economic,' and 'political' are merely convenient categories to the historian who seeks to lay bare its processes of change."[104] Rostovtzeff's basic conclusion is that the decay of society is inevitable because of unchangeable traits of human nature.

It is no wonder, then, that, as Laski has noted,[105] Rostovtzeff is overwhelmed with pessimism in contemplating the history of the ancient world. The decay of the Hellenistic world "is another melancholy instance in the history of mankind of the antinomy of destructive and creative forces within one and the same great people."[106] The decline of the world empire of the Romans inspires in him the now classic gloomy paradox: "Our civilization will not last unless it be a civilization not of one class, but of the masses. . . . Is not every civilization bound to decay as soon as it begins to penetrate the masses?"[107] He says specifically of us moderns: "We on our part have greatly developed what we inherited from antiquity or independently created, but are we sure that our economic progress will last forever, that it will never be terminated by events brought about not by economy but by the development of our mentality and our emotions?"[108]

But it would be a mistake to deny the pioneering greatness of Rostovtzeff. His methodological and conceptual deficiencies do not alter the fact that, by his astounding genius and realism in marshaling the documentary evidence of the economic and social conditions of Hellenistic and Roman societies, his great care in the periodization and generative presentation of the evidence, his masterly elucidation of countless aspects of classical civilization, he made possible for the first time a scientific description of the evolution of the ancient world.[109]

Notes

ABBREVIATIONS

AA = *Antike und Abendland*
AJA = *American Journal of Archaeology*
BCH = *Bulletin de Correspondence Hellénique*
CAH = *Cambridge Ancient History* (first edition)
CR = *Classical Review*
DS = Daremberg-Saglio, *Dictionnaire des Antiquités Greques et Romaines*
HAW = Michael Rostovtzeff, *A History of the Roman World* (Oxford, 1928–30) 2 vols.
HSCP = *Harvard Studies in Classical Philology*
JRS = *Journal of Roman Studies*
L&R = Naphtali Lewis and Meyer Reinhold, eds., *Roman Civilization* (New York, 1966)
    2 vols. (first edition)
LCL = *Loeb Classical Library*
MAAR = *Memoirs of the American Academy in Rome*
MN = *Mnemosyne*
PAPS = *Proceedings of the American Philosophical Society*
PBA = *Proceedings of the British Academy*
RE = *Paulys Realencyclopädie der Classischen Altertumswissenschaft*
RSI = *Rivista di Studi Italiani*
SEHHW = Michael Rostovtzeff, *The Social and Economic History of the Hellenistic World*
    (Oxford, 1941) 3 vols.
SEHRE = Michael Rostovtzeff, *The Social and Economic History of the Roman Empire*
    (Oxford, 1926)
TAPA = *Transactions of the American Philological Association*
WS = *Wiener Studien*

FOREWORD

1. William M. Calder III, Foreword to *Classica Americana*, by Meyer Reinhold (Detroit: Wayne State University Press, 1984), p. 10.

2. *Marcus Agrippa: A Biography* (Geneva, N.Y.: 1933; repr. Rome: 1965; rev. ed., Chicago: Ares, 1981).

3. *CR* (1934): 151; *Classical Journal* 30 (1935): 557.

4. *Bollettino di Filologia Classica* 40 (1934): 228. On its current value, see *Oxford Classical Dictionary*, ed. Simon Hornblower and Antony Spawforth (Oxford, 1996), s.v. "Vipsanius Agrippa, M."

5. *Roman Civilization: Selected Readings* (New York, 1966; 3rd ed., 1990). 2 vols.

6. *CW* 46 (1952–53): 59.

7. See, for example, R. J. Hopper, *CR* (1953): 214.

8. *The Classical Drama* (1959); *Barron's Teen-Age Summer Guide* (1960; 3rd ed., 1965); *A Simplified Approach to Plato and Aristotle* (1964); *Barron's Simplified Approach to Ten Greek Tragedies* (1965); *Barron's Simplified Approach to Vergil: Eclogues, Georgics, Aeneid* (1966); *Barron's Simplified Approach to "The Iliad": Homer* (1967); and *Barron's Simplified Approach to "The Odyssey": Homer* (1967; rev. ed., 1987).

9. *Collection Latomus* 116 (Brussels: Latomus, 1970).

10. *Past and Present* (Toronto, 1972); *The Classick Pages* (University Park, 1975); *Classica Americana* (Detroit, 1984).

11. *Thomas Jefferson* (New York, 1986).

CHAPTER 1

This chapter, originally appearing in the *Proceedings of the American Philosophical Society* 114 (1970): 347–65, was published as the introduction for *The Conflict of Generations in Ancient Greece and Rome*, ed. S. Bertman (Amsterdam: 1976), pp. 15–54. For recent work on the subject (beyond that volume), see B. S. Strauss, *Fathers and Sons in Athens: Ideology and Society in the Era of the Peloponnesian War* (Princeton, N.J.: 1993), and L. Nash, "Concepts of Existence: Greek Origins of Generational Thought," *Daedalus* 107.4 (1978): 1–21.

1. L. S. Feuer, *The Conflict of Generations* (New York: 1969), p. 28. On Freud's concept of primordial patricide as the "original sin" of mankind, presupposing a stage of intense generational conflict between fathers and sons based on sexual rivalry, see, e.g., E. Wellisch, *Isaac and Oedipus* (London: 1954), pp. 9–10. Rejecting father-son conflict as a universal human phenomenon stemming from the libido, E. Fromm, "The Oedipus Myth," *Scientific American* 180 (January 1949): 22–27, considers the main theme of the myth of the father slayer the struggle against paternal authority in patriarchal societies. I do not deem it profitable to elaborate here on the lack of historical evidence for Freud's universalist theory in antiquity.

2. M. Eliade, *Cosmos and History. The Myth of the Eternal Return* (New York: 1954); R. C. Dentan, *The Idea of History in the Ancient Near East* (New Haven, Conn.: 1955); J. J. Finkelstein, "Mesopotamian Historiography," *PAPS* 107 (1963): 461–472; S. H. Hooke, *Middle Eastern Mythology* (Baltimore: 1963); E. O. James, "The Nature and Function of Myth," *Folk-Lore* 68 (1957): 474–482; C. Kluckhohn, "Myths and Rituals: A General Theory," *Harv. Theol. Rev.* 35 (1942): 45–79; J. Fontenrose, *The Ritual Theory of Myth* (Berkeley: 1966); P. M. Kaberry, "Myths and Ritual: Some Recent Theories," *Bull. Inst. Class. Stud., Univ. Lond.* 4 (1957): 42–54.

3. Margaret Mead, "The Generation Gap," *Science* 164 (April 11, 1969), believes that for the first time in world history there exists today a worldwide generation gap and revolt of young people against the adults who control the societal mechanisms. Mead's study *Culture and Commitment. A Study of the Generation Gap* (Garden City, N.Y.: 1970) sheds little light on ancient cultures.

4. Ptah-hotep, *Wings of the Falcon. Life and Thought of Ancient Egypt*, trans. J. Kaster (New York: 1968), pp. 166, 169, 172–173; *cp.* Feuer, *Conflict of Generations*, p. 30. Text of the "Maxims of Ptah-hotep" also in J. H. Breasted, *The Dawn of Conscience* (New

York: 1939), pp. 129, 130, 134; *Ancient Near Eastern Texts*, ed. J. B. Pritchard (Princeton, N.J.: 1950), pp. 412–414; Z. Žaba, *Les Maximes de Ptahhotep* (Prague: 1956).

5. Cp. Feuer, *Conflict of Generations*, p. 25.

6. It is possible that a new generation of army recruits, age twenty, is meant.

7. Pritchard, *Ancient Near Eastern Texts*, pp. 414–418; A. Scharff "Der historische Abschnitt der Lehre für König Merikcare," *Sitz. Bayer. Akad. Wiss., Philos. Hist. Abt.* 1936, Heft 8: 11, 15–16, 21; A. H. Gardiner, "New Literary Works from Egypt," *Jour. Eg. Arch.* 1 (1914): 20–36; W. C. Hayes, "The Middle Kingdom in Egypt," *CAH* (1961), 1, chap 20, p. 5.

8. On the Hittite-Hurrian, Ugaritic, and Phoenician myths of generational conflict, see A. Lesky, "Hethitische Texte und griechischer Mythos," *Anz. Öst. Akad. Wiss., Philos.-Hist. Kl.* 87 (1950): 137–160; idem, "Griechischer Mythos und vorderer Orient." *Saeculum* 6 (1955): 35–52; H. G. Güterbock, "The Hittite Version of the Hurrian Kumarbi Myth," *AJA* 52 (1948): 123–134; B. C. Dietrich, "Some Eastern Traditions in Greek Thought," *Acta Classica* 8 (1965): 11–30; M. L. West, *Hesiod. Theogony* (Oxford: 1966), pp. 18–31.

9. Hesiod, *Theogony*, pp. 156–182; 453–506. Cp. M. L. West, *Hesiod. Theogony*, pp. 1–31: A. Heubeck, "Mythologische Vorstellungen des alten Orients im archaischen Griechentum," *Gymnasium* 62 (1955): pp. 508–525 ; H. Otten, "Vörderasiatische Mythen als Vorläufer griechischer Mythenbildung," *Forschungen und Fortschritte* (1949): 145–147; U. Bianchi, "Teogonie Greche e Teogonie Orientali," *Studi e Materiali di Storia delle Religioni* 24–25 (1953–1954): 64–75; P. Walcot, *Hesiod and the Near East* (Cardiff, Wales: 1966); E. R. Dodds, *The Greeks and the Irrational* (Berkeley: 1951), p. 61 n. 103, who probes the psychology of the Greeks in adopting the Hittite-Hurrian Kumarbi succession myth, finds in the father-castration theme "a reflex of unconscious human desires" reflecting "the son's attainment of sexual freedom through removal of his father-rival."

10. Homer, *Iliad* 9.448–477. According to some versions of the myth, Phoenix was blinded by his father as punishment. Blinding was a frequent penalty for sexual crimes.

11. *Iliad* 9.527–573. Cp. W. Kraus, "Meleagros in der Ilias," *WS* 63 (1948): 8–21; W. Wolfring, "Ilias und Meleagrie," *WS* 66 (1953): 24–49.

12. *Iliad* 1.259.

13. Hesiod, in T. A. Sinclair, *Hesiod, Works and Days* (Hildesheim: pub, 1966), pp. 182, 185–189, 331–332. In his commentary on these passages, Sinclair associates Hesiod's pessimism concerning parent-children relationships with the later tradition of apocalyptic literature. Cp. Mark 13.12: "Now . . . children shall rise up against their parents, and shall cause them to be put to death"; *Sibylline Oracles* 1.74, A. Rzach, "Sibyllinische Weltalter," *WS* 34 (1912): 114–122.

14. Exod. 20.12: "Honor thy father and mother, that thy days may be long." Cp. Prov. 1.8; 23.22: "Hearken to thy father who begat thee, and despise not the words of thy mother."

15. Exod. 21.15, 17. Cp. Mark 7.10; Matt. 15.4.

16. Cp. S. W. Baron, *A Social and Religious History of the Jews*, vol. 1 (New York: 1952), p. 361; J. Gaudemet, *Institutions de l'Antiquité* (Paris: 1967), pp. 121–122; *Reallexikon für Antike und Christentum*, "Eltern," 4: pp. 1198–1203; S. J. Feigen, "Disrespect toward Parents in the Torah and the Near Eastern Laws" [in Hebrew], *Sefer ha-Shanah li-Yehude Amerika* (10–11): 301–315, was not available to me.

17. Deut. 21.18–21. Stoning to death for filial disobedience is a unique penalty, and we are properly reminded that, "the present law will hardly, however, have often been

carried into practice," by S. R. Driver, *Critical and Exegetical Commentary on Deuteronomy* (New York: 1895), p. 248.

18. Deut. 27.16.

19. Lev. 20.9; Prov. 30.17.

20. Job 30.1, 9, 10.

21. The text appears to isolate here the very poor and low-class youths (perhaps shepherd boys or brigands).

22. Job 32.6, 9. Cp. 32.20.

23. Stobaeus, *Anthology* 4.25 *passim*. cp. Isocrates, *Demonicus* 14, 16. Stobaeus (4.25.5) quotes the tragedian Cleaenetus: "It is beautiful to die for one's parents." On parent-children relationships in Greece, cp. *Reallexikon für Antike und Christentum*, 4: 1191–1194.

24. Pseudonym of author of work written first century B.C./first century A.D. See K. von Fritz, "Perictyone," *RE* 19: cols. 794–795.

25. L. Lerat, "Un Loi de Delphes sur les Devoirs des Enfants envers leurs Parents," *Revue de Philologie* 17 (1943): 68–86; Th. Thalheim, article Κάκωσις in *RE* 10: cols. 1526–1528; G. Glotz, *La Solidarité de la famille . . . en Grèce* (Paris: 1904), pp. 359–360; R. Flaceliere, *Daily Life in Greece at the Time of Pericles* (New York: 1966), p. 80; B. E. Richardson, *Old Age among the Ancient Greeks*, Johns Hopkins Univ. Studies in Archaeology, no. 16 (1933), pp. 48–54; W. K. Lacey, *The Family in Classical Greece* (London: 1968), pp. 116–118. Cp. Vitruvius VI, Praef. 3: "The laws of all the Greeks provide that parents be fed by children, but among the Athenians not all, only those who have taught them a trade."

26. An Orphic fragment (Stobaeus, *Anthology* 4.25.28); Euripides, frag. *Alcmaeon* (Stobaeus 4.25.15); Plato, *Laws* 880E; Euripides, frag. *Heraclidae* (Stobaeus 4.25.2); Antiphanes, frag. 262 (Kock = Stobaeus 4.25.7a); Menander, frag. 805 (Edmonds = Stobaeus 4.25.26); Pempelos of Thurii (cp. K. von Fritz, *RE* 19: col. 416), frag. of a pseudo-Pythagorean work, "Concerning Parents" (Stobaeus 4.25.52); Hierocles, frag. (Stobaeus 4.25.53).

27. Plato, *Phaedo* 113E; Von Fritz, "Perictyone" (see n. 24 above): "If anyone despises his parents . . . , the sin is written down among the gods; both while alive and in death he is hated by men, and under the earth, together with the sinners there, he is for all eternity justly afflicted by the gods below who have been assigned as overseers of these matters."

28. Plato, *Laws* 931C. On curses and their significance in antiquity, see E. Ziebarth, "Fluch," *RE* 6: cols. 2771–2773; J. Th. Kakridis, 'Αραί (Athens: 1929); E. Kagarov, *Griechische Fluchtafeln*, in *Eos Suppl.* 4 (Paris: 1929). Cp. E. R. Dodds, *The Greeks and the Irrational*, pp. 46, 60, n. 102. Dodds would date the origin of Greek myths concerning curses of fathers to a period when the position of the father was being undermined among the Greeks by allegiance to the polis, that is, the post-Homeric period.

29. E.g., Menander, frag. (Stobaeus, Flor. 2.25.14 = Edmonds 586): "I am only ashamed before my father, Cleitophon. I shall not be able to face him if I do wrong"; Timocles, writer of Middle Comedy, frag. (Stobaeus 4.25.17): "Whoever fears his father and feels shame before him, that man will be a good citizen"; Antiphanes, Middle Comedy, frag. 261 (Kock = Stobaeus, 4.25.7): "Whoever at such an age still blushes in the presence of his parents is not evil."

30. R. Sealey, "On Coming of Age in Athens," *CR* 71 (1956): 195–197; G. Glotz, *La Solidarité*, p. 359; P. Girard, *L'Education Athenienne* (Paris: 1891), pp. 270–327.

31. H. Schaefer, "Partheniae," *RE* 18: cols. 1884–1886; *CAH* 3: 537, 674; G. L. Huxley, *Early Sparta* (Cambridge, Mass.: 1962), pp. 37–38.

32. Feuer, *Conflict of Generations*, p. 29, acknowledges generational balance in some periods of modern times, but characterizes generational friction in antiquity as continuing "with its bitterness unrelieved by any safety valve such as a developing technology or new world."

33. L. Beauchet, "Patria Potestas," *DS* 4: 342–343.

34. Cp. E. R. Dodds, *The Greeks and the Irrational*, pp. 45–46; G. Aigrisse, *Psychoanalyse de la Grèce antique* (Paris: 1960), p. 17; Lacey, *Family in Classical Greece*, pp. 16, 20.

35. The phrase is A. W. Gouldner's in *Enter Plato. Classical Greece and the Origins of Social Theory* (New York: 1965), p. 74.

36. Ibid., p. 73; V. Ehrenberg, *The People of Aristophanes. A Sociology of Old Attic Comedy* (Oxford: 1951), p. 208.

37. Xenophon, *Memorabilia* 1.2.33 35.

38. Gouldner, *Enter Plato*, pp. 356–358, has a valuable analysis of this social problem in slave societies.

39. The Greeks did not glorify the elderly in their art. See Richardson, *Old Age*, pp. xiii. 16, 31.

40. Aristotle, *Politics* 1269A.

41. Aeschylus, *Persians* 744.

42. Aeschylus, *Suppliant Women* 361.

43. Aeschylus, *Eumenides* 150, 162, 728–729, 731, 778–779, 808–809, 848–850, 883–884. Cp. A. J. Podlecki, *The Political Background of Aeschylean Tragedy* (Ann Arbor: 1966), p. 79.

44. Sophocles *Antigone* 639–648.

45. Ibid., 635–636, 701–702.

46. Ibid., 718–723, 728–729, 743, 755.

47. Ibid., 734–735, 742.

48. Ibid., 726–727.

49. See *supra*.

50. Euripides, *Alcestis* 679.

51. Ibid., 629–672, 737–738.

52. Pherecrates (Old Comedy), frag. 145 (Kock): "youth is impulsive, elders deliberate." Euripides, frag. 115.5 (Nauck): "There is an old proverb—the power of youth is in deeds, of the older generation in counsel."

53. E.g., Dodds, *The Greeks and the Irrational*, pp. 47, 61, n. 104; V. Ehrenberg, *People of Aristophanes*, p. 209; E. B. Castle, *Ancient Education and Today* (Baltimore: 1961), pp. 53–54; F. A. G. Beck, *Greek Education, 450–350 B.C.* (New York: 1964), pp. 147–187, 304–305; W. Jaeger, *Paideia* (New York: 1945): vol. 1, pp. 286–331; H. I. Marrou, *Histoire de l'Éducation dans l'Antiquité* (Paris: 1965), pp. 87–106.

54. Cp. G. Glotz, *La Solidarité*, pp. 415, 606–607; Castle, *Ancient Education*, p. 49.

55. Feurer, *Conflict of Generations*, p. 19.

56. Cp. S. Luria, "Väter und Söhne in den neuen literarischen Papyri," *Aegyptus* 7 (1926): 244–245.

57. Cp. Eupolis (writer of Old Comedy, fl. 430–410 B.C.), frag. 310 (Edmonds): "The young lads stand up and speak before the men."

58. H. Diels, *Die Fragmente der Vorsokratiker*, ed. W. Kranz (Berlin: 1960), vol. 2: pp. 322–324; K. Freeman, *Ancilla to the Pre-Socratic Philosophers* (Oxford: 1948), p. 141. Cp. K. Oppenheimer, "Thrasymachus," *RE Zw* R., 6: cols. 584–592; Luria, "Väter," pp. 250–251.

59. P. Oxy. 11, 1364, lines 135–139; cp. pp. 92–93. Cp. Luria, "Väter," p. 268; E. Wellmann, *RE* 1: col. 2529.

60. Ehrenberg, *People of Aristophanes*, p. 208.

61. Ibid., pp. 210–211.

62. Aristophanes, *Clouds* 963, 993–994, 998–999. Cp. Ehrenberg, *People of Aristophanes*, pp. 210–211.

63. A. Bork, *Der junge Grieche* (Zurich: 1961), pp. 65–67; Dodds, *The Greeks and the Irrational*, p. 61.

64. Aristophanes, *Clouds* 1321–1436.

65. Aristophanes, *Birds* 755–759, 1347–1352. Cp. F. Wehrli, *Motivstudien zur griechischen Komödie* (Zurich, 1936), pp. 56–69.

66. Luria, "Väter," pp. 243–268; Ehrenberg, *People of Aristophanes*, pp. 209–211. Cp. P. Oxy. 13, 1608, a fragment of the dialogue *Alcibiades* of Aeschines Socraticus, one of Socrates's most devoted pupils. In this work (lines 1–6, 34–51), Themistocles's unfilial relations with his parents, which lead to his disinheritance, are discussed.

67. Eupolis, frag. 122b–c (Edmonds) πανούργων ... νεωτέρων. The reference is to Diognetus, a brother of Nicias. In 411 B.C. he was between fifty and sixty years of age.

68. Aristophanes, *Wasps* 1099–1100.

69. Thucydides, *History* 6.12.2, 13.1. Cp. K. J. Dover, *Thucydides Book VI* (Oxford: 1961), p. 20.

70. Thucydides *History* 6.17,1, 18.6. On Nicias's conflict with Alcibiades and the generational conflict of the time, cp. Ehrenberg, *People of Aristophanes*, p. 210; J. de Romilly, *Thucydide et l'Imperialisme Athénien* (Paris: 1947), pp. 174–176.

71. On the rhetorical cliché "youthful folly" see Dover, *Thucydides Book VI*, p. 20. In Ps-Andocides, *Against Alcibiades* 22 (a forgery of late date), the failure of the Athenians to punish the insolence of the youthful Alcibiades resulted in moral decline. "The young men," taking Alcibiades as their model, "spend their days not in the gymnasium but in the courts. And while the older men are on military campaigns, the younger make speeches."

72. Thucydides, *History* 6.38.5. Cp. Dover, *Thucydides Book VI*, p. 50; Lenschau, "Hermokrates," *RE* 8: cols. 883–887.

73. Xenophon, *Memorabilia* 1.2.33–35.

74. Luria, "Väter," p. 268; Castle, *Ancient Education*, p. 51.

75. E.g., Stobaeus, *Anthology* 4.25.42: "One must adapt oneself to a senseless father as to a harsh law"; Xenophon, *Memorabilia* 2.2.3, 13.

76. Xenophon, *Memorabilia* 1.2.53, 2.55; *Apology* 19.

77. Xenophon, *Memorabilia* 1.2.49, 51–52; *Apology* 19–21.

78. Xenophon, *Memorabilia* 1.2.55.

79. Musonius (*ca.* 30–102 A.D.) was the teacher of Epictetus. In the fragment of his teaching preserved in Stobaeus, *Flor.* 4.26.51, Musonius reasons that while obedience to parents is a general principle, even on the assumption that parents are basically well-intentioned to their children, if a father acts willfully in ignorance or orders his son to steal or betray a trust, or commit a shameful act for pay, then a son is wise if he disobeys his father. In the pseudo-Platonic *Theages* (123B), probably of the second century

B.C., Socrates is made to say to Theages after he has quarreled with his father, who does not want him to continue an intellectual education, "What wisdom do you lack, when you blame your father for being unwilling to place you with people who would enable you to become wise?"

80. Isocrates, *Antidosis* 285–287 (the date is 354/353 B.C.). On the degeneracy and dissipation of the Athenian youth in the fourth century B.C., see also Athenaeus 12.532D; cp. Bork, *Der junge Grieche*, pp. 54–55. Athenaeus *Deipnosophistai*, (4.165–166) records the story that Ctesippos, son of the Athenian general Chabrias in the middle of the fourth century B.C., in order to indulge his prodigality, actually sold one by one the stones of a monument to his father that had been erected with public funds. Unfortunately, we do not know the ages of the four Athenians, Cinesias (dithyrambic poet *ca.* 450–390 B.C.), Apollophanes, Mystalides, and Lysitheos, who called themselves κακοδαιμονισταί ("Devil's Club") and feasted together on religiously forbidden days (Lysias, frag. 53.2 [Thalheim] from Oration against Cinesias).

81. Isocrates, *Areopagiticus* 49–51.

82. Ibid., 25, 43, 48–49. Cp. S. Cecchi, *Isocrate Antologia delle Orazioni* (Milan: 1960), pp. 127–128; R. C. Jebb, *Attic Orators* (New York: 1962) vol. 2: pp. 202–213; Bork, *Der junge Grieche*, pp. 53–54; W. Jaeger, *Paideia* 3: pp. 48–49, 119–123; Münschner, *RE* 9: cols. 2206–2208, G. Norlin, *Isocrates* (LCL) vol. 2: p. 100, warns that we must be on guard against exaggerations in Isocrates and the philosophers of the fourth century in their depiction of the degeneracy of Athens.

83. Isocrates, *Demonicus* 14–16.

84. Xenophon, *Anabasis* 1.9.5.

85. Xenophon, *Memorabilia* 3.5.14–15.

86. G. Busolt, *Die griechische Staats-und Rechtsaltertümer* (Munich: 1892), pp. 306–307; J. Oehler, *RE*, Zw. Reihe, 3: cols. 1104–1106.

87. Plato, *Laws* 881A.

88. Plato, Stobaeus, *Anthology*, 4.25.43; *Laws* 879B, 880E, 881B–C, 930A, 931E, 932A; *Seventh Letter* 331C. On the authenticity of Plato's *Seventh Letter*, see, e.g., L. Edelstein, *Plato's Seventh Letter* (Leiden: 1966), pp. 167–169; F. Solmsen, *Gnomon* 41 (1969): 29–34.

89. Plato, *Laws* 717–718A.

90. Ibid., 879C.

91. Cp. Plato *Euthyphro* 4D–E, 5D, 6A.

92. Plato, *Laws* 718A, 879B–C, 880E, 881A–B, 931C.

93. Ibid., 928D–E.

94. Ibid., 879B–C.

95. Ibid., 881D.

96. Ibid., 932A–C.

97. Feuer, *Conflict of Generations*, pp. 27–30.

98. Ibid., pp. 27–28.

99. Plato, *Republic* 549C–550B.

100. Ibid., 560B–E, 561A–E. Cp. Bork, *Der junge Grieche*, pp. 52–53.

101. Plato, *Republic* 562D–563A.

102. E.g., Plato, *Seventh Letter* 328B; *Laws* 716A.

103. Aristotle, *Rhetoric* 2.12.3–16.16.

104. Ibid., 2.12.3–14.

105. Ibid., 2.13.6, 9, 13–14. Cp. 1.5.6, on self-restraint and courage as the *aretai* of the youth.

106. Cp. Feuer, *Conflict of Generations*, p. 30. I fail to see as evidence for "the immense political significance of generational struggle in the Greek towns" the political struggles for office in the oligarchic cities of Massilia, Ister Heraclea, and Cnidos, cited by Aristotle, *Politics* 5.5. Rather than involving generational confrontations, the passage deals with provision made to prevent members of the same families—older and younger brothers, fathers and sons—from holding magistracies at the same time. In *Nicomachean Ethics* 7.6.2, Aristotle tells of a man who when indicted for beating his father defended himself by testifying that it ran in the family: his father beat his father, and he fully expects his own son to beat him. Dinarchus's *Against Aristogeiton* (338 B.C.) involves a case in Athens of a man accused of mistreating his father.

107. P. S. Dunkin, *Post-Aristophanic Comedy. Studies in the Social Outlook of Middle and New Comedy* Studies in Language and Literature, No. 21 (3–4) (Urbana: 1946), pp. 24–30, 52–54, 106–137. F. Wehrli, *Motivstudien*, pp. 56–69. Cp., e.g., Diphilus, frag. 93 (Edmonds; Kock=Stobaeus, *Anthology* 4.25.16): "If I appear to speak better than my father, I wrong myself and am no longer reverent to the gods, for I harm my sire and do not love him."

108. D. L. Page, *Greek Literary Papyri* (LCL), No. 56 (4). Cp. Menander, frag. 663 (Edmonds; Koch): "He who gladly makes himself a proper and true guardian for his son will not have someone around waiting for him to die," Ariston (Peripatetic philosopher of the third century B.C. [*RE* 2: cols. 952–957], frag. (Stobaeus, *Anthology* 4.25.44): "Those who have recently studied philosophy, and question all, beginning with their parents, are like new born puppies. Not only do they bark against outsiders, but also those inside."

109. R. C. Forbes, *Neoi* (Middletown, 1933=Amer. Philol. Assn., Monographs, No. 2): F. Poland, *Neoi, RE* 16: cols. 2401–2409; P. F. Girard, *Neoi, DS* 4: 59. R. F. Willetts, *Aristocratic Society in Ancient Crete* (London: 1955), pp. 188–190.

110. Insc. Cret. 4.162, 163, 164; H. Schaefer, "Neotas," *RE* 16: col. 2477; Willetts, *Aristocratic Society*, pp. 187–190.

111. Polybius, *Universal History* 4.53.7–9.

112. Insc. Cret., 1: pp. 84–88, lines 10–14; Willetts, *Aristocratic Society*, 119–120, 182–183; H. van Effenterre, "A propos du serment des Dreriens," *BCH* 61 (1937): 327–332. Scholars disagree on whether the oath of the Drerian youth was a new oath for the occasion or recopied at the time from a much older archetype.

113. R. Thapar, *Asoka and the Decline of the Mauryas* (Oxford: 1961), p. 213.

114. D. Schlumberger and L. Robert, "Une Bilingue Greco-Arameenne d'Asoka," *Journal Asiatique* 246 (1958): 2–3. The Aramaic text of the same edict (p. 22) is slightly different: in place of "contrary to what had been the case previously," it reads "in conformity with the obligations which fate has imposed upon each."

115. Rock Edicts II, III, IV, XI, XIII; Pillar Edict VII. On the texts and significance of Asoka's edicts see *The Edicts of Asoka*, ed. and trans. N. A. Nikam and R. McKeon (Chicago: 1959); J. Bloch, *Les Inscriptions d'Asoka* (Paris: 1950); V. A. Smith, *Asoka, The Buddhist Emperor of India* (Oxford: 1920), pp. 149–230; R. Thapar, *Asoka and the Decline of the Mauryas* (Oxford: 1961), pp. 147, 164, 180, 213–217, 250–266 (texts in English); B. G. Gokhale, *Asoka Maurya* (New York: 1966); G. Woodcock, *The Greeks in India* (London: 1966), pp. 47–61.

116. Gaius 1.55. On *potria potestas*, see, e.g., R. Paribeni, *La Famiglia Romana* (Rome: 1948), pp. 11, 31–33, 45, 46; M. Borda, *Lares La Vita Familiare Romana* (Rome: 1947), pp. 2–3; M. Pellison, *Roman Life in Pliny's Time* (New York: 1897), pp. 19–20, L. Beauhet, "Patria Potestas," *DS* 4: 344–347; M. Johnston, *Roman Life* (Chicago: 1957), pp. 106–109; M. Kaser, "Der Inhalt der Patria Potestas," *Zeitschrift der Savigny-Stiftung für Rechtsgeschichte, Rom. Abt.* 58 (1938): 62–87; Reallexikon für Antike und Christentum, vol. 4: 1194–1198.

117. Cicero, *De officiis* I, 122.

118. Ibid.

119. C. Koch, "Pietas," *RE* 20: cols. 1221–1232; R. Heinze, "Zum römischen Moral," in *Vom Geist des Römertums* (Stuttgart: 1960), pp. 82–86.

120. K. Müller, ed. *Festus, De Verborum significatione* (Leipzig, 1839), p. 230. W. M. Lindsay, ed. *Festus, De Verborum significatione* (Leipzig, 1913) p. 260.

121. Dunkin, *Post-Aristophanic Comedy*, pp. 64–102; Wehrli, *Motivstudien* pp. 56–69.

122. Quoted by Cicero, *De Senectute* 6.60.

123. See, e.g., A. Gwynn, *Roman Education from Cicero to Quintilian* (Oxford: 1926), pp. 12–21.

124. Plutarch, *Cato Maior* 20.3–8.

125. The collapse of traditional Roman moral standards in the first century B.C. is too well known to require documentation here. A good example is Cicero's son Marcus. Cp. J. Carcopino, *Cicero, The Secrets of His Correspondence* (London: 1951) vol. 1: pp. 151–177; F. F. Abbott, "The Career of a Roman Student," in *Society and Politics in Ancient Rome* (New York: 1963, reprint), pp. 200–213. On the nonconformism and retreat from national commitment on the part of many of the Roman youth in the first century B.C. in both politics and literature see the suggestive comments of J. Granarolo, "La jeunesse au siècle de César d'apres Catulle et Cicéron," *Assoc. G. Budé, Congrés de Lyon, Actes* (Paris: 1960), pp. 483–519.

126. Cicero, *De officiis* 2.13.46: "And if they associate constantly with such men they inspire in the public the expectation that they will be like them, seeing that they have themselves selected them for imitation."

127. Cicero, *De Senectute* 6.20.

128. Sallust, *Catiline* 12.1.

129. Ibid., 37.7.

130. Ibid., 3.3–5, 12.1–2, 13.4–5; *Epistula I ad Caesarem* 5.5–6.

131. Sallust, *Catiline* 38.1; cp. 52.26.

132. Ibid., 14.1–4.

133. Sallust, *Epistula I ad Caesarem* 6.1.

134. Ibid., 5.6, 6.4, 7.2.

135. On Sallust's views, see, e.g., K. Vretska, *C. Sallustius Crispus: Invektiven und Episteln* (Heidelberg: 1961) 1: p. 70; 2: pp. 224, 239. The genuineness of Sallust's letters to Caesar seems well established in contemporary scholarship.

136. Horace, *Odes* 3.6.21–32, 45–48.

137. See, e.g., Zeibarth, "Iuvenes," *RE* 10: cols. 1357–1358; C. Jullian, "Iuvenes," *DS*, vol. 3, pp. 782–785; "Iuvenes," *Dizionario Epigrafico di Antichità Romane*, vol. 4, pp. 317–320, S. L. Mohler, "The Iuvenes in Roman Education" *TAPA* 68 (1937): 442–479, M. Rostovtzeff, *Römische Bleitesserae, Klio*, Beiheft 3 (1905); idem, *The Social and*

Economic History of the Roman Empire, rev. by P. M. Fraser (Oxford: 1962), pp. 103, 107, 127–128. Rostovtzeff considered the *collegia iuvenum* as "seminaries of future soldiers" which provided military preparation for future officers, soldiers, and local militia. By contrast, Mohler regarded these associations as clubs of schoolboys for the promotion of sports and social activities for school youth.

CHAPTER 2

Originally published in *Historia* 20 (1981), 275–302. For a recent treatment of many related topics, see J. E. Lendon, *Empire of Honour* (Oxford, 1997).

　　1. The vast variety of social forms and gradation in local situations throughout the Roman Empire—and hence the necessity of avoiding generalizations—is well represented in *The Conflict between Paganism and Christianity in the Fourth Century*, ed. A. Momigliano (Oxford: 1963), p. 4.

　　2. M. A. Levi, *Political Power in the Ancient World* (New York: 1965), p. 172; cp. also p. 143.

　　3. Pliny, *Natural History* 33:12.41, calls social distinction *differentia*.

　　4. On the technical concept *usurpare, usurpatio* see, e.g., Suetonius, *Claudius* 25; E. Cuq, in *DS*, 5: 610. In Ammianus Marcellinus (15,6,3) we find *praesumere fortunae superioris insignia*.

　　5. Paul, *Sententiae* 5, 25,12, Qui insignia altioris ordinis utuntur militiamque confingunt, quo quem terreant vel concutiant, humiliores capite puniuntur, honestiores deportantur. The Latin term for "status symbols" is *insignia dignitatis* (e.g., Apuleius, *Apologia* 50: 75). Diodorus (31.15.2) speaks of white togas and special shoes; Dio Chrysostom (4.61) refers to tiaras and purple ("extrinsic symbols"). Aristotle (*Politics* 1324b) notes that in many societies military decorations are the primary status symbols: "There are many such practices, varying from people to people, some sanctioned by laws, some by custom." On the intensity of the Roman passion for such badges and distinctions, cp. S. Dill, *Roman Society from Nero to Marcus Aurelius* (London: 1905), pp. 210, 214–215. On the gradual encroachment, despite interdicts, by unauthorized persons on distinctive badges and costumes of upper ranks in antiquity, cp. Herbert Spencer, *Principles of Sociology* (New York: 1880), bk. 2, pt. 4 (*Ceremonial Occasions*), pp. 187–189. Herbert Spencer was the first to subject to systematic analysis status symbols, mostly of primitive peoples. Rousseau, deploring the disappearance of many status symbols in his day, comments: "Que d'attention chez les Romains à la langue des signes!" *Emile* (Paris: 1860), p. 389.

　　6. On such abuses in general and the difficulty of controlling them cp. Th. Mommsen, *Römisches Staatsrecht* (Leipzig: 1887–1888), 3: 514,517; R. Taubenschlag, *The Law of Greco-Roman Egypt in the Light of the Papyri* (New York: 1944), pp. 362–364; J. Gagé, *Les Classes Sociales dans l'Empire Romain* (Paris: 1964), pp. 143–146.

　　7. A. H. M. Jones, *The Later Roman Empire* (Oxford: 1964), vol 1: p. viii.

　　8. See below.

　　9. Cp., e.g., Livy 41:8.11; 9.9–11 on evasions, fraud, and the flouting of the law by Italian allies bent on securing individual transfers of Roman citizenship in the second century B.C., *imaginibus iuris spretis, promiscue sine lege*. During the civil wars of 68–69 A.D. numerous slaves and freedmen were catapulted into higher status (cp. Tacitus, *History* 1:13; 1:76; 2:57). Cp. also C. G. Starr, *The Roman Imperial Navy* 2nd ed. (New York: 1960), pp. 81, 188.

10. Tacitus, *Annals* 3:53–54 (22 A.D.).

11. The frequent repetition of sumptuary laws among the Romans is evidence for the persistent flouting of such statutes. See, e.g., C. Lécrivain, *DS* 4:1563; B. Kübler, *RE*, Zw. Reihe, 4:901–908. Cp. F. E. Baldwin, *Sumptuary Legislation and Personal Regulation in England* (Baltimore: 1926). Cp. also the frequent reissuance of sumptuary laws in seventeenth-century Japan, the universal violation of these laws, and the many retreats of the authorities before widespread infractions; see D. H. Shively, "Sumptuary Regulation and Status in Early Tokugawa Japan," *Harvard Journal of Asiatic Studies* 25 (1964/1965): 123–164.

12. See note 107 below.

13. Valerius Maximus, 3:4, 5 (the text is somewhat garbled, but the basic facts are clear). Cp. F. Münzer, *RE* 19: 893–894; *Römische Adelsparteien und Adelsfamilien* (Stuttgart: 1963), pp. 95–97.

14. See E. Badian, "Quaestiones Variae," *Historia* 18 (1969): 489–490.

15. Cicero's speech *Pro Archia*, despite the political motivations underlying the challenge to the Roman citizenship of the Greek poet Archias, must be read against the background of suspicion of widespread individual usurpation of Roman citizenship at this time.

16. *Verr.* 2: iii, 80, 185, 187.

17. Macrobius, *Saturnalia* 3:14.13.

18. Suetonius, *Julius* 39.2; Macrobius, *Saturnalia* 2:7.2; Seneca, *Controversies* 7.3.9. Cp. W. Kroll, *RE* 12:246–247.

19. Cicero, *Letters to Friends* 10:32.2.

20. R. Syme, *The Roman Revolution* (Oxford: 1939), p. 368, calls Augustus "a small-town bourgeois, devoted and insatiable in admiration of social distinction."

21. K. Hopkins, "Elite Mobility in the Roman Empire," *Past and Present* 32 (1962): 12–13.

22. Gagé, *Les Classes Sociales*, p. 40.

23. Cassius Dio 56:33.3, describes Augustus's social policy as directed to keeping "a wide distance between Romans and the subject peoples." On Augustus's social policies see Gagé, *Les Classes Sociales*, pp. 66–77; Syme, *Roman Revolution*, pp. 349–386, 490–508; H. Last, *CAH* 10:183–189, 425–434; H. T. Rowell, *Rome in the Augustan Age* (Norman, Okla.: 1962), pp. 68–99; R. Paribeni, *L'eta di Cesare et di Augusto* (Bologna: 1950), pp. 451–459; M. Rostovtzeff, *SEHRE* (Oxford: 1957), pp. 46–51; A. D. Winspear and L. K. Geweke, *Augustus and the Reconstruction of Roman Government and Society* (Madison: 1935), pp. 86–123; N. A. Maschkin, *Zwischen Republik und Kaiserreich. Ursprung und sozialer Charakter des Augusteischen Prinzipats* (Leipzig: 1954), pp. 418–448.

24. Cassius Dio 53:27.6.

25. K. Hopkins, "Elite Mobility," p. 17: "So long as an aristocracy depends on birth alone it can remain exclusive; when it admits complementary criteria of achievement, whether money or political skill, it opens the way to *arrivistes*."

26. *Epodes* 4: 15–16: sedilibusque magnus in primis eques / Othone contempto sedet. Cp. E. Fraenkel, *Horace* (Oxford: 1957), 57–58, who dates the epode in 37/36 B.C., during the Sicilian War between Octavian and Sextus Pompey.

27. Scholl in *Juvenal* 5: 3; Porphyry on Horace, *Satires* 1. 5: 51–55; Plutarch, *Antony* 59.4.

28. Cicero, *Philippics*. 2:18.44.

29. Suetonius, *Augustus* 40.

30. Suetonius, *Gaius* 26.

31. Suetonius, *Domitian* 8. Cp. A. Stein, *Der römische Ritterstand* (Munich: 1927; Münch. Beitr. z. Papyrusforsch. und Ant. Rechtsgesch. X), pp. 22–28.

32. Martial, *Epigrams* 5:8. Other instances of the use of expensive clothing to ape equestrian wealth and thus usurp a seat are given in Martial 5: 23, 35.

33. Martial, *Epigrams* 5:14. Cp. also 3:95; 5:25, 27.

34. Seneca, *De Clementia* 1:24; *Historia Augusta, Severus Alexander* 27. The jurists Ulpian and Paul dissuaded Alexander Severus from establishing a hierarchy of distinctive official garbs for all classes, including slaves, as a dangerous social innovation. On clothing as status symbols among the Romans cp. Mommsen, *Römisches Staatsrecht*, 3:215–223.

35. *Digest* 49:14, 32; Pliny, *Epistles* 4:11.3. A defendant in a case involving alleged usurpation of citizenship (*reus peregrinitatis*) was permitted by the Emperor Claudius to change from Greek pallium to Roman toga frequently during the trial, depending on whether he was being accused or defended at the moment (Suetonius, *Claudius* 15).

36. Of course, the usurpation of distinctive class clothing insignia, such as the senatorial *latus clavus* and shoe, and the equestrian *angustus clavus* were not likely to go unchallenged.

37. Cassius Dio 49:16. Diodorus (36:7.4) records the usurpation by Tryphon, leader of the slave revolt in the Second Servile War (104–101 B.C.) of purple toga, and tunic with *latus clavus*, as well as other symbols of holders of the imperium in the Roman government.

38. Cassius Dio 57:13.4–5.

39. M. Reinhold, *History of Purple as a Status Symbol in Antiquity* (Bruxelles: 1970. Collection Latomus, 116), pp. 48–73.

40. Ibid., pp. 62–67. On purple garments as status distinctions in the Roman Empire see articles *purpura* by M. Besnier, *Daremberg-Saglio* 4: 776–778; K. Schneider, *RE* 12:2018–2020.

41. *Cod. Theod.* 10:21.3 (*Cod. Just.* 11:9). Cp. R. S. Lopez, "Silk Industry in the Byzantine Empire," *Speculum* 20 (1945): 1–10. Lopez's perspective is incorrect when he analyzes the flouting of restrictions on the use of purple as a struggle on the part of private citizens against the efforts by the later emperors to establish a "hierarchy of clothing."

42. Ammianus Marcellinus 14:9.7.

43. *Cod. Theod.* 10:20.18 (436 A.D.).

44. *Cod. Just.* 4:40.1: fortunarum se suarum et capitis sciat subiturum esse discrimen. Cp. Lactantius, *Div. Inst.* 4:7, 6: Romanis indumentum purpurae insigne est regiae dignitatis assumptae. One should recall in this connection the purple garment put on Christ as "king" by Roman soldiers (Mark 15.17; Matt. 27.28; John 19.23).

45. Cp. L. Friedländer, *Roman Life and Manners under the Early Empire* (New York: 1965), 2: 131–230; also K. Polanyi, C. Arensberg, and H. W. Pearson, *Trade and Politics in the Early Empires* (Glencoe, Ill.: 1957), pp. 335–338, for conspicuous spending as a prestige symbol in Roman society.

46. Cp. Martial, *Epigrams* 4:61; 5:39; 8:6; 9:59; 10:87; 12:69. There was a lucrative industry engaging in the manufacture of imitation gems; manuals containing instructions for making fake gems existed. See Pliny, *Natural History* 37: 75–76, 197–200.

47. Pliny, *Natural History* 33:6.23; cp. Petronius, *Satyricon* 32.3 (in this case the motive may also have been to pass as a free person). For the practice of plating rings of

inferior metals with gold and the numerous gilded bronze rings which have come down to us see F. H. Marshall, *Catalogue of the Finger Rings . . . in the British Museum* (London: 1907), pp. xx, xxxii.

48. Martial, *Epigrams* 2:29.

49. On the status and status symbols of the Equestrian Order see Stein, *Der römische Ritterstand*, pp. 21–49; Kübler, *RE* 6:286–288, 2972–2999; R. Cagnat, *Daremberg-Saglio* 2: 771–789; Mommsen, *Römisches Staatsrecht* 3: 476–569; H. Hill, *The Roman Middle Class in the Republican Period* (Oxford: 1952), pp. 215–216.

50. Martial, *Epigrams* 5: 38.

51. Ibid., 1:103.2; 4:67.4; 9:49. Mommsen, *Römisches Staatsrecht* 3: 514, 517, declares that usurpation of equestrian title and dress was widely practiced and tolerated.

52. Pliny, *Natural History* 33:8.32.

53. Ibid., 33.8.33.

54. Ibid.

55. *Cod. Just.* 9:21; 9:31; 10:33.1; *Cod. Theod.* 9:20. Cp. Ineditum Vaticanum 226: Ius anulorum ingenuitatis imaginem praestat salvo iure patronorum patronique liberorum. It is interesting to note that when Claudius's freedman Pallas (Pliny, *Epistles* 7:29; 8:6) was granted *ornamenta praetoria* and the *anulus aureus* by the Roman Senate, he resisted acceptance of the gold ring. He did this because he desired to retain the advantages of an imperial freedman, and so declined even fictive liberation through grant of *ingenuitas* from ties with the emperor. Cp. A. N. Sherwin-White, *The Letters of Pliny. A Historical and Social Commentary* (Oxford: 1966), pp. 453–454. On *ingenuitas* in general see Kübler, *RE* 9:1544–1552; on aspects of social mobility in the early empire, P. R. C. Weaver, "Social Mobility in the Early Roman Empire: The Evidence of the Imperial Freedmen and Slaves," *Past and Present* 37 (1967): 1–20; C. Nicolet, *L'Ordre Equestre à l'Epoque Républicaine* (Paris: 1966), pp. 140–142, 457–464.

56. Suetonius, *Claudius* 25; Pliny, *Natural History*, 33:8, 33. Cp. *Historia Augusta, Severus Alexander* 19, 4: libertinos numquam in equestrem locum redegit adserens seminarium senatorum equestrem locum esse.

57. See Mommsen, *Römisches Staatsrecht* 2:.

58. Herodian 3: 8, 5.58.

59. Mommsen, *Römisches Staatsrecht* 1: 455–467. See also articles *ornamenta* by Lécrivain, *DS* 4: 238–239; Borsák, *RE* 18: 1110–1122. The display of freedmen's wealth as a status symbol in Rome, Italy, and the provinces is a well-known phenomenon.

60. See, e. g., Dill, *Roman Society*, pp. 100–137; A. M. Duff, *Freedmen in the Early Roman Empire* (Oxford: 1928), pp. 50–71; Rowell, *Rome in the Augustian Age*, pp. 8–98; Gagé, *Les Classes Sociales*, pp. 138–143.

61. See note 59.

62. Suetonius, *De Grammaticis* 18; Martial, *Epigrams* 6:17. On the substitution of Latin names by freedmen see Duff, *Freedman in the Early Roman Empire*, pp. 55–58; Friedlander, *Roman Life*, pp. 56–57. In Ptolemaic Egypt we have evidence in the papyri of numerous Egyptians assuming Greek names, beginning about the middle of the second century B.C. See S. Davis, *Race-Relations in Ancient Egypt. Greek, Egyptian, Hebrew, Roman* (New York: 1952), p. 55. For Egyptians assuming Greek names in Roman Egypt, see J. G. Winter, *Life and Letters in the Papyri* (Ann Arbor: 1933), pp. 24–25.

63. Suetonius, *Claudius* 25: peregrinae condicionis homines vetuit usurpare Romana nomina dumtaxat gentilicia. Cp. also Claudius's edict on the citizenship of some

Alpine tribes, below. The enforcement of this law was difficult and not carefully policed. Cp. Starr, *Roman Imperial Navy*, p. 72. Eventually massive uncontrollable inroads destroyed the purity of the Roman nomenclature. In Roman Egypt it is not possible to determine legal status from name alone, for some persons using non-Roman names were Roman citizens, while others with Roman names were not. Cp. J. F. Oates, "Philadelphia in the Fayum during the Roman Empire," *Atti dell'XI Congresso Internazionale di Papirologia* (Milan: 1965), 453–458.

64. Paul, *Sententiae* 5:25, 11: [Ad Legem Corneliam Testamentariam] Qui sibi falsum nomen imposuerit, genus parentesve finxerit, quo quid alienum interciperet caperet possideret, poena legis Corneliae de falsis coercetur; *Gnomon Idiologi* 42: "Persons who improperly describe themselves and persons who knowingly concur in such descriptions incur confiscation of one-fourth of their property."

65. Cassius Dio 78:13.3–4; Fluss, *RE* 14: 1547–1549.

66. Suetonius, *Claudius* 25; Arrian, *Epictetus* 3:24.42.

67. *Corpus Inscriptionum Latinarum* 5: 5050; *Fontes Iuris Romani Antejustiniani* 1, no. 71; Dessau, *Inscriptionum Latinae Selectae*, no. 206; N. Lewis and M. Reinhold, *Roman Civilization*, rev. ed. (New York: 1966), 2: 130–131. Cp. V. Scramuzza, *The Emperor Claudius* (Cambridge, Mass.: 1940), pp. 129–133; A. Momigliano, *Claudius the Emperor and His Achievement*, rev. ed. (New York: 1961), 67.

68. Cp. Scramuzza, *Emperor Claudius*, p. 277, note 11. Scramuzza cites, among others, the case of Latins usurping Roman citizenship in 195 B.C. (Livy 34: 42, 5–6): cum ob id se pro civibus Romanis ferrent, senatus iudicavit non esse eos cives Romanos.

69. Cassius Dio 60:17.6–8. Cp. Tacitus, *Annals* 14:50.

70. Acts 22.27–28. See A. N. Sherwin-White, *Roman Society and Roman Law in the New Testament* (Oxford: 1963), pp. 154–156.

71. See F. Schulz, "Roman Registers of Birth and Birth Certificates," *JRS* 32 (1942): 78–91; 33 (1943): 55–64.

72. Cp. Sherwin-White, *Roman Society and Roman Law*, pp. 147–148.

73. Cp. Petronius, *Satyricon* 57, where a freedman, claiming to be a king's son, states: ipse me dedi in servitutem, et malui civis Romanus esse quam tributarius.

74. Tacitus, *Annals* 14: 50.

75. Cp. N. Lewis, "On Official Corruption in Roman Egypt," *PAPS* 98 (1954): 153–158; H. Braunert, *Die Binnenwanderung. Studien zur Sozialgeschichte Ägyptens in der Ptolemäer— und Kaiserzeit* (Bonn: 1964; Bonn. Hist. Forsch., Bd. 26), pp. 165–186.

76. For Augustus's policy toward Hellenes and his social organization of Egypt, see G. W. Bowersock, *Augustus and the Greek World* (Oxford: 1965); *CAH*, 10:294–300; Winspear and Geweke, *Augustus and the Reconstruction*, pp. 235–242; A. H. M. Jones, *The Cities of the Eastern Roman Provinces* (Oxford: 1937), pp. 311–318.

77. Cp. V. A. Tcherikover, *Hellenistic Civilization and the Jews* (Philadelphia: 1961), pp. 20–21; H. I. Bell, *Egypt from Alexander the Great to the Arab Conquest* (Oxford: 1948), p. 386; Davis, *Race-Relations*, pp. 52–57.

78. Josephus, in a personal attack on Apion (*Against Apion* 2: 29), asserts that Apion was unquestionably of Egyptian status but falsely declared himself to be an Alexandrian, thereby disowning the ignominy of his origin; but Josephus also concedes that Apion was granted citizenship rights by the Alexandrians (2: 32, 41).

79. *Gnomon Idiologi* 42, 43, 46, 55, 56. See A. S. Hunt and C. C. Edgar, *Select Papyri*, no. 212; Lewis and Reinhold, *Roman Civilization*, pp. 366–369; *Corpus Papyrorum*

Judaicarum, ed. V. A. Tcherikover, A. Fuks, and M. Stern (Cambridge, Mass.: 1957–1964), 1: 56–74; 2: 1–5, 36–55.

80. *Giessen Papyrus* 40, 3–4.

81. There is a vast bibliography on the Jews in Roman Alexandria. See, e.g., Tcherikover, *Hellenistic Civilization and the Jews*, pp. 311–332; idem, "The Decline of the Jewish Diaspora in Egypt in the Roman Period," *Journ. Jewish Stud.* 14 (1963): 1–32; *CPJud* 2: 154–159; H. Musurillo, *Acts of the Pagan Martyrs* (Oxford: 1954), passim; Momigliano, *Claudius*, pp. 96–98; A. Segré, "The Status of the Jews in Ptolemaic and Roman Egypt. New Light from the Papyri," *Jewish Soc. Stud.* 6 (1944): 375–400; Davis, *Race-Relations*, 93–112; Scramuzza, pp. 64–79; H. I. Bell, "Anti-Semitism in Alexandria," *JRS* 31 (1941): 1–18; Braunert, *Die Binnenwanderung*, pp. 195–200.

82. *CPJud*, 2: 153.

83. *PSI* 1160, col. ii; *CPJud*, no. 156; Musurillo, *Acts of Pagan Martyrs*, pp. 1–3, 8092. Musurillo dates the "Boule Papyrus" in the first half of the first century A.D.; it may belong to the end of the Augustan Age. Cp. Rostovtzeff, *SEHRE*, 2:560–561. In the "Acts of Isidore" (*PBerl* 8877; Musurillo, 23–26), the Alexandrian Isidorus is given this speech: "They [the Jews] are not of the same temperament as the Alexandrians, but after the fashion of the Egyptians. . . . Are they not on a level with those paying the tax?"

84. *Gnomon Idiologi* 40, 44, 47, 55, 67. Juridically all Egyptians were *dediticii*, the lowest stratum of peregrines. Enrollment in even such low-ranking military units as the fleets at Misenum and Ravenna entailed advancement of status. Augustus may have allowed enrollment in the Italic fleets to the *laoi* of Egypt so as to afford Egyptian peasants at least one military outlet. Cp. A. H. M. Jones, *JRS* 26 (1936): 232, n. 37; Starr, *Roman Imperial Navy*, p. 77. Egyptians continued to be denied entry into the Roman legions and the other Roman military forces until the third century A.D., when the auxiliary units were opened to them.

85. Paul, *Sententiae* 5: 25,12 (see note 5 above).

86. See, e.g., Starr, *Roman Imperial Navy*, pp. 68–69; W. L. Westermann, *The Slave Systems of Greek and Roman Antiquity* (Philadelphia: 1955), pp. 37, 67.

87. *Digest* XLLX, 16,11.

88. Cassius Dio, *Epit.* 67: 13, 1.

89. Pliny, *Epistles* 10:29–30. Cp. Lewis and Reinhold, *Roman Civilization*, 2: 495–496, Sherwin–White, *The Letters of Pliny*, pp. 598–602.

90. *Theodosian Code* 7:21, 1 (313 A.D.).

91. Ibid., 14:10 (382 A.D.).

92. Ibid., 7:20, 12.

93. See, e.g., O. Seeck, *Geschichte des Untergangs der antiken Welt* (Berlin: 1901), 2: 301; F. Lot, *The End of the Ancient World and the Beginnings of the Middle Ages* (New York: 1931), pp. 124–125.

94. On the degree and variety of social mobility in the later empire see R. MacMullen, *Enemies of the Roman Order. Treason, Unrest, and Alienation in the Empire* (Cambridge, Mass.: 1966), pp. 199–200; idem, "Social Mobility in the Theodosian Code," *JRS* 54 (1964): 49–53; M. K. Hopkins, "Social Mobility in the Later Empire: The Evidence of Ausonius," *CQ* 11 (1961): 239–249; K. Hopkins, "Elite Mobility in the Roman Empire," *Past and Present* 32 (1965): 12–26; A. H. M. Jones, "The Social Background of the Struggle between Paganism and Christianity," in *The Conflict between Paganism and Christianity in the Fourth Century*, ed. A. Momigliano (Oxford, 1963), pp. 26–35.

95. A. H. M. Jones, *The Later Roman Empire*, 2:543.

96. On the Senatorial Order of the later empire, and on the fraud, bribery, and collusion practiced to obtain admission to this class, see, e.g., Abbott-Johnson, 103–104; A. H. M. Jones, *The Greek City from Alexander to Justinian* (Oxford: 1940), 193–197; idem, *The Later Roman Empire*, 2:523–562; Gagé, *Les Classes Sociales* 366–376; Momigliano, *The Conflict between Paganism and Christianity in the Fourth Century*, 8–9.

97. Cp. e.g., J. Vogt, *Der Niedergang Roms. Metamorphose der antiken Kultur* (Zurich: 1965), pp. 63, 134.

98. Jones, *Later Roman Empire*, 2: 740; Westermann, *Slave Systems*, p. 148.

99. On the curial class of the Roman Empire see, e.g., A. E. R. Boak, *Manpower Shortages and the Fall of the Roman Empire in the West* (Ann Arbor: 1955), pp. 79–83; P. Petit, *Libanius et la vie municipale à Antioche au IVe siècle ap. J. C.* (Paris: 1955); Gagé, *Les Classes Sociales*, pp. 376–383; S. Dill, *Roman Society in the Last Century of the Western Empire* (London: 1905), pp. 228–258; Jones, *The Greek City*, 192–209; idem, *Later Roman Empire*, 2: 724–763; W. Seyfarth, *Soziale Fragen der spätrömischen Kaiserzeit im Spiegel des Theodosianus* (Berlin: 1963).

100. On the extent of such evasion, see, e.g., Gagé, *Les Classes Sociales*, 339–341, 415–439; Jones, *The Greek City*, pp. 192–209.

101. Jones, *Later Roman Empire*, 2:754.

102. *Novels of Theodosius* 15.2.

103. *Theodosian Code* 6:22.1.

104. Ibid., 6:22.2.

105. Ibid., 6:22.7.3 (383 A.D.).

106. Ibid., 6:5.1 (383 A.D.).

107. Ibid., 6:5.2 (384 A.D.).

108. *Nov. Theod.* 22.2 (443 A.D.). Cp. *Nov. Theod.* 8 (439 A.D.).

CHAPTER 3

Originally published in *The Craft of the Ancient Historian: Essays in Honor of Chester G. Starr*, J. W. Eadie and J. Ober, eds. (Lanham, Md., 1985), pp. 21–40. For the views of human nature discussed, see E. O. Wilson, *On Human Nature* (Cambridge, Mass., 1978), and B. F. Skinner, *Beyond Freedom and Dignity* (New York, 1971), and *The Behavior of Organisms* (New York, 1938). On human nature in Thucydides, cf. G. Crane, *Thucydides and the Ancient Simplicity* (Berkeley and Los Angeles, 1998), pp. 295–303.

1. A. W. H. Adkins, *From the Many to the One: A Study of Personality and Views of Human Nature in the Context of Ancient Greek Society, Values, and Beliefs* (Ithaca, N.Y.: 1970), p. ix.

2. D. Hume, *An Enquiry concerning Human Understanding*, ed. L. A. Selby-Bigge (Oxford: 1927), p. 16.

3. W. Jaeger, *Paideia: The Ideals of Greek Culture* (New York: 1945): vol. 1, pp. 306, 307. On human nature in pre-Socratic thought, see, e.g., John W. Beardslee, Jr., *The Use of ΦΥΣΙΣ in Fifth Century Greek Literature* (Chicago: 1918), pp. 10–16; W. K. C. Guthrie, *History of Greek Philosophy* III (Cambridge, 1969), pp. 63–65; Adkins, *From the Many*, 92–101.

4. See, e.g., Beardslee, *Fifth Century Greek Literature*, pp. 31–42; W. H. S. Jones, *Philosophy and Medicine in Ancient Greece* (Baltimore: 1946), pp. 23–24, 31–32, 47; Jae-

ger, *Paideia* vol. 1, p. 477, n. 56; Josef-Hans Kuhn, *System- und Methoden-probleme im Corpus Hippocraticum* (Wiesbaden: 1956), pp. 20–23, 26–28, 57, 102; Charles Lichtenthaeler, *Thucydide et Hippocrate: vus par un historien-médicin* (Geneva: 1965), passim; Guthrie, *History of Greek Philosophy*, vol. 2 (Cambridge: 1965), pp. 351–353; Adkins, *From the Many*, 101–109; Jacques Jouanna, ed., *Hippocrate, La nature de l'homme* (Berlin: 1975; *Corpus Medicorum Graecorum*, I, i, part 3), pp. 38–39, 45–50, 59–61, 223–225.

5. On human nature in the thought of the Sophists see, e.g., Beardslee, *Fifth Century Greek Literature*, pp. 31–42; Louis Gernet, ed., *Antiphon, Discours* (Paris: 1923, Budé text), pp. 172–177; Mario Untersteiner, *The Sophists*, trans. Kathleen Freeman (Oxford: 1954), pp. 284, 288–289; Guthrie, *History of Greek Philosophy*, vol. 3, pp. 63–65, 107–110; Adkins, *From the Many*, pp. 110–126; George B. Kerferd, *The Sophistic Movement* (Cambridge: 1981), pp. 111, 114, 157–158.

6. Herodotus was the first to use the term, but he employed it merely to indicate the limits of human beings: 3.6.53, 8.38, 8.83.1.

7. On Thucydides's relationship to the pre-Socratics, Sophists, and the Hippocratic school, see, e.g., Jaeger, *Paideia*, vol. 1, pp. 306–307; D. L. Page, "Thucydides' Description of the Great Plague at Athens," *Classical Quarterly* n.s., 3 (1953): 98; André Rivier, "Pronostic et prevision chez Thucydide," *Museum Helveticum* 26 (1969): 129; Klaus Weidauer, *Thukydides und die Hippokratischen Schriften* (Heidelberg: 1954), pp. 32–46; Lichtenthaeler, *Thucydide*, pp. 154–156, 238; Kurt von Fritz, *Die griechische Geschichtsschreibung* (Munich: 1967), pp. 545–546; A. Geoffrey Woodhead, *Thucydides on the Nature of Power* (Cambridge, Mass.: 1970), pp. 15–16, G. E. M. de Ste. Croix, *The Origins of the Peloponnesian War* (Ithaca, N.Y.: 1972), p. 12 n. 2n. 20; Hunter R. Rawlings, *A Semantic Study of Prophasis to 400 B.C.* (Wiesbaden: 1975), pp. 76–81.

8. Peter R. Pouncey, *The Necessities of War: A Study of Thucydides' Pessimism* (New York: 1980), pp. xi, 20–23. Cp. de Ste. Croix, *Origins*, p. 29; Jaeger, *Paideia* vol. 1, p. 106; vol. 3, p. 6; Harald Patzer, *Das Problem der Geschichtsschreibung des Thukydides und die thukydideische Frage* (Berlin: 1937), pp. 91–97; Weidauer, *Thukydides*, pp. 32–46; Adkins, *From the Many*, pp. 101–106.

9. Thucydides, *History of the Peloponnesian War*, 1.76.2–3 (speech of Athenians at conference of Corinth); 3.84.2; 4.61.5 (speech of Hermokrates of Syracuse); 5.105.2 (speech of Athenians at Melos). Cp. Paul Shorey, "On the Implicit Ethics and Psychology of Thucydides," *TAPA* 24 (1893): 66–88; Wilhelm Nestle, "Thukydides und die Sophistik," *Neue Jahrb. Klass. Altertum* 33 (1914): 662–663, 668–669, 684; August Grosskinsky, *Das Programm des Thukydides* (Berlin: 1936), pp. 61–70; John H. Finley, *Thucydides* (Cambridge, Mass.: 1942), pp. 98–99; Jaeger, *Paideia* vol. 1, 306–307, 389, 485–486, n. 21; II, 6; Hans Peter Stahl, *Thucydides: Die Stellung des Menschen im geschichtlichen Prozess* (Munich: 1966), pp. 15–16; Adkins, *From the Many*, pp. 78, 82; Giovanni Casertano, *Natura e istituzioni umane nelle dottrine dei Sofisti* (Naples: 1971), pp. 24–27, Pouncey, *Necessities*, pp. 33–38.

10. Thucydides, *History* 1.76.2, 3.39.5 (Cleon's speech), 4.61.5, 5.89 (speech of Athenians at Melos), 5.105.2. Cp. Democritus, frag. 287: φύσει τὸ ἄρχειν οἰκήιον τῷ κρέσσονι. In 3.84.2 man's ungovernable *physis* is depicted as based on self-interest and aggression, and as giving revenge and thirst for power priority over religion, law, and justice. This passage is usually bracketed as a gloss (cp. A. W. Gomme, *A Historical Commentary on Thucycides* (Oxford, 1956), vol. 2; pp. 382–386, but Edgar Wenzel, "Zur Echtheitsfrage von Thukydides 3.84," *WS* 81 (1968): 18–27, argues cogently for the genuineness of the passage. Cf. Ernest

Toptisch, "Ανθρωπεία, φύσις und Ethik bei Thukydides," WS 61–62 (1943–1947): 59–61; Stahl, *Thukydides*, pp. 114, 122–124, 166–71.

11. Thucydides, *History* 3.45.3 (Diodotus's speech); cp. 3.40.2 (Cleon's speech).

12. E.g., in Sophocles, *Antigone* 1023–1024 (ἀνθρώποισι γὰρ/τοῖς πᾶσι κοινόν ἐστι τοὐξημαρτάνειν), Euripides, Xenophon, Cicero, Lucian. On the proverbial *errare est humanum* see August Otto, *Die Sprichwörter und sprichwörterlichen Redensarten der Römer* (Leipzig: 1890), pp. 155–156.

13. On prognosis in Thucydides, see, e.g., Nestle, "Thukydides," 655; Rivier, "Pronostic," p. 129; Lichtenthaeler, *Thucydide*, pp. 155–157, 167, 238–240; Lowell Edmunds, *Chance and Intelligence in Thucydides* (Cambridge, Mass.: 1975), pp. 145, 154.

14. Thucydides, *History* 1.22.4, 3.82.2.

15. Cf. Woodhead, *Thucydides*, p. 19; Pouncey, *Necessities*, p. 35; G. E. M. de Ste. Croix, *The Class Struggle in the Ancient Greek World* (Ithaca, N.Y.: 1981), p. 27.

16. Shorey, "Implicit Ethics," pp. 75, 77–78; Nestle, "Thukydides," 661–662; Pierre Huart, *Le Vocabulaire de l'analyse psychologique dans l'oeuvre de Thucydide* (Paris: 1968), pp. 491–505.

17. W. Müri, "Beitrag zum Verständnis des Thukydides," *Museum Helveticum* 4 (1947): 273. Cp. Rawlings, *Semantic Study*, p. 77.

18. Rivier, "Pronostic," pp. 136–138.

19. Edmunds, *Chance*, p 154.

20. Marc Cogan, *The Human Thing: The Speeches and Principles of Thucydides' History* (Chicago: 1981), pp. 185–186, 188–190, 197–198, 237–238.

21. For Thucydides's basic concern with collective behavior, see Arnaldo Momigliano, *The Development of Greek Biography* (Cambridge, Mass.: 1971), p. 39; K. J. Dover, *Greek Popular Morality in the Time of Plato and Aristotle* (Berkeley, Calif.: 1974), pp. 81–83; de Ste. Croix, *Class Struggle*, p. 27.

22. Pouncey, *Necessities*, pp. 142–144. On ethnocentric influence on conceptions of human nature, Cp. Ellsworth Faris, *The Nature of Human Nature* (New York: 1937), pp. 13–15, 18; Clyde Kluckhohn, *Anthropology and the Classics* (Providence, R.I.: 1961), p. 41.

23. See the valuable discussion of Wesley E. Thompson, "Individual Motivation in Thucydides," *Classica et Mediaevalia* 30 (1969): 171–172. Cp. Weidauer, *Thukydides*, p. 37; Michael C. Mittelstadt, "Thucydidean Psychology and Moral Value Judgement in the History: Some Characteristics," *Rivista di Studi Classici* 25 (1977): 31–35, 55.

24. See, e.g., Pouncey, *Necessities*, p. 23; cp. R. G. Collingwood, "Human Nature and Human History," *PBA* (May 1936): 98–99, 101, 108–109, 115.

25. Claus Meister, *Die Gnomik im Geschichtswerk des Thukydides* (Winterthur: 1955), pp. 60–61, 75–77; Patzer, *Das Problem*, pp. 91–97; Pouncey, *Necessities*, p. 23. Cp. Merle E. Curti's acute observation in *Human Nature in American Thought: A History* (Madison, Wis.: 1980), p. 409, that most views of human nature are generalizations made up of traditional beliefs and inferences from random observations; idem, *Human Nature in American Historical Thought* (Columbia, Mo.: 1970), pp. v–vi.

26. Thucydides, *History*, 2.50.1, 3.82.2.

27. Cp. E. R. Dodds, *The Greeks and the Irrational* (Berkeley, Calif.: 1951), pp. 191–192; Curti, *Human Nature in American Thought*, p. xi.

28. See, e.g., Hans Drexler, "Die Entdeckung des Individuums: Probleme antiker Menschendarstellung," *Gymnasium* 63 (1956): 402–403.

29. Shorey, "Implicit Ethics," pp. 66–68; Nestle, "Thukydides," p. 663; Finley, *Thucydides*, p. 54; Jacqueline de Romilly, "L'Utilité de l'histoire selon Thucydide," in *Histoire et Historiens dans l'Antiquité* (Vandoeuvres-Geneve: 1956, Fondation Hardt, IV), pp. 55–56; Thompson, "Individual Motivation," pp. 163, 171.

30. See Kluckhohn, *Anthropology*, pp. 30, 41.

31. Cp. Huart, "Vocabulaire," 491–494.

32. In the dedication to the earl of Devonshire of his translation of Thucydides. On Hobbes's congenial attitude to Thucydides's view of the aggressive, selfish appetites in human nature see *Hobbes' Thucydides*, ed. Richard Schlatter (New Brunswick, N.J.: 1975), pp. xx–xxi; Pouncey, *Necessities*, 151–157 ("Human Nature in Hobbes").

33. Thus in Xenophon's historical works we do not find any concern for the influence of human nature. For the factors of causation in the works of Xenophon, Ephorus, Anaximenes, and Theopompus see Paul Pédech, *La Méthode historique de Polybe* (Paris: 1964), pp. 59–64, 70–75; cp. William E. Higgins, *Xenophon the Athenian: The Problem of the Individual and the Society of the Polis* (Albany, N.Y.: 1977), p. 120.

34. 16.28.5–7; cp. 7.11.1–2, 10–12. On Polybius' historiography see W. Warde Fowler, "Polybius's Conception of Τύχη," *CR* 17 (1903): 445–449; E. J. Tapp, "Polybius' Conception of History," *Prudentia* 9 (1972): 31–41; Pédech, *Methode*, pp. 213–215, 331–356; F. W. Walbank, *A Historical Commentary on Polybius I* (Oxford: 1957), pp. 6–26; Kenneth Sacks, *Polybius on the Writing of History* (Berkeley, Calif.: 1981), esp. p. 137 n. 32.

35. 4.8.7. Cf. Ivo Bruns, *Die Persönlichkeit in der Geschichtsschreibung der Alten* (Berlin: 1898), pp. 85–86; 94–95; Carl Wunderer, *Die psychologischen Anschauungen des Historikers Polybius* (Erlangen: 1905), p. 58.

36. Polybius 7.11.1–2, 18.33.6–7. Cf. Walbank, *A Historical Commentary II* (Oxford: 1967), pp. 231, 538.

37. Cp. Wunderer, *Psych. Ansch.*, pp. 38–52.

38. Polybius, *Universal History* 1.81.7. Walbank, *A Historical Commentary*.

39. Polybius 1.81.5–9.

40. E.g., ibid. 2.7.1–4; it is the human condition to suffer misfortunes caused by *tyche* or the inhumanity of other men; 10.40–48; it is the tendency of human beings (*anthrōpinē physis*) who have achieved great success to become overweening.

41. Polybius 10.4; Plutarch, *Alexander* 1.2.

42. Cf. P. G. Walsh, *Livy: His Historical Aims and Methods* (Cambridge: 1961), pp. 22–27; Momigliano, *Development of Biography*, pp. 43–64.

43. See, e.g., Heinrich Gottlieb Strebel, *Wertung und Wirkung des thukydideischen Geschichtswerkes in der griechisch-römischen Literatur* (Ph.D. Diss. Munich: 1935), p. 27; Hans Drexler, *Die Entdeckung des Individuums* (Salzburg: 1966), pp. 253–257.

44. See, e.g., Walsh, *Livy*, pp. 27, 34–39; Louis H. Feldman, *Cicero's Conception of Historiography* (Ph.D. Diss. Harvard, 1951), esp. 115; P.A. Brunt, "Cicero's Historiography," *Miscellanea di Studi Classici in onore di Eugenio Manni*, vol. 1 (Rome: 1980), pp. 311–340; Erich Burck, "Grundzüge römischer Geschichtsauffassung und Geschichtsschreibung," in *Vom Menschenbild in der römischen Literatur* (Heidelberg: 1981), pp. 72, 78, 81. Caesar's two mentions of human nature (*Gallic War* 3.10.3; *Civil War* 2.4.4) are moralizing comments.

45. On the influence of Thucydides on Sallust see Strebel, *Wertung*, pp. 31–32; Paul Perrochat, *Les Modèles grecs de Salluste* (Paris: 1949), pp. 1–39, esp. 15.

46. Frag. *Histories* 1.7; cp. frag. 1.11. On this key passage in Sallust and its relation to Thucydidean thought on human nature see Karl Büchner, *Sallust* (Heidelberg: 1960), pp. 68, 309, 334, 339–341; Wilhelm Avenarius, "Die griechische Vorbilder des Sallust," *Symbolae Osloenses* 33 (1957): 52–53; L. Stock, *Die Geschichtsauffassung bei Thukydides und Sallust* (Ph.D. Diss. Freiburg, 1946), 113–117; Thomas Francis Scanlon, *The Influence of Thucydides on Sallust* (Heidelberg: 1980), pp. 23–27, 196–198, 218–219.

47. Cp. S. L. Uttschenko, *Der Weltanschaulichpolitische Kampf in Rom am Vorabend des Sturzes der Republik* (Berlin: 1956, trans. from Russian), 102–103.

48. Cp. Büchner, *Sallust*, 341–342.

49. Sallust, *Catiline*, prologue, 1.2.

50. Cp. Sallust, *Jugurtha* 2.4: ingenium (the mind) quo neque melius neque amplius aliud in natura mortalium est. See M. Rambaud, "Les Prologues de Salluste et la demonstration morale dans son oeuvre," *Revue des Études Latines* 24 (1946): 118–119, 121.

51. Cp. Hans Oppermann, "Des Menschenbild Sallusts," *Gymnasium* 65 (1958), pp. 190, 195.

52. Sallust, *Jugurtha* 1.1; cp. Sallust, *Catiline* 2.7.

53. Sallust, *Jugurtha* 1.4.

54. Sallust, *Catiline* 2.7; *Jugurtha* 1.1.

55. Etienne Tiffou, *Essai sur la pensée morale de Salluste à la lumière de ses prologues* (Paris: 1973), pp. 314–316.

56. Walsh, *Livy*, pp. 53–55, 61–62.

57. Livy 3.68.10; 24.25.8; 28.23.4, 25.14.

58. Walsh, *Livy*, pp. 21–22, 108–109.

59. H. Oldfather, *Diodorus* (London: 1933), Loeb vol. I, p. xx; Massimiliano Paven, "La Teoresi Storica di Diodoro Sicolo," *Atti della Accademia Nazionale dei Lincei, Rendiconti* 16 (1961): 19, 22, 134, 147–148; Anne Burton, *Diodorus Siculus, Book I. A Commentary* (Leiden: 1972), pp. 35–36.

60. Though Dionysius of Halicarnassus in his *Roman Antiquities* knew Thucydides's work and could quote him on human nature (his *Thuc.* 3.7; *De Comp.* 22.108.1–2; *Ep. ad Pomp.* 1), he remains a rhetorical historian without knowledge of human personality. For him the gods and divine providence were the principal causal forces in history. Cp. W. Kendrick Pritchett, ed., *Dionysius of Halicarnassus on Thucydides* (Berkeley, Calif.: 1979), p. xxviii, and commentary on chaps. 3 and 7.

61. Cp. Strebel, *Wertung*, pp. 32–33.

62. Tacitus *Histories* 1.22.6, 55.1; 2.20.2, 38.1; *Agricola* 42.3; *Dialogue* 31.

63. Tacitus *Histories* 2.38.1.

64. Ibid., 1.55.1.

65. Ibid., 2.20.

66. Ibid., 1.22.6 (said of Otho's belief in prophecies about his future power).

67. Tacitus, *Agricola* 42.3: proprium humani ingenii est odisse quem laeseris; Seneca, *De Ira* 2.33.1: hoc habent pessimum animi magna fortuna insolentes: quos laeserunt et oderunt.

68. Cp. W. H. Alexander, "The Psychology of Tacitus," *Classical Journal* 47 (1952): 327.

69. Viktor Pöschl, "Die römische Auffassung der Geschichte," *Gymnasium* 63 (1956): 191, 202–205; idem, "Der Historiker Tacitus," *Die Welt als Geschichte* 22 (1962): 10.

70. E.g., Joseph Lucas, *Les Obsessions de Tacite* (Leiden: 1974), pp. 4–7; Jean-Marie Engle, *Tacite et l'étude du comportement collectif* (Ph.D. diss., Dijon, 1972), 297–307, 722–747, 772.

71. A. Michel, "La Causalité historique chez Tacite," *Revue des Études Anciennes* 1 (1959): 96–106; Peter v. Kloch-Kornitz,"Geschichtsauffassung und Darstellung bei Tacitus," *Die Welt als Geschichte* 21 (1961): 158–161.

72. Barry Baldwin, *Studies in Lucian* (Toronto: 1973), p. 90.

73. Lucian, *How to Write History*, chaps. 15, 25, 40–42.

74. Cassius Dio, *History of Rome* 1.5.12; 2.7.3; 3.12.3; 4.17.7, 14; 5.20.4; 6.24.1; 8.36.1, 14; 12.50.2; 13.55.1; 14.57.18; 36.20.1, 31.4; 38.7.2, 18.3; 39.6.1; 52.2.6, 18.1, 34.6–8; 55.14.4; 56.2.3, 45.1; 76[77].5.1; 78[79].15.3. Cp. Strebel, *Wertung*, pp. 55–68.

75. Fergus Millar, *A Study of Cassius Dio* (Oxford: 1964), p. 76.

76. On the relation of this passage to Thucydides, cf. note 10 above regarding the *History* 3.84. Gomme, commenting on Thucydides *History* 3.84 states that the similarity of Dio's comments here do not prove imitation. They seem to be "commonplaces that Dio could have got from one of a dozen writers or have thought of for himself, and to have nothing to do with this chapter."

77. Cp. Thucydides, *History* 3.82.2.

78. Adkins, *From the Many*, pp. 1–2.

79. Cf. Eugene A. Miller, "Political Philosophy and Human Nature," *Personalist* 52 (1972): 209.

80. Hume, *An Enquiry Concerning Human Understanding*, pp. 85–86.

81. José Ortega y Gasset, *Toward a Philosophy of History* (New York: 1941), p. 217.

CHAPTER 4

Originally published in the *Classical Journal* 77 (1981/2), 97–103. Work on the period of Octavian's rise and Augustus' reign continues unabated (see final note next chapter). On the war of Actium, see C. Pelling in the *Cambridge Ancient History*, Vol. X (2nd ed., Cambridge, 1996), pp. 36–65, and on its aftermath and representation, R. Gurval, *Actium and Augustus: the Politics and Emotions of Civil War* (Ann Arbor, 1995).

1. Cassius Dio, *History of Rome* 50.5.5, 6.1, 26.3–4; Plutarch, *Antony* 60.1. Cp. Viktor Gardthausen, *Augustus und seine Zeit* (Leipzig: 1891–1904) vol. 1, p. 364; J. Kromayer, "Kleine Forschungen zur Geschichte des zweiten Triumvirats," *Hermes* 33 (1898): 33–35, 46; Fritz Blumenthal, "Die Autobiographie des Augustus," *WS* 36 (1914): 87; Stahelin, *RE, s.v.* "Kleopatra," no. 20, Halbband 21: 766, 770; M. P. Charlesworth, *CAH*, vol. 10, 82–83, 98–99; Hans Volkmann, *Cleopatra. A Study in Politics and Propaganda* (New York: 1958), pp. 170–171; Michael Grant, *Cleopatra* (London: 1972), pp. 201–202; Hermann Bengtson, *Marcus Antonius, Triumvir und Herrscher des Orients* (Munich: 1977), pp. 225–226; Eleanor G. Huzar, *Mark Antony. A Biography* (Minneapolis: 1978), pp. 208–209.

2. Vergil, *Aeneid* 8.696–700; Horace, *Carmina* 1.37.6–14; Propertius 3.11.30–58; *Elegia in Maecenatem* 1.53–4; use Becher, *Das Bild der Kleopatra in der griechischen und lateinischen Literatur* (Berlin: 1966), pp. 23–58.

3. Cassius Dio, *History of Rome* 50.4.3, 6.1, 26.2–4. But he was not formally declared a *hostis* by the Senate, though a vote was taken. Appian *Bella Civilia* 4.45 reports that a certain Sergius (proscribed in 43 B.C. but spared through Antony's intercession) cast the only *open* negative vote on the motion. Suetonius's *Augustus* 17.1 is careless with

his *hosti iudicato*; Augustus (*RGDA* 24) is realistic with his reference to Antony, as is *cum quo bellum gesseram*.

4. Cf. Jean Béranger, "L'Accession d'Auguste et l'Idéologie du 'Privatus,'" in *Principatus* (Geneva: 1973), pp. 243–258; Meyer Reinhold, "Augustus' Conception of Himself," *Thought* 55 (1980): 42.

5. Cassius Dio, *History of Rome* 50.6.1. Despite urgent advice from a group of his adherents that he separate himself from her by sending her back to Egypt from his headquarters, he did not do so (Plutarch, *Antony* 56.2–3, 59.3).

6. Though Cassius Dio's *History of Rome* 50.26.3 put this into a "speech" by Octavian to his troops before the Battle of Actium, he has him state that Cleopatra was declared an enemy εὐθὺς οἷς ἔπραττεν, "*precisely* for her acts." Cp. Charlesworth, *CAH*, vol. 10, 98.

7. M. P. Charlesworth, "The Fear of the Orient in the Roman Empire," *Cambr. Hist. Journ.* 2 (1926): 9–16; W. W. Tam, "Alexander Helios and the Golden Age," *JRS* 22 (1932): 135–160; *Sibylline Oracles* 3.350–361, 367–380, for Cleopatra as Eastern warrior queen leading an anti-Roman crusade.

8. Cassius Dio, *History of Rome* 50.5.4; Prop. 3.11.45–46; *Anthologia Latina* 1.462.3; Ovid, *Metamorphoses* 15.826–828; *Elegia in Maecenatem*. I.53–54; Florus 4.11.2; Eutropius, 7.7.1.

9. P. C. Sands, *The Client Princes of the Roman Empire under the Republic* (Cambridge: 1908; rpt. New York, 1975), pp. 55, 165–173; Cf. *CAH*, vol. 10: 34 n. 3.

10. E.g., Plutarch, *Antony* 25–27. On Cleopatra's correct conduct as Roman client see Sands, *Client Princes*, pp. 172–173.

11. See, e.g., *Oxford Classical Dictionary* (2nd edn) *s.v.* "Cleopatra VII," 251.

12. Sands, *Client Princes*, pp. 56–57; *CAH*, vol. 10: 34. Herod's accountability to Rome from 40 B.C. to his death extended even to his will, which required the approval of Augustus (Sands, 226–228).

13. Plutarch, *Antony* 56.7, 61.1–3; Cassius Dio, *History of Rome* 51.1.5, 2.1–3. Cp. Hans Buchheim, *Die Orientpolitik des Triumvir M. Antonius* (Heidelberg: 1960. *Abh. Heidelb. Akad. Wiss., Philosoph.-Hist. Kl.*, no. 3[1960]): 11–28, 49–83.

14. Cicero, *Deiotarus* 13.22. Cp. Richard A. Bauman, *The Crimen Maiestatis in the Roman Republic and Augustan Principate* (Johannesburg: 1967), pp. 149–151.

15. A. Hirtius, *Bellum Alexandrinum* 67; cp. Cicero, *Deiotarus* 9, 11–12, on Deiotarus's service to Pompey, "a man whom we all followed."

16. Cicero, *Deiotarus* 13–16, on Deiotarus as loyal to his responsibilities as *socius et amicus*, and his contributions to other commanders, as well as to Caesar.

17. A. Hirtius, *Bellum Alexandrinum* 68.1.

18. Cicero, *Deiotarus* 11. Cp. Raphael Giomini, *Bellum Alexandrinum* (Rome, no date), 209.

19. In 42 B.C. he responded to the *evocatio* of Brutus, but after Philippi went over to the triumvirs. Cp. F. E. Adcock, "Lesser Armenia and Galatia after Pompey's Settlement of the East," *JRS* 27 (1937): 12–17; E. Badian, *OCD* (2 refs to 2nd edition), *s.v.* "Deiotarus"; *Kleine Pauly*, 1: 1431–1432.

20. E. Badian, *Foreign Clientelae* (264–70 B.C.) (Oxford: 1958), pp. 271–272.

21. Sands, *Client Princes*, pp. 55–56.

22. Cp. Bauman, *Crimen Maiestatis*, pp. 150–151, on Deiotarus.

23. Cicero, *Deiotarus* 22.

24. For the concept and implementation of *maiestas populi Romani* see, e.g., the treaty with the Aetolians in 187 B.C. (Livy 38.11.2; Polybius 21.32.3; N. Lewis and M. Reinhold, *Roman Civilization* [New York: 1966], vol. 1: 178–179); treaty with Gades in 78 B.C. (sic. *Balb.* 35; Ascon. *Scaur.* 22C); treaty with Astypalaea, 105 B.C. (*IGRR*, vol. 4, no. 1028; Lewis and Reinhold, *Roman Civilization*, vol. 1: 331–332); on the Lex Julia Maiestatis, Lewis and Reinhold, vol. 2: 29–31.

25. Donald McFayden, "The Rise of the Princeps' Jurisdiction within the City of Rome," *Wash. Univ. Stud., Hum. Ser.* 10 (1923): 208; Pandas M. Schisas, *Offences against the State in Roman Law* (London: 1926), pp. 3, 13; Hans G. Gundel, "Der Begriff Maiestas im politischen Denken der römischen Republik," *Historia* 12 (1963): 289–291, 294, 315; Sands, *Client Princes*, pp. 49–57; Kübler, *RE*, *s.v.* "Maiestas," vol. 14: 542–549; Bauman, *Crimen Maiestatis*, pp. 1–8.

26. Cicero, *Deiotarus* 1.

27. Tacitus, *Annals* 2.42.2–3; Josephus, *Antiquities of the Jews* 17.342–344; *Bellum Judaicum* 2.111–112; Strabo 16.2.46; cass. Dio 55.25. Cp. Schisas, 14, n. 3.

28. Servius *ad. Aeneidem* 8.696; Cassius Dio, *History of Rome* 50.5.1.

29. Cassius Dio, *History of Rome* 50.26.2, 28.5.

30. Plutarch, *Antony* 36.2; cp. Anna E. Glauning, *Die Anhängerschaft des Antonius und ders Octavia* (Ph.D. diss., Leipzig, 1936): 42.

31. On the territorial gifts of Antony to Cleopatra and her children see M. P. Charlesworth, *CAH*, vol. 10: 80–81; Joseph Dobiaš, "La Donation d'Antoine à Cléopatre en l'an 34 av. I.-C.," *Mélanges Bidez. Univ. Libre de Bruxelles, Annuaire de l'Inst. de Philol. et d'Hist. Orient.* 2 (1934): 287–313; R. Syme, *The Roman Revolution* (Oxford: 1939), pp. 260–261; H. U. Instinsky, "Bemerkungen ueber die ersten Schenkungen des Antonius an Cleopatra," *Studies Presented to David Moore Robinson* (St. Louis: 1953), vol. 2: 974–979; Glauning, *Die Anhängerschaft*, pp. 39–43; Buchheim, *Die Orientpolitik*, pp. 68–74; Grant, *Cleopatra*, 162–168; Huzar, *Mark Antony*, pp. 196–200.

32. Livy 1.32.4–14.

33. Cf. Cicero, *Republic* 3.23.35.

34. Livy 1.32.4–14. Cp. Cassius Dio, *History of Rome* 50.5.4–5; R. M. Ogilvie, *A Commentary on Livy Books 1–5* (Oxford: 1965), pp. 127–129; DS vol. 2: 1095–1101; J. W. Rich, *Declaring War in the Roman Republic in the Period of Transmarine Expansion* (Bruxelles: 1976. *Collection Latomus*, vol. 149), pp. 17, 56–60, 104–107.

35. Cassius Dio, *History of Rome* 50.26, 28.3 ("speech" of Octavian), "against those in revolt against us."

36. Following the traditional formula of declarations of war according to the fetial rite (Livy 1.32.13), the formal declaration against Cleopatra may, in part, be reconstructed thus: Quod Cleopatra, Aegyptiorum regina, adversus populum Romanum Quiritium fecit, deliquit, quod populus Romanus Quiritium bellum cum Cleopatra, Aegyptiorum regina, iussit esse senatusque populi Romani Quiritium censuit consensit conscivit ut bellum cum Cleopatra, Aegyptiorum regina, fieret, ob eam rem ego [i.e., the head or *pater patratus* of the college of fetials, at this time Octavian] populusque Romanus Cleopatrae, Aegyptiorum reginae, bellum indico facioque.

CHAPTER 5

This chapter originally appeared in *Thought Quarterly* 55 (1980), 1–18. A good deal of work on Augustus and the Augustan Age has appeared in the last two decades. Important contributions appear in F. Millar and E. Segal, eds., *Caesar Augustus: Seven Aspects* (Oxford, 1984), and in K. A. Raaflaub and M. Toher, eds., *Between Republic and Empire: Interpretations of Augustus and his Principate* (Berkeley and Los Angeles, 1990). Z. Yavetz's contribution to the latter volume, "The Personality of Augustus: Reflections on Syme's *Roman Revolution,*" pp. 21–41, is especially relevant to this subject. Cf. also K. M. Girardet, "'Traditionalismus' in der Politik des Oktavian/Augustus—mentalitätsgeschichtliche Aspekte," *Klio* 75 (1993), 202–18.

1. John B. Firth, *Augustus Caesar and the Organisation of the Empire of Rome* (New York: 1903), p. v; T. Rice Holmes, *The Architect of the Roman Empire, 27 B.C.–A.D. 14* (Oxford: 1931), pp. 2, 73; *CAH* (vol. 10, p. 590; Donald Earl, *The Age of Augustus* (New York: 1968), p. 191; Karl Loewenstein, *The Governance of Rome* (The Hague: 1973), p. 311; Meyer Reinhold, *The Golden Age of Augustus* (Toronto: 1978), pp. ix–xii.

2. *De Vita Sua Libri XIII*, carried down to about 25 B.C. See Fritz Blumenthal, "Die Autobiographie des Augustus," *WS* 35 (1913): 113–130; 36 (1914): 84–103. It was ransacked by Augustus's contemporary Nicolaus of Damascus in his *Life of Augustus*.

3. For the much-edited and glossed *Res Gestae*, see, e.g., Jean Gagé, *Res Gestae Divi Augusti*, 2nd ed. (Paris: 1950); P. A. Brunt and J. M. Moore, *Res Gestae Divi Augusti* (London: 1967).

4. Pliny, *Natural History* 7.147–150, gives a lengthy, gloomy catalog of them.

5. E.g., Harold D. Lasswell, *Power and Personality* (New York: 1948); James D. Barber, *The Presidential Character*. 2nd ed. (Englewood Cliffs, N.J.: 1977); James MacGregor Burns, *Leadership* (New York: 1978).

6. On Augustus's origins and early years, Suetonius, *Augustus* 1–8.1; Nicolaus of Damascus, *Life of Augustus* 2–5.

7. On the *ignobilitas* of his family see Cicero, *Philippics* 3.6.15–17. In the *Res Gestae* Augustus was silent about his father, mother, and ancestors because he was ashamed of the family connection.

8. Suetonius, *Augustus* 94.4–5; Cassius Dio, *History of Rome* 45.1; Donatus, *Vita Vergilii*, ed. A. Reifferscheid, p. 56.

9. Pliny, *Natural History* 2.94.

10. Augustus valued greatly the glamour of this highest social status in Roman society. As *princeps* later he elevated many of his plebeian adherents to patrician status both to reward them and to ensure the survival of this elite class. See Edward Togo Salmon, "Augustus the Patrician," *Essays on Roman Culture: The Todd Memorial Lectures*, ed. A. J. Dunston (Toronto: 1976), pp. 3–33.

11. Nicolaus of Damascus, *Life of Augustus* 18.

12. Cp. Lasswell, *Power and Personality*, p. 39; Barber, *Presidential Character*, p. 100; Burns, *Leadership*, pp. 58, 101–104, 113.

13. Nicolaus of Damascus, *Life of Augustus* 6, 9–10; Pliny, *Natural History* 7.148–149; Suetonius, *Augustus* 59, 72.2, 80–82; Albert Esser, *Cäsar und die Julisch-Claudischen Kaisern im biologisch-ärtzlichen Blickfeld* (Leiden: 1958 = *Janus*, Suppldbd. I,), pp. 45–66.

14. Cp. Esser, *Cäsar*, p. 69.

15. Cited by Barber, *Presidential Character*, p. 101.

16. Suetonius, *Augustus* 73, 79–80.

17. E.g., *CAH*, vol. 10, pp. 557–559.

18. Cicero, *Philippics* 13.11.24–25.

19. Mario Attilio Levi, "Ottaviano e la Memoria de Giulio Cesare," *Acme* 5 (1952): 485–491; Richard Heinze, *Die Augusteische Kultur* (Leipzig: 1930), pp. 14–15.

20. Suetonius, *Augustus* 18.1; Cassius Dio, *History of Rome* 51.16.5.

21. Suetonius, *Augustus* 50. Suetonius tells us that he previously used an image of a sphinx on his seal ring, and that after 23 B.C. he replaced Alexander's image with his own portrait.

22. Vergil, *Aeneid* 1.279.

23. Plutarch, "Sayings of Romans," *Moralia* 207D.

24. On the *imitatio Alexandri* by Augustus see Emanuele Ciaceri, "L'Impero universale di Augusto," *Nuova Antologia* 399 (1938): 164–168; Hans Ulrich Instinsky, *Die Siegel des Kaisers Augustus* (Baden-Baden: 1962), pp. 31–36; Tonio Hölscher, *Victoria Romana* (Mainz am Rhein: 1967), pp. 6–47; Dietmar Kienast, "Augustus und Alexander," *Gymnasium* 76 (1969): 430–456; Andreas Alföldi, *Oktavians Aufstieg zur Macht* (Berlin: 1976), pp. 9–11.

25. Cassius Dio, *History of Rome* 56.36.3.

26. Suetonius, *Augustus* 12; cp. Cicero, *Philippics* 13.11.24.

27. It is noteworthy that Augustus arranged that his beloved grandsons (his adopted sons) Gaius and Lucius Caesar, were not to become consuls until they were twenty.

28. *Res Gestae*, ch. 1; Cassius Dio, *History of Rome* 53.5.2.

29. Cp. Mario Attilio Levi, "La composizione della 'Res Gestae Divi Augusti,'" *Rivista di filologia Classica* 75 (1947): 189–210; T. D. Barnes, "The Victories of Augustus," *JRS* 64 (1974): 21–26.

30. Seneca, *On Anger,* 3.23.4–8; Suetonius, *Augustus,* 51, 55; Seneca the Elder, *Controversies,* 2.4.12–13.

31. *Res Gestae*, chs. 9, 34, 35. Cp. Velleius Paterculus, *History of Rome* 2.91.

32. Hans Ulrich Instinsky, "Consensus Universorum," *Hermes* 75 (1940): 265–278; Lothar Wickert, "Princeps," in *RE* vol. 22, part 2 (1954), col. 2264.

33. Suetonius, *Augustus* 58. See Andreas Alföldi, *Der Vater des Vaterlandes im römischen Denken* (Darmstadt: 1971); Jean Béranger, *Recherches sur l'Aspect Idéologique du Principat* (Basel: 1953), pp. 276–278.

34. *Res Gestae*, chs. 13, 30, 32. Cp. Suetonius, *Augustus* 31.5, 42.1.

35. Hendrik Wagenvoort, "Princeps," *Philologus* 91 (1936): 206–221, 323–345; Wickert, "Princeps," cols. 2057–2071.

36. Cicero, *Republic* 2.46: "Lucius Brutus, a man preeminent in native ability and bravery, although a private citizen, sustained the whole burden of government."

37. On Augustus's emphasis on his voluntary personal intervention with help and contributions see *Res Gestae*, chs. 1, 5, 15–18; cp. Livy, *Periocha* 118; Velleius Paterculus, *History of Rome* 2.61.1; Cicero, *Letters to Friends* 11.7.2; Cicero, *Philippics* 3.2.3, 5; Jean Béranger, "L'Accession d'Auguste de l'Idéologie du 'Privatus,'" in *Principatus* (Geneva: 1973), pp. 243–258.

38. *Res Gestae* ch. 34.3.

39. Ernst Hohl, "Des Selbstzeugniss des Augustus über seine Stelling im Staat," *Museum Helveticum* 4 (1947): 101–115; Chaim Wirszubski, *Libertas as a Political Idea at Rome during the Late Republic and Early Principate* (Cambridge: 1950), pp. 112–118; Béranger, *Recherches*, pp. 114–131; Luca Canali, "Il 'Manifesto' del Regime Augusteo," *Rivista di Cultura Classica e Mediaevale*, 15 (1973): 171–173.

40. Suetonius, *Augustus* 7.2; Cassius Dio, *History of Rome* 53.16.6–8.

41. The multifaceted association of "augustus" with sanctity, augury, and "increase" is emphasized by Ovid, *Fasti* 1.609–616.

42. On "Augustus," see Kenneth Scott, "The Identification of Augustus with Romulus-Quirinus," *TAPA* 56 (1925): 62–105; Lily Ross Taylor, *The Divinity of the Roman Emperor* (Middletown: 1931), pp. 158–160; Jean Gagé, "Romulus-Augustus," *Mélanges d'Archéologie et d'Histoire* 47 (1930): 138–181; F. Muller, "Augustus," *Mededeelingen der Koninklije Akademie van Wetenschappen Afdeeling Letterkunde* 63, Ser. A, no. 11 (1927): 275–347.

43. Hieronymus Markowski, "De quattuor virtutibus Augusti in clipeo aureo ei dato inscriptis," *Eos* 37 (1936): 109–128; M. P. Charlesworth, "The Virtues of a Roman Emperor. Propaganda and the Creation of Belief," *PBA* 73 (1937): 111–114; Inez Scott Ryberg, "Clupeus Virtutis," in *The Classical Tradition. Literary and Historical Studies in Honor of Harry Caplan,* ed. Luitpold Wallach (Ithaca: 1966), pp. 232–238.

44. Harold D. Lasswell, *Psychopathology and Politics,* rev. ed. (New York: 1960), pp. 75–76. Lasswell points out that "the private motives may be entirely lost from the consciousness of the political man, and he may succeed in achieving a high degree of objective validation from his point of view."

45. For Stoic influence on Augustus: V. Gardthausen, *Augustus und seine Zeit* (Leipzig: 1891), vol. 2, pp. 1313–1314; Henry Bardon, *Les Empereurs et les lettres latines d'Auguste à Hadrien* (Paris: 1940), pp. 10–11; Béranger, "L'Accession d'Auguste," pp. 243–258.

46. *CAH* vol. 10, pp. 591, 594.

47. Aulus Gellius, *Noctes Atticae* 15.7.3; Velleius Paterculus, *History of Rome* 2.124.2; Erich Köstermann, "Statio Principis," *Philologus* 87 (1932): 358–368, 430–444.

48. Cassius Dio, *History of Rome* 53.5.3–4.

49. Vitruvius, *On Architecture,* Book 1, preface 2.

50. Cassius Dio, *History of Rome* 54.3.2–3.

51. Paulus *Digesta Justiniani Augusti* 1.15.1–2.

52. Victor Ehrenberg and A. H. M. Jones, *Documents Illustrating the Reigns of Augustus and Tiberius,* 2nd ed. (Oxford: 1955), p. 141; Reinhold, *Golden Age,* p. 191. On Augustus's devotion to duty, see Ronald Syme, *The Roman Revolution* (Oxford: 1939), p. 520; Béranger, *Recherches,* pp. 169–175.

53. *Res Gestae,* ch. 5; Suetonius, *Augustus* 52; Velleius Paterculus, *History of Rome* 2.89.5. See Jean Béranger, "Le Refus du pouvoir," *Museum Helveticum* 5 (1948): 181–185; Geza Alföldy, "Die Ablehnung der Diktatur durch Augustus," *Gymnasium* 79 (1972): 1–12.

54. Suetonius, *Augustus* 28.1.

55. Seneca, *On the Shortness of Life* 4.2–3.

56. Suetonius, *Augustus* 58.2.

57. Pliny, *Natural History* 7.149.

58. Suetonius, *Augustus* 28; cp. Velleius Paterculus, *History of Rome* 2.91.2; Gellius, *Noctes Atticae* 15.7.3.

59. *Res Gestae,* chs. 15–22 (an appendix, not part of the original document, characterizes Augustus's expenditures as *innumerabilis*); Suetonius, *Augustus* 28–29, 41, 43, 49; Vitruvius, *On Architecture,* book 1, preface 2; Cassius Dio, *History of Rome* 54.30,3, 56.40,4–5.

60. Suetonius, *Augustus* 66.4.

61. Ibid., 101.3; Cassius Dio, *History of Rome* 56.41.5. For Augustus's public uses of his private fortune see Hans Kloft, *Liberalitas Principis* (Cologne: 1970), pp. 73–84.

Robert Etienne, *Le Siècle d'Auguste* (Paris: 1970), pp. 50–56; Israel Shatzman, *Senatorial Wealth and Roman Politics* (Bruxelles: 1975), pp. 357–371.

62. Suetonius, *Augustus* 53.2, 72–73, 76–77; Cassius Dio, *History of Rome* 56.40.4, 41.5; Macrobius, *Saturnalia*, 2.4.14; Nevio Degrassi, "La dimora di Augusto sul Palatino e la base di Sorrento," *Rendiconti della Pontificia Accademia Romana di Archeologia* 39 (1966/1967): 77–116.

63. Suetonius, *Augustus* 25.4; Gellius, *Noctes Aticae* 10.11.5; Polyaenus, *Stratagems* 8.24.4.

64. Suetonius, *Augustus* 84.

65. Ibid., 82.

66. Konrad Kraft, "Der Sinn des Mausoleum des Augustus," *Historia* 16 (1967): 189–206; Joseph Vogt, "Caesar und Augustus im Angesicht des Todes," *Saeculum* 23 (1972): 3–14 (=*Gymnasium* 80 [1973]: 421–437).

67. Suetonius, *Augustus* 99.2.

68. Ibid., 99.1; Cassius Dio, *History of Rome* 56.30.4.

69. Suetonius, *Augustus* 52; Cassius Dio, *History of Rome* 51.20.5–8.

70. Lily Ross Taylor, *Divinity*, pp. 166–167, 236–239; Christian Habicht, "Die augusteische Zeit und das erste Jahrhundert nach Christi Geburt," in *Le Culte des Souverains dans l'Empire Romain*, ed. Willem den Boer (Vandoeuvres-Genève, 1972), pp. 76–85; M. P. Charlesworth, "The Refusal of Divine Honours. An Augustan Formula," *Papers of the British School at Rome*, 15 (1939): 1–10.

71. Tacitus, *Annals* 4.37–38. Augustus also forbade undue adulation of any sort, including use of the term *dominus* (lord) for him (Suetonius, *Augustus* 53.1).

72. *Res Gestae* 8.4: ipse multarum rerum exempla imitanda posteris tradidi ("I myself handed down models in many matters for imitation by posterity").

73. Vitruvius, *On Architecture*, book 1, preface 3.

74. Henry T. Rowell, "The Forum and the Funeral *Imagines* of Augustus," *Memoirs of the American Academy in Rome* 17 (1940): 131–143; Paul Zanker, *Forum Augustum* (Tübingen: Wasmuth, 1968).

75. Suetonius, *Augustus* 31.5; cp. 71.3 ("my generosity will elevate me to heavenly glory").

76. Mason Hammond, "The Sincerity of Augustus," *Harvard Studies in Classical Philology* 69 (1965): 139–162; Loewenstein, *Governance*, pp. 241, 315–317.

77. *CAH*, vol. 10, p. 596.

78. Cited by Ernst Hohl, "Augustus," *Das Altertum* 2 (1956): 241.

CHAPTER 6

This chapter was originally published as the Introduction to M. Reinhold, *From Republic to Principate: An Historical Commentary on Cassius Dio's* Roman History Books 49–52 (36–29 B.C.) (Atlanta, 1988), pp. 5–15. For further work on Dio and his value as a source for the early empire, see also M. Reinhold and P. M. Swan, "Cassius Dio's Assessment of Augustus," in Raaflaub and Toher (opening note previous chapter), pp. 155–73, J. W. Rich, "Dio on Augustus," in Averil Cameron, ed., *History as Text* (Chapel Hill, 1989), pp. 86–110, and id., *Cassius Dio, the Augustan Settlement* (Roman History 53.1–55.9) (Warminster, 1990).

1. East Apthorp, *Letters on the Prevalence of Christianity before Its Civil Establishment* (London: 1788), pp. 33–34.

2. Jean Béranger, *Recherches sur l'Aspect Idéologique du Principat* (Basel: 1953), p. 97.

3. Cp. R. S. Rogers, "Ignorance of the Law in Tacitus and Dio: Two Instances from the History of Tiberius," *TAPA* 64 (1933): 18–27.

4. On Dio's methods of compression see M. J. Moscovich, "Historical Compression in Cassius Dio's Account of the Second Century B.C.," *Ancient World* 8 (1983): 137–143.

5. E. Gabba, "The Historians and Augustus," in F. Millar and E. Segal, eds. *Caesar Augustus: Seven Aspects* (Oxford, 1984), pp. 70–71.

6. F. Millar, *A Study of Cassius Dio* (Oxford, 1964) pp. vii, 28, 34–38, 84–85, 91.

7. Cassius Dio, *History of Rome* 44.35.3, citing Augustus's autobiography.

8. Millar, *Study,* p. 35.

9. See G. T. Griffith, in *Fifty Years (and Twelve) of Classical Scholarship* (Oxford: 1968), p. 208.

10. Schwartz *RE* 3.1697–1705 (= *Geschichtschreiber* 415–426); M. Levi "Appunti sulle fonti augustee" *Athenaeum* 15 (1937): 3–11 (= *Tempo* 414–423 [appendix 6: "Dione Cassio, fonte per l'età auguste"]); R. Syme, "Livy and Augustus," *HSCP* 64 (1959): 73–74, 86 n. 293 (Syme believes that, beginning with 29 B.C., Livy was deserted by Dio); H. J. Mette, "Livius und Augustus," *Gymnasium* 68 (1961): 281–284; Jesse D. Harrington, Cassius Dio: A Reexamination (Ph.D. diss. University of Kentucky 1970) pp. 57–60; Harrington *Dio*, 35–44. V. Fadinger, *Die Begründung des Prinzipats. Quellenkritische Untersuchungen zu Cassius Dio und die Parallelüberlieferung* (Bonn, 1969) 29, 131–133.

11. See, e.g., H. Petersen, "Livy and Augustus," *TAPA* 92 (1961): 440–452.

12. H. Tränkle, "Augustus bei Tacitus, Cassius Dio und dem älteren Plinius," *WS* 82 (1969): 126 n. 29.

13. B. Manuwald *Cassius Dio und Augustus* (Weisbaden, 1979) pp. 168–254 (especially pp. 223–239), 281.

14. Schwartz, *RE* 3.1697–1705 (= *Geschichtschreiber* 414–426).

15. See, e.g., M. P. Charlesworth, *CAH* 10.875–876; H. Tränkle *WS* 82 (1969): 114–115, 126, 128; Dieter Flach, "Dios Platz in der kaiserlichen Geschichtschreibung," *AA* 18 (1973): 138–139; Manuwald, *Dio*, "Appunti sulle Fonti Augustee" 168–254, 275–277; Levi, 14–17 (= *Tempo* 424–427), who would put the shift in source at Dio's 53.17–19, where Levi detects a suture.

16. R. Syme, *Tacitus* (Oxford: 1958), 1.273; 2.691.

17. Millar, *Study,* pp. 85–91.

18. F. Wilmans, *De Dionis Cassii fontibus et auctoritate* (Berlin: 1836); G. Vrind, "De Cassii Dionis historiis," *MN* 54 (1926): 321–347.

19. Cf Harrington, *Dio,* pp. 45–47.

20. See, e.g., Schwartz *RE* 3.1705, 1714–1715 (= *Geschichtschreiber* 426, 438–439); Millar, *Study,* pp. 85–87; Harrington, *Dio,* pp. 40–43, 47–54 (who argues that Dio used Suetonius directly beginning with book 52); Syme, *Tacitus,* 2.690; Manuwald, *Dio,* pp. 258–268.

21. Manuwald, *Dio,* pp. 254–258; Wirth, *Dio,* pp. 39–43.

22. Hans A. Andersen, *Cassius Dio und die Begründung des Principates* (Berlin, 1938) pp. 9–48, followed by Millar, *Study,* p. 90.

23. See D. R. Stuart, "The Attitude of Cassius Dio toward Epigraphic Sources," *Roman Historical Sources and Institutions,* University of Michigan Studies, Humanistic

Series I (New York: 1904), pp. 102–112. On Dio's sources in general, see Schwartz *RE* 3.1692–1716 (= *Geschichtschreiber* pp. 406–441); Millar, *Study*, pp. 32–38; Harrington, *Dio*, passim; Manuwald, *Dio*, passim; Wirth, *Dio*, pp. 39–43.

24. Cp. Millar, *Study*, pp. 83, 92.

25. G. Zecchini, *Cassio Dione e la guerra gallica di Cesare* (Milano: 1978), especially pp. 106–108, 150, treats again the much-litigated problem of the relationship of Dio's account of the Gallic War and Caesar's *Commentaries*, and concludes that Dio was completely independent of Caesar and the Livian vulgate, and used, rather, an anti-Caesarian source (perhaps Q. Aelius Tubero). His conclusions, however, are highly questionable.

26. Zecchini, *Cassio Dione*, pp. 14, 199; cp. M. Grasshof, *De Fontibus et Auctoritate Dionis Cassii Cocceiani* (Ph.D. diss., Bonn, 1867), 38–43.

27. Cassius Dio, *History of Rome* 53.19.4, 6; cp. Flach, "Dios Platz," pp. 138–139.

28. Wirth, *Dio*, pp. 19–20; Z. Rubin, *Civil-War Propaganda and Historiography*, Collection Latomus, vol. 173 (Bruxelles: 1980), 9.

29. See, e.g., Millar, *Study*, p. 90; Fadinger, *Begründung*, p. 334; Bleicken *Hermes* 90 (1962): 445–446; Flach, "Dios Platz," pp. 134–135. On the similar literary methods of Plutarch in the use of sources—conflation of related matters, compression, telescoping of events, transfer of details from one person to another, even fabrications—see C. B. R. Pelling, "Plutarch's Adaptation of his Source-Material," *Journal of Hellenic Studies* 100 (1980): 127–140.

30. Cp. C. Questa, "Tecnica biografica e tecnica annalistica nei libri LIII-LXIII di Cassio Dione," *StudUrb* 31 (1957): 37–53.

31. Zecchini, "Modelli e problemi teorici della storiografia nell'età degli Antonini," *Critica Storica* 20 (1983): 29–31.

32. See especially E. Litsch, *De Cassio Dione imitatore Thucydidis* (Ph.D. diss. Freiburg, 1893), passim; Harrington, *Dio*, pp. 57–60; Flach, "Dios Platz," pp. 130–131; Manuwald, *Dio*, pp. 75, 283–284. See also Reinhold, *From Republic to Principate*, appendix 1, "'Human Nature' in Dio."

33. W. Ameling, "Cassius Dio und Bithynien," *Epigraphica Anatolica* 4 (1984): 126–128; Gabba, "Historians and Augustus," pp. 64–65; L. Zgusta, "Die Rolle des Griechischen im römischen Kaiserreich," in *Die Sprachen im römischen Reich der Kaiserzeit*, Beihefte der Bonner Jahrbücher 40 (Köln: 1980), pp. 121–145 (including "Der Einfluss des Lateinischen," 131–135).

34. T. D. Barnes, "The Composition of Cassius Dio's *Roman History*," *Phoenix* 38 (1984): 240–255.

35. For the date of composition of book 52, see introduction to Maecenas's speech before Octavian (52.14–40).

36. M. M. Eisman, "Dio and Josephus: Parallel Analyses," *Latomus* 36 (1977): 657–673.

37. Schwartz *RE* 3.1716; cp. E. Gabba, "Storici Greci dell' Impero Romano da Augusto ai Severi" *RSI* 71 (1959): 376–378; Manuwald, *Dio*, pp. 8–12, 21–26.

38. See, e.g., Andersen, *Dio*, pp. 49–64; Fadinger, *Begründung*, pp. 27–28; Wirth, *Dio*, pp. 30–31.

39. Cp. Flach, "Dios Platz," pp. 141–143.

40. Cp. Mason Hammond, "The Significance of the Speech of Maecenas in Dio Cassius, Book LII," *TAPA* 63 (1932): 88–102; M. F. A. Brok, review of Millar, *Study*, in *MN* 20 (1967): 194–195.

41. Cp. Manuwald, *Dio*, pp. 6–7, 25–26, 275.

42. See Fadinger, *Begründung*, pp. 333–336; N. A. Maschkin, *Zwischen Republik und Kaiserreich* (Leipzig: 1954), pp. 328–330; Tränkle, "Augustus" p. 128; cp. Millar, *Study*, pp. 83–102.

43. M. A. Giua, "Augusto nel libro 56 della Storia romana di Cassio Dione," *Athenaeum* 61 (1983): 441–450, 455–456.

44. Manuwald, *Dio*, pp. 12–21, 273–284.

45. G. Alföldy, "The Crisis of the Third Century as Seen by Contemporaries," *Greek, Roman, and Byzantine Studies* 15 (1974): 92–93, 102; Gabba, "Historians and Augustus," pp. 70–71; cp. M. Stern, ed., *Greek and Latin Authors on Jews and Judaism*, vol. 2 (Jerusalem: 1980), p. 347.

46. See, e.g., Fadinger, *Begrüdung*, pp. 27–28; Millar, *Study*, pp. 83–118; Manuwald, *Dio*, pp. 279–282.

47. The third-century concerns of Dio have been admirably isolated by R. Bering-Staschewski *Römische Zeitgeschichte bei Cassius Dio* (Bochum, 1981). See also Millar, *Study*, pp. 119–173 ("The History of His Own Time").

48. Bering-Staschewski has identified several contemporary figures implicit in Dio's parallels.

CHAPTER 7

This chapter originally appeared in *L'Antiquité Classique* 55 (1986), 213–22. For recent bibliography, see note at the beginning of the previous chapter.

1. Schwartz, *Cassius Dio*, in *RE* 111, col. 1716; Hans A. Andersen, *Cassius Dio und die Begründung des Principates* (Berlin: 1938), pp. 49–64; Emilio Gabba, "Storici Greci dell' Impero Romano da Augusto ai Severi," *RSI* 71 (1959): pp. 376–378; Volker Fadinger, *Die Begründung des Prinzipats. Quellenkritische Untersuchungen zu Cassius Dio und die Parallelüberlieferung* (Bonn: 1969), pp. 27–28, 334–336; F. Millar *A Study of Cassius Dio* (Oxford 1964) p. 83; Bernd Manuwald, *Cassius Dio und Augustus* (Weisbaden: 1979), pp. 6–8, 12, 21, 25–26, 275.

2. Cp. Manuwald, *Cassius Dio und Augustus*, p. 273. Dio here is undoubtedly following the thinking of Thucydides, who posited an innate "human nature" driving men to aggression and desire to dominate. Dio likewise seeks to read "human nature" into historical events, using the term more frequently than any other ancient historian, and with great variety in nuance. In general Dio tends to be pessimistic about "human nature," and most frequently broods on the dark side of human behavior. E.g., men are selfish and resort to violence for self-aggrandizement (52.2.6); ambition for sole power is not inconsistent with human nature (52.18.1). Millar's passing judgment (*Study*, p. 76) that most of his comments on human nature are "no more than commonplaces," is too dismissive and overlooks the complexity of his usage.

3. See *CAH*, vol. 10, pp. 90–99; Kenneth Scott, "The Political Propaganda of 44–30 B.C.," *MAAR* 11 (1933), pp. 7, 37–49.

4. On Agrippa as imperial role model for a subordinate, see Meyer Reinhold, *Marcus Agrippa. A Biography* (Geneva, N.Y.: 1933), pp. 149–152; Jean-Michel Roddaz, *Marcus Agrippa* (Rome: 1984), (*Bibl. des Écoles Françaises d'Athènes et de Rome*, 253), pp. 496–511.

5. Cassius Dio, *History of Rome* 49.2.1–4.1; 49.8.5–10.4; 50.12.13–14.2; 50.31.1–35.

6. Ibid., 49.19.1–22.1.

7. Ibid., 52.19.4–5; 52.33.5–6. Cp. Clinton W. Keyes, *The Rise of the Equites in the Third Century of the Roman Empire* (Princeton, N.J.: 1915); Arthur Sten, *Der römische Ritterstand* (Munich: 1927), pp. 166–167, 170–171; Jochen Bleicken, "Der politische Standpunkt Dios gegenüber der Monarchie," *Hermes* 90 (1962): 451–453, 458–460, 465; Fergus Millar, *The Emperor in the Roman World (31 BC–AD 337)* (Ithaca, N.Y.: 1977), pp. 69–110.

8. Cassius Dio, *History of Rome* 49.23–33. Plutarch's extended account (*Antony* 37.3–50.4) is more reliable. Cp. August Bürcklein, *Quellen und Chronologie der römisch-parthischen Feldzüge in den Jahren 713–718 d. St.* (Berlin: 1897), pp. 6–46; Hermann Bengtson, *Zum Partherfeldzug des Antonius* (*Sitzungsberichte Bayer. Akad. Wiss., Philosoph.-Hist Kl*, 1974, Heft 1), pp. 9–13; Manuwald, *Cassius Dio and Augustus*, pp. 222–223.

9. Johannes Kromayer, "Kleine Forschungen zur Geschichte des zweiten Triumvirats, VII: Der Feldzug von Actium und der sogenannte Verrath der Cleopatra," *Hermes* 34 (1899): 1–54; also Johannes Kromayer "Actium: ein Epilog," *Hermes*, 68 (1933): 361–383; Aldo Ferrabino, "La Battaglia d'Azio," *Riv. Filolog.* 52 (1924): 433–472; T. Rice Holmes, "The Object of Antony and Cleopatra in the Battle of Actium," in *The Architect of the Roman Empire* (Oxford: 1928), pp. 253–258; Jacqueline Leroux, Les Problèmes stratégiques de la Bataille d'Actium," *Recherches de Philologie et de Linguistique* 2 (1968): 29–37, 55; John M. Carter, *The Battle of Actium* (London: 1970), pp. 200–214.

10. Cp., e.g., W. W. Tarn, "The Battle of Actium," *JRS* 21 (1931): 192–197; Hans Volkmann, *Cleopatra: A Study in Politics and Propaganda* (New York: 1958) (= *Kleopatra: Politik und Propaganda*, Munich: 1953), pp. 193–196; W. R. Johnson, "A Queen, a Great Queen? Cleopatra and the Politics of Misrepresentation," *Arion* 6 (1967): 387–402. This is not to deny that Dio, in his selective manipulation of the sources, did not elsewhere introduce (50.33) a number of anti-Cleopatra propaganda themes. Here Cleopatra is said to have made a dash for safety out of the battle because of womanly fear. And in 51.6.5–10.9, he highlights, like Plutarch, the weaknesses of Antony, and also Cleopatra's "treachery" to him.

11. See Plutarch, *Antony* 86.5; *Cicero* 49.4. Cp. Andersen, *Dio und die Begründung*, pp. 35–36; Fadinger, *Begründung*, p. 247 n. 2.

12. On the consul Sextus Pompey see Miliner, *Pompeius* 19, in *RE* 21.2 (1952), col. 2060.

13. Cassius Dio, *History of Rome* 36.4.

14. See, e.g., T. Mommsen, *Römisches Staatsrecht* (Leipzig, 1888) vol. 1, pp. 67–70; L. Wickert, *Princeps*, in *RE* 12 cols. 2283–2286; Hugh Last, "On the *Tribunicia Potestas* of *Augustus*," *Rend. Inst. Lomb.* 84 (1951): 93–110; Béranger, *Recherches*, pp. 97–101; Mason Hammond, *The Augustan Principate* (Cambridge, Mass.: 1968), pp. 79–84.

15. See, e.g., Millar, *Study*, pp. 102–118; Mason Hammond, "The Significance of the Speech of Maecenas in Dio Cassius Book LII," *TAPA* 63 (1932): 88–102; Bleicken, "Der politische Standpunkt," pp. 444–453; Emilio Gabba, "Progetti di riforme economiche e fiscali in uno storico dell'età dei Severi," in *Studi in onore di Amintore Fanfani*, vol. 1 (Milan: 1962), pp. 39–68.

16. Georges Méautis, *Une Métropole égyptienne sous l'empire romain. Hermoupolis-la-Grande* (Lausanne: 1918), pp. 152–155, 199–203; Luigi Moretti, *Iscrizioni agonistiche greche* (Rome: 1953), passim; N. Lewis and M. Reinhold, *Roman Civilization II: The Empire* (New York: 1966), pp. 232–237; Gabba, "Progetti di riforme."

17. Gabba, "Progetti di riforme"; Millar, *Study*, p. 11.

18. See, e.g., Rostovtzeff, *SEHRE*, pp. 142–149, 387–388; R. F. Newbold, "Cassius Dio and the Games," *L'Antiquité Classique*, 44 (1975): 589–604.

19. See Tom B. Jones, "A Numismatic Riddle: The So-Called Greek Imperials," in *PAPS* 107 (1963): 308–347; Jean-Pierre Callu, *La politique monétaire des empereurs romaine de 238 à 311* (Paris: 1969) (*Bibl. Éc. Fr. d'Ath. et de Rome*, 214); "Approches numismatiques de l'histoire du III siècle (238–311)," *ANRW* 11, 2: 594–613; Michael Crawford, "Finance, Coinage and Money from the Severans to Constantine," *ANRW* 11:2 pp. 560–593.

20. Cassius Dio, *History of Rome* 52.35.5. Dio's views on emperor worship are analyzed as "a most remarkable text on the imperial cult," by G. W. Bowersock, "Greek Intellectuals and the Imperial Cult in the Second Century A.D.," in *Le Culte des Souverains dans l'empire romain*, ed. Willem Den Boer (Vandoeuvres-Genève: 1973) (*Entretiens sur l'Antiquité Classique*, 19), pp. 202–206; D. M. Pippidi, "Dion Cassius et la religion des empereurs," in *Rev. Hist. du Sud-Est européen* 19 (1942): 407–418.

21. Millar, *Study*, p. 72. Cp. Harold R. Mattingly's review of Millar in *History* 50 (1965): 207: Dio is there appreciated as "capable of real political insights," and "an under-prized historian."

22. For extensive treatment of the merits and faults of Cassius Dio, see my work "From Republic to Principate: A Historical Commentary on Cassius Dio's *Roman History* Books 49–52," published in the Monograph Series of the American Philological Association, 1988.

CHAPTER 8

This chapter originally appeared in *Science and Society* 10 (1946), 361–91; this article was excerpted by M. Chambers, ed., *The Fall of Rome* (New York, 1963), pp. 76–84. For Rostovtzeff's bibliography, see C. B. Wells, "Bibliography—M. Rostovtzeff," *Historia* 5 (1956), 351–88. For further work on Rostovtzeff, see J. Rufus Fears, in W. W. Briggs and W. M. Calder III, eds., *Classical Scholarship: A Biographical Encyclopedia* (New York, 1990), pp. 405–18 (with bibliography), and K. Christ, *Von Gibbon zu Rostovzeff* (Darmstadt, 1989), pp. 334–49. For an introduction to the debate over the nature of the ancient economy, see M. I. Finley, *The Ancient Economy* (Berkeley and Los Angeles, 1973) and, Finley, ed., *The Bucher-Meyer Controversy* (New York, 1979).

1. It is not my purpose to provide the reader with a concordance to the verbal contradictions and minor inconsistencies in Rostovtzeff's writings, but rather to lay bare the profound antitheses in his thinking. I am indebted for valuable suggestions especially to Prof. N. Lewis of Columbia University. Documentation of Rostovtzeff's views has been limited, for the most part, to the sources of direct quotations.

2. N. Lewis, review of M. Rostovtzeff *SEHHW* in *Classical Weekly* 36 (1943): 187.

3. V. G. Childe, *What Happened in History* (New York: 1946); B. Russell, *A History of Western Philosophy* (New York: 1945). I may cite here also, for example, R. F. Arragon, *The Transition from the Ancient to the Medieval World* (New York: 1939); H. J. Haskell, *The New Deal in Old Rome* (New York: 1939); R. M. Geer, *Classical Civilization: Rome* (New York, 1940); J. Day, *An Economic History of Athens under Roman Domination* (New York: 1942).

4. Rostovtzeff, "The Decay of the Ancient World and its Economic Explanations," *Economic History Review* 2 (1929–1930): 197.

5. HAW, vol. 1, p. 6.

6. Ibid., p. 6n.

7. T. Frank, "Recent Work on the Economic History of Ancient Rome," *Journal of Economic and Business History* 1 (1928): 114; R. Turner, *The Great Cultural Traditions: The Foundations of Civilization* (New York: 1941), vol. 2 p. 935 n. A dualistic tendency in Rostovtzeff has been observed by A. Momigliano, "Rostovtzeff's Twofold History of the Hellenistic World," *Journal of Hellenic Studies* 43 (1943): 116 n. Cp. Momigliano, "Aspetti di Michele Rostovzev," *La Nuova Italia* 4 (1933): 160–164.

8. Rostovtzeff, *HAW*, vol. 1, p. 10. Cp. *Zeitschrift für die gesamte Staatswissenschaft*, 92 (1932), p. 334 n. 1.

9. This is somewhat less true of his last great work, *The Social and Economic History of the Hellenistic World*, where there is incidentally a special note of caution, in criticism of Meyer, Beloch et al. against the tendency to interpret the facts from modern points of view (p. 1327 n. 25).

10. Rostovtzeff, "The Decay of the Ancient World," pp. 204–208. Despite his awareness, at the time of the publication of his pioneering *Social and Economic History of the Roman Empire* (1926), that "there is no identity between the economic development of the modern and that of the ancient world" (p. 483), he nevertheless speaks unreservedly in that work of capitalists, a capitalistic system of agriculture, capitalistic methods in trade, city-capitalism, commercial capitalism, the methods of pure capitalistic economy. At that time he was prepared to concede only that "the ancient world never reached the economic stage in which we live, the stage of industrial capitalism" (p. 482 n.).

11. Rostovtzeff, *SEHHW*, p. 1303.

12. Rostovtzeff, "The Hellenistic World and Its Economic Development," *American Historical Review* 41 (1935–1936): 250.

13. See L. M. Hacker, *The Triumph of American Capitalism* (New York: 1940), pp. 16–27; G. Mickwitz, "Zum Problem der Betriebsführung in der antiken Wirtschaft," *Vierteljahrschrift für Sozial- und Wirtschaftsgeschichte* 32 (1939): 1–25; F. Lot, *The End of the Ancient World and the Beginnings of the Middle Ages* (London: 1931), pp. 55–85; A. Rochester, *The Nature of Capitalism* (New York: 1946), pp. 17–25; O. von Zwiedineck, "Was macht ein Zeitalter kapitalistisch?," *Zeitschrift für die gesamte Staatswissenschaft* 90 (1931): 482–524.

14. "The Problem of the Origin of Serfdom in the Roman Empire," *Journal of Land and Public Utility Economics* 2 (1926): 203: "The economic evolution of a prosperous world Empire based on private property tended naturally towards capitalism"; *SEHRE*, p. 167: "The purchasing power of the country population and the lower classes of the city residents was very small. But their numbers were large. The existence of such conditions was bound to give rise to mass production and factory work."

15. *SEHRE*, p. 18 n. and 55; "Decay of Ancient World," p. 206: "Hence the peculiar form of 'capitalism' (concentration of goods in the hands of few people) in Rome, which has no parallels either in the ancient or in the modern world."

16. N.B. Rostovtzeff's comment on Ps.-Aristotle, *Oeconomica*, vol. 2 (*SEHHW*, p. 445 n.): "The fact that in his view [Ps-Aristotle's] the income of a private person is chiefly derived from land is interesting as an indication of the mainly agricultural character of the economic system of his time."

17. *SEHHW*, pp. 1252 and 1270 n.; *SEHRE*, 145, 161, and 474 n. What is the proof? See *SEHRE*, p. 145: "Unfortunately, we have no learned work dealing with this problem [sources of wealth of Roman 'capitalists' of the second century A.D.]. No scholar

has endeavored to collect the evidence about the rich men of the second century, about the sources of their income, and about the character of their economic activity. . . . Our information is fairly abundant. As far as I can judge from the evidence I have got together, the main source of large fortunes, now as before, was commerce." The reader is referred to p. 530, n. 16, but no supporting evidence is cited there. But see p. 292: "In every case where we can trace the origin of the large fortunes of wealthy municipal nobles [in Africa during the early Roman Empire], we find them to have been derived from ownership of land."

18. *SEHRE*, p. 1, 3, and 482 f.

19. *SEHHW*, p. 1200: "Whether it ever came to resemble modern mass production for an indefinite market . . . I am afraid no conclusive answers can be given"; cp. pp. 1211 and 1230. This is not to deny that there existed in antiquity simple, precapitalistic commodity production serving largely the military and building requirements, and the luxury demands of the upper classes.

20. *HAW*, vol. 2, p. 301; *SEHRE*, pp. 165–169; *SEHHW*, pp. 100, 306 n., 317, 564 n., and 1210 n. He has relinquished his earlier view on the existence of textile factories in Hellenistic Egypt—see "A Large Estate in Egypt in the Third Century B.C.: A Study in Economic History," *University of Wisconsin Studies in the Social Sciences and History*, no. 6 (Madison: 1922), pp. 53, 115, and 135; also *SEHHW*, pp. 1227–1229. But he is still confident that factories for the manufacture of military equipment existed in both the Hellenistic world and the Roman Empire (*SEHHW*, p. 1220).

21. *SEHRE*, p. 305; *HAW*, vol. 1, p. 374. Cp. *SEHRE*, pp. 302–305; *SEHHW*, pp. 1204, 1230.

22. *HAW*, I, p. 375. But cf. *SEHRE*, p. xi f., where Rostovtzeff assumes sweepingly that the working classes were the chief consumers of industrial goods.

23. K. Wiedenfeld, "Transportation," *Encyclopedia of the Social Sciences*, vol. 15, p. 83.

24. *AHR*, "Hellenistic World Economic Development," p. 248; *SEHHW*, p. 132, 134 n., 654, 737, and 1019. Yet he admits that the Hellenistic states enjoyed only partial economic unity (*SEHHW*, pp. 185 and 1098); that the Hellenistic Greek leagues possessed no such unity (*SEHHW*, p. 204); that the Seleucid Empire "never could be welded into anything like an economic unit" (*SEHHW*, p. 430). The notion of "economic unity" is confused with political unity, uniformity of currency, commercial relations, and especially with cultural uniformity in the mode of life of the Greco-Macedonian ruling class in the Hellenistic world.

25. G. Mickwitz, "Economic Rationalism in Graeco-Roman Agriculture," *English Historical Review* 52 (1937), pp. 577–589.

26. *SEHHW*, p. 1357 n. 53.

27. N.B. *SEHHW*, p. 536: "Nevertheless the reigns of Seleucus and his early successors were without doubt a period of prosperity," despite evidence of the existence of general misery and distress cited in the pages immediately preceding.

28. *SEHRE*, p. ix, 100, 178, 414, and 451; *SEHHW*, pp. 94 n., 163, 610–612, 625, 938, 1031, 1121, and 1128.

29. For the bourgeois middle class of pre-Soviet Russia, see L. Tikhomirov, *Russia, Political and Social*, trans. A. Aveling (London: 1888), vol. 1, pp. 247–259; D. S. Mirsky, *Russia, a Social History* (London: 1931), pp. 267–270; J. Mavor, *An Economic History of Russia* (London and New York: 1925), pp. 155 and 588.

30. L. Corey, *The Crisis of the Middle Class* (New York: 1935), p. 140 n.

31. Ibid., pp. 42 and 168; E. Grünberg, *Der Mittelstand in der kapitalistischen Gesellschaft* (Leipzig: 1932), pp. 124, 165–167; C. Brinkmann, "Bourgeoisie," *Encyclopedia of the Social Sciences*, vol. 2, p. 654 ff.; A. Meusel, "Middle Class," ibid., pp. x, 407ff. The terms "middle class" and "bourgeoisie" are used carelessly and interchangeably by F. C. Palm, *The Middle Classes Then and Now* (New York: 1936).

32. *SEHHW*, p. 1115f.

33. Ibid., pp. 163 and 625. Cp. pp. 1145–1148 and 1204f.

34. Cp. A Segré, *Il mercantilismo nel mondo antico* (Catania: 1931), p. 10. F. Lot, *End of Ancient World*, p. 74f.

35. A. Meusel, "Middle Class," p. 410f.

36. *SEHRE*, p. 103. Cp. pp. 115, 399, 405f., 448, and 616 n. 31. The term "educated classes" is often used synonymously with "bourgeoisie." But note p. 177: "The low standards of intellectual culture among even the richest families of the city bourgeoisie . . . all sections of it, including the higher . . ."

37. *SEHHW*, pp. 1122 and 1125.

38. Ibid., p. 1027; *SEHRE*, pp. 100, 293, and 298; "The Near East in Hellenistic and Roman Times," *Dumbarton Inaugural Lectures* (Cambridge, Mass.: 1941), p. 29f.

39. A. Meusel, "Middle Class," p. 410.

40. *HAW*, vol. 1, p. 209; *SEHRE*, p. xii; "Hellenistic World Economic Development," p. 238; *SEHHW*, pp. 273f., 291, 565, and 1301.

41. *HAW*, vol. 1, p. 316f.

42. First elaborated by him in his now famous article, "The Foundations of Social and Economic Life in Egypt in Hellenistic Times," *Journal of Egyptian Archaeology* 6 (1920): 161–178. Cp. *SEHHW*, pp. 81, 279, 302, 332f., 1101, and 1309.

43. *SEHHW*, p. 273.

44. Ibid., p. 406. Cp. pp. 289–291, 330, and 1098. In his "Foreign Commerce of Ptolemaic Egypt," *Journal of Economic and Business History* 4 (1931–1932), pp. 758–761, Rostovtzeff has admitted that he had overdrawn the *étatization* of trade in Egypt.

45. See W. Lippman, *An Inquiry into the Principles of the Good Society* (Boston: 1943), p. 101f.

46. *SEHHW*, pp. 316 and 892.

47. Ibid., pp. 81, 407, 706, and 1017.

48. Ibid., p. 412.

49. Ibid., p. 1101.

50. Ibid., pp. 414f, 894–896, 913f, and 1102.

51. *SEHRE*, p. 571 n. 38. Cp. *HAW*, vol. 1, p. 47.

52. *SEHHW*, p. 911.

53. See N. Lewis, "article name," p. 189.

54. *SEHHW*, p. 1028f.

55. *HAW*, vol. 2, p. 115. Cp. *SEHRE*, p. 24.

56. *SEHRE*, p. viii.

57. *SEHHW*, pp. 755, 1031, and 1107. Rostovtzeff's view of the inevitability of class struggle is called into question by F. W. Walbank, review of Rostovtzeff, *SEHHW*, in *CR* 56 (1942): 84.

58. *SEHHW*, p. 1107.

59. J. E. Cairnes, *The Slave Power* (New York: 1863), p. 47.

60. *SEHRE*, p. xi. Cp. p. 300f.

61. Ibid., p. 588.

62. Ibid.; cp. p. 344.

63. Ibid., p. 333.

64. Ibid., pp. ix and 444: "The antagonism between the city and the country was the main driving force of the social revolution of the third century." See also Rostovtzeff, "Cities in the Ancient World," Institute for Research in Land Economics: *Urban Land Economics* (Ann Arbor: 1922), pp. 17–58; Rostovtzeff, "Les Classes rurales et les classes citadines dans le Haut Empire Romain," *Mélanges d'histoire offerts à Henri Pirenne*, vol. 2 (Brussels: 1926), pp. 419–434. For the same emphasis on antagonism between town and country in the Hellenistic world see *SEHHW*, p. 1105f.

65. Rostovtzeff, "La Crise sociale et politique de l'Empire Romain au IIIe siècle après J.-C.," *Le Musée Belge* 27 (1923): 238; *SEHRE*, pp. ix, xi, 441–453, and 480. Cp. *SEHHW*, p. 1128. Rostovtzeff even attributes (*SEHRE*, p. 627 n. 63) the aggressive mood of the peasants in the third century A.D., after centuries of "dull submissiveness," to the paternalistic social policy of the emperors and to the rise in the standard of culture among the masses. But note p. 451: "the tillers of the soil, on whom the economic prosperity of the Empire rested and whose toil and travail never brought them any share in the civilized life of the cities or in the management of local affairs."

66. See, e.g., H. Last, review of M. Rostovtzeff, *SEHRE*, in *JRS* 16 (1926): p. 126f, who denies the existence of evidence for an alliance between the peasants and the army.

67. *SEHRE*, p. 487.

68. R. Turner, *Great Cultural Traditions*, vol. 2, p. 935 n.

69. "Hellenistic World Economic Development," p. 252.

70. M. Dobb, *Political Economy and Capitalism* (London: 1937), p. 79.

71. See N. Lewis, review, p. 190.

72. *SEHHW*, p. 618, 622f., and 825.

73. Ibid., p. 622f.

74. Ibid., pp. 911 and 913.

75. Ibid., pp. 912f.

76. Ibid., p. 1031.

77. Ibid. Cp. p. 1028f.

78. Ibid., p. 1311. Elsewhere, too, he presents the chief cause of the decay of the Hellenistic world as political (*SEHHW*, p. 1096; "Hellenistic World Economic Development," p. 252).

79. See Walbank, review, pp. 82–84.

80. *SEHRE*, p. 190.

81. "The Problem of the Origin of Serfdom in the Roman Empire," p. 203.

82. *SEHRE*, p. xi. Cp. pp. 190 and 332f.

83. *HAW*, vol. 2, p. 365.

84. Ibid., p. xii.

85. Ibid., p. 33. Cp. pp. ix and 322; *HAW*, vol. 2, pp. 311 and 365.

86. *SEHRE*, p. ix.

87. *HAW*, vol. 2, p. 366.

88. *SEHRE*, p. 480.

89. *HAW*, vol. 2, pp. 366. Cp. p. 360 and 364.

90. *SEHRE*, p. 482.

91. "Decay of Ancient World," pp. 197–214; SEHRE, pp. 302f., 482f.; *Zeitschrift für die gesamte Staatswissenschaft*, 92 (1932), pp. 333–339.

92. I cannot trace here the ramifications of this controversy—the most important in the study of ancient economic history—which has attracted the attention of Bücher, E. Meyer, M. Weber, Beloch, Póhlman, Salin, Salvioli, Hasebroek, Sanna, Rostovtzeff, Mickwitz, Ziebarth, Schwahn, Sundwall, Reichardt, Gummerus, Francotte, Sigwart, Heichelheim, Oertel, and Bolkestein. Though he claims to hold a middle position between Bücher and Meyer (SEHHW, p. 1327), Rostovtzeff is actually one of the leading "modernizers."

93. SEHRE, p. 482; "Decay of Ancient World," pp. 200 and 203f. See K. Kautsky's introduction to G. Salvioli, *Der Kapitalismus im Altertum*, trans. by K. Kautsky, Jr. (Stuttgart and Berlin: 1922), p. VIII, where Kautsky criticizes Bücher's theory as a distortion of Marxism.

94. See e.g., N. H. Baynes, review of F. Lot, *La Fin du monde antique et le début du Moyen Âge*, in *JRS* 19 (1929): 230; J. H. Clapham, *The Study of Economic History* (Cambridge: 1929), p. 27.

95. E.g., SEHHW, p. viii: "While appreciating the importance of the social and economic aspect of human life in general, I do not overestimate it, in the Marxian fashion."

96. Cp. Rostovtzeff's ideas with the *Communist Manifesto*, ed. D. Ryazanoff (New York: 1930), section 1 ("Bourgeois and Proletarians"), pp. 25f., 31, and 35. See also K. Marx and F. Engels, *The German Ideology*, parts 1 and 3 (New York: 1939), pp. 8 and 43f., where the antagonism between town and country is stressed as running throughout all history.

97. Rostovtzeff, "The Near East in Hellenistic and Roman Times," p. 27.

98. SEHRE, pp. xi, xii, and 484; SEHHW, p. viif.

99. SEHRE, pp. x and 455.

100. HAW, vol. 1, pp. 197 and 204; vol. 2, 98f. and 295. SEHRE, p. x; Cp. SEHRE, p. 174: "A history of the different systems of law which prevailed in the Empire would form the basis of a study of the economic conditions which underlay them."

101. SEHRE, chs. 2 and 10. HAW, vol. 1, chs. 4, 10, 12, 14, 15, 21, and 25; vol. 2, chs. 9–13, 16–20; SEHHW, passim.

102. Cp. SEHHW, p. 1032: "In the first part of my survey I shall address myself to the social aspect of the period, and proceed to the economic aspect in the second."

103. F. Walbank, review, p. 83. Cp. R. Turner, *Great Cultural Traditions*, vol. 2, p. 934 n.

104. Walbank, review, p. 84.

105. H. J. Laski, *Faith, Reason and Civilization* (New York: 1944), 162f.

106. SEHHW, p. 1312.

107. SEHRE, p. 486 f.

108. "Hellenistic World Economic Development," p. 252.

109. F. W. Walbank's article "The Causes of Greek Decline," *Journal of Hellenic Studies* 64 (1944): 14–20, containing a critique of some of Rostovtzeff's basic views and substantially in agreement with the position taken here, arrived too late for consideration.

Index

Achilles, 6, 7

Actium, Battle of, 55, 57, 74, 75, 77
    soundness of Dio's account of, 78–79

"Acts of Isidore," 115n.83

Acts of Pagan Martyrs, 39

Acts of the Apostles, 35

Adkins, A. W. H., 45, 53

Admetus, 12

Aeneas, 68

Aeschines Socraticus, 106n.66

Aeschylus, 11

Aetolia, 6–7

Afghanistan, 21

afterlife, 9, 17

Against Aristogeiton (Dinarchus),
    108n.106

Agamemnon, 7

Agathon, 8

Age of Augustus. *See* Augustus

aggression, 46, 48, 53, 130n.2

agriculture, 84, 85, 88, 95, 96

Agrippa, Marcus, 34, 71, 78, 79–80

Akkad dynasty, 3

Alalu, 5

Alcestis (Euripides), 12

Alcibiades, 14

Alcibiades (Aeschines Socraticus),
    106n.66

Alexander Helios, 57

Alexander Severus, Emperor, 112n.34

Alexander the Great, 19, 61–62, 93–94

Alexandria, 36–39, 67

Aloades, 6

Alpine tribes, 34–35

Althaea, 6–7, 9

Althaemenes, 7

altruism, 53, 74

Amyntor, 6, 9

Anaunians (tribe), 34–35

Anaximenes of Lampsacus, 8, 119n.33

ancesters cult, 21

Andersen, Hans A., 72

Antigone, 11–12

Antigone (Sophocles), 11–12,
    118n.112

Antiochus of Commagene, 56

Antiphanes, 8

Antiphon, 46

Antoninus Pius, Emperor, 36

Antony, Mark, 61, 62, 72
    Actium strategy of, 78–79
    Cleopatra and, 54, 55, 56–57, 58
    Parthian defeat of, 78
    tomb of, 67

Anu, 5

anulus aureus, 27, 33, 113n.55

Apion, 114n.78

apocalyptic literature, 103n.13

apokeruxis, 14

Apollo, 11, 60

Apollophanes, 107n.80

appearance vs. reality, 74

Appian, 51, 74, 79

apprenticeship systems, 4

Arabia Nabataea, 57

Archelaus of Cappadocia, 56

Archelaus of Judea, 56

Archias, 111n.15

Areius of Alexandria, 64

Areopagiticus (Isocrates), 16

Areopagus, 16

arete, 12

Argos, 7

aristocracy
    decline of Roman Empire attributed
        to, 98

aristocracy (*continued*)
  Greek generational disequilibrium in,
    17
  Hellene provincial, 28
  Roman social mobility and, 24, 28
  Senatorial Order as, 33, 41
Aristonicus, 27
Aristophanes, 13–14
Aristotle, 11, 17, 18–19, 50
Armenia, 55–56, 57
Arrian, 51, 74
Artavasdes, 57
artisans, 84
Asoka, 20–21
Athena, 6, 11
Athenaeus, 107n.80
Athenagoras, 14
Athenodorus of Tarsus, 64
Athens, 9, 10–20
athletic contests, 24
Atia (mother of Augustus), 60
Atreus, 9
Augustus (formerly Octavian), 59–69
  basic temperament of, 69
  bestowal of "Augustus" title on, 64
  consensus building by, 63
  deification of, 26, 67–68
  dictatorship refusal by, 65–66
  Dio's assessment of, 77
  Dio's changed conception of, 75–76
  Dio's history of, 57, 65, 66, 70–72, 74–
    76, 78–79
  early years of, 60–61
  fame as motivation of, 68
  as father figure, 24
  frugal lifestyle of, 67
  longevity of, 59
  lost autobiography of, 59, 71
  "make haste slowly" dictum of, 67
  mythmaking by, 59, 64
  philosopher-teachers of, 64–65
  physical appearance of, 61
  political mission of, 65
  poor health of, 61, 67
  power as *princeps*, 24, 63, 75, 77, 79
  psychology of, 60–61, 62, 66, 69
  refusal to retire by, 66
  repression of Egypt by, 35–36
  Rostovtzeff's view of, 91
  self-esteem problems of, 60–61
  self-obituary by, 59, 62, 63, 65, 68, 72,
    124n.7
    social structure under, 25, 28, 29, 32,
      33, 35, 37, 38, 115n.84
    sumptuary laws of, 26
    tomb of, 67, 68
    as triumvir, 30, 54–58, 62, 72, 75, 78
    war against Cleopatra by, 54, 56–58,
      78–79
    war against Sextus Pompey by, 40
augustus clavus, 31
authoritarianism
  Greek parental, 10, 16–18
  of Hellenistic world, 19
  human nature viewed as tending
    toward, 46
  Roman parental, 10, 21–24

Babylonian captivity, 7–8
Balbus, L. Cornelius, 27
bankruptcy, 29
Barachiel the Buzite, 8
Barnes, T. D., 74
Bassus, Aufidius, 71, 72
behavior. *See* human nature
Beloch, Julius, 98
Bering-Staschewski, R., 130n.47
biography, 51–52
  conceptions of Augustus, 59–69
  inception of, 49
Birds (Aristophanes), 14
birth records/certificates, 35
Bithynia, 40, 74
Blumenthal, Fritz, 124n.2
"Boule Papyrus," 39
bourgeoisie, 83, 86–92, 94–100
bribery, 35, 40, 41, 42
bronze coins, 81
Brutus, Lucius, 62
Buddhism, 20

Caesar, Gaius (adopted son of Augustus),
  125n.27
Caesar, Julius, 23, 57, 58, 68, 72
  Augustus as adoptive heir of, 60, 61,
    62, 69, 75
  client rulers and, 55–56
  Commentaries, 129n.25
  dicatorship of, 66
  dynamism of, 67
  social leveling by, 27, 28
Caesar, Lucius (adopted son of
  Augustus), 125n.27
Caligula, Emperor, 29, 38

Calliodorus, 31
Calydon, 6–7
Cannae, Battle of, 40
capitalism, applied to ancient world, 83–100
capital punishment, 34, 40
Caracalla, Emperor, 34, 37, 39, 80
Carcabus, 7
cardinal virtues, 64
caste system, 41
castration (mythical), 5, 6
Cataline, 23
catastrophic crises, 93, 100
Catiline (Sallust), 50
Cato the Elder, 22
Catreus, 7
causality, 51
Chandragupta, 20
change, fear of, 4
chariot races, 81
Childe, V. Gordon, 82
Cicero, Marcus Tullius (father), 27, 52, 58, 109n.125, 111n.15
  on Caesar's adoption of Octavian, 61
  on cardinal virtues, 64
  defense of client ruler by, 55, 56
  generational relations and, 22, 23
Cicero, Marcus Tullius (son), 79, 109n.125
Cilicia, 57
Cinesias, 107n.80
Cinna, 32
Cinna (Corneille), 59
Circe, 7
citizenship, Roman
  in Alexandria, 38
  Caracalla's extension of, 39
  freedman restricted, 33
  illegal assumption of, 27, 34–35, 36–37
  military service and, 39–40
  provinicial avenues to, 36–37
  Roman names and, 34
  toga as Roman symbol of, 30
civil war, Roman (48–49 B.C.), 55–56, 58
civil war, Roman (68–69 A.D.), 40
class. *See* social class; social mobility; specific classes
class struggle, 90, 91, 98
Claudius, Emperor, 32, 34, 35, 38–39, 112n.35, 113n.55, 113–14n.63

Cleaenetus, 103n.23
Cleisthenes, 16
Cleopatra, 56–58, 61
  Actium battle and, 78–79
  propaganda campaign against, 54, 57–58, 78, 79
  tomb of, 67
Cleopatra Selene, 57
clothing
  ban on assumed military garb, 40
  as status symbol, 30–31, 112n.34
  sumptuary laws, 26, 30–31
Cloudcuckooland (fictional place), 14
Clouds (Arisophanes), 13–14
Cnossus, 7, 20
Cogan, Marc, 47
consensus senatus, 63
collective behavior. *See* group behavior analysis
collegia invenum, 24
colonies, Greek, 10
colonies, Roman, 22
coming of age, 9
comites order, 41
Commentaries (Caesar), 129n.25
commerce, 84, 85, 94
Commodus, Emperor, 33, 76, 80
Conflict of Generations, The (Feuer), 102n.1
consensus universorum, 63
conspicuous consumption. *See* luxury consumption
Constantine, Emperor, 40, 41, 42, 43
Constantius Gallus, 31
Constitutio Antoniniana (213 A.D.), 37, 41
constitutional monarchy, 75
consular rank
  Augustus's early election to, 62, 65
  first non-Roman *nomen,* 27
Cordus, Cremutius, 72
Corneille, 59
cosmogonic myths, 5–6, 17
Crassus, M. Licinius, 79
Creon, 11–12
Crete, 20, 57
crisis behavior, 48
Cronus, 6, 17
Ctesippos, 107n.80
Curetes of Pleuron, 6–7
curiales, 42–43
curse, parental, 9, 22

Curtius Rufus, Quintus, 51
Cyprus, 57
Cyril of Alexandria, 39
Cyrus of Persia, 16

damnatio memoriae decree, 79
Darius of Persia, 11
Darwinism, 98
death penalty. *See* capital punishment
dediticius status, 30
Deiotarus of Armenia, 55–56, 58
Deiphantes, 7
Delphi, 9
demi-noblesse, 28
democracy
    as challenge to parental authority, 10–
        11, 13, 15, 16, 17–18
    execution of Socrates under, 15
    Hellenistic decline of, 19
    Rostovtzeff's view of Greek, 88
Democritus of Abdera, 45
Demonicus, 16
determinism, 47, 51
Deuteronomy, 8
"Devil's Club," 107n.80
dharma, 20, 21
dialectical materialism, 98
Dicaeogenes, 8
dictatorship
    Augustus's refusal of, 65–66
    generational tensions and, 18
Didymus, 64
Dinarchus, 108n.106
Dio, Cassius, 70–76, 77–81, 111n.23
    achievements of, 77–81
    on Augustus at Actium, 57, 74, 75, 77,
        78–79
    on Augustus's political mission, 65, 78
    on Augustus's public dedication, 66
    on Augustus's reign, 74–76, 77
    background of, 76
    composition date of books 49 through
        52, 74
    crisis in Roman Empire and, 76
    economic proposal by, 80–81
    emulation of Thucydides by, 51–52,
        70, 76, 130n.2
    human nature viewed by, 52, 74, 76,
        78, 130n.2
    methods and style of, 72–74
    on sale of Roman citizenship, 35
    shortcomings of, 70

sources for books 49 through 52, 71–
    74
    third century reportage by, 76, 77, 80
Diocletian, Emperor, 41
Diogenes of Apollonia, 45
Dionysius of Halicarnassus, 51
Dionysus, 6
Diphilus, 8, 19
disownment, 14
dissipation, Roman youth, 23
divine intervention, 49
divine origins, 5, 60
divine retribution, 17
divine rule, 81
divine succession, 6, 17
Domitian, Emperor, 29–30, 40
"Donations of Alexandria" (34 B.C.), 57
Drerus (Crete), 20
dress. *See* clothing
dynastic struggles (mythical), 5–7

economic analysis
    by Dio, 80–81
    by Rostovtzeff, 82–100
Edmunds, Lowell, 47
"educated classes," 135n.36
education
    early Roman, 22
    in Roman Alexandria, 38, 39
egalitarianism, 12
Egypt, 37, 38, 113n.62
    Antony in, 56–58, 61, 77–78
    generational conflict in, 5
    right conduct formulation in, 4–5
    as Roman client state, 54–55, 88
    Roman propaganda campaign against
        Cleopatra, 54, 57–58, 78, 79
    Roman war against, 54–58, 61, 77–78
    Rostovtzeff's economic theories and,
        88–90, 92, 94
    social divisions under Rome, 28,
        35–40
Eisman, M. M., 74
El (deity), 5
elder respect, 4–5
    Athenian democracy as challenge to,
        10–11, 13, 15, 16, 17–18
    Greek cultural, 8–10, 15, 16
    growth of Greek disequilibrium in, 12–
        20
    Indian dharma and, 21
    Jewish commandmant, 7–8

Plato on, 16–18
as Roman generational basis, 10, 21–24
Elihu, 8, 12
emperor worship, 26, 81
Ennius, 64
ephebate, 38, 39
Ephorus, 119n.33
Epictetus, 106n.79
Epicureanism, 23, 24
equality, elder authority vs., 10, 18
eques (title). *See* Equestrian Order
eques Romanus, 28
Equestrian Order
    Augustus and, 32, 63
    creation of, 28
    eques title, 28, 31
    forged status symbols of, 31–32
    late Republic entrants into, 27
    membership restriction, 31–32, 33
    Roman youth and, 24
    Senatorial Order vs., 33, 41
    social mobility and, 78
    status symbols of, 31
    status usurpation, 29–33, 34
    theater seating and, 27, 28, 29, 31, 32
equus publicus, 28
equus Romanus, 31
Erinyes, 9, 11
estate system, 28
Eteocles, 9
Eumenides (Aeschylus), 11
Euripides, 8–9, 12, 67
Euthyphro (Plato), 16–17
Eutropius, 72
evolutionists, 98
executions. *See* capital punishment
exiles, 30

factories, 83, 84–85
family relations. *See* elder respect; father-son conflict
fatalistic forces, 49
"father beater" (stock comedic figure), 14
father-son conflict
    curses on sons, 9, 22
    disownment of sons, 14
    divine mythical, 5–7
    Greek backlash, 16–18
    Greek New Comedy stock characters, 19

Greek Old Comedy stock characters, 13–14
    Greek vs. Roman authority, 10
    incompetence charges against fathers, 14
    Jewish commandment against, 7–8
    Roman lack of, 21–24
    Socrates's position on, 15
fatum, 49, 50
Favonius, M., 29
Ferrabino, 78
fertility rites, 64
fetial rite, 58, 123n.36
Feuer, L. S., 17, 102n.1
fictive offices and honors, Roman, 33–34
filial duty. *See* elder respect
First Messenian War, 9–10
five ages of man, 7
Flavian, Emperor, 92
florus, 72
forged status symbols, 31
fortuna, 49, 50, 51
Forum, Roman, 68
franchise, Roman, 27, 38
    extension of, 37, 41
Frank, T., 82
fraud, Roman social mobility through, 25–26, 35, 37, 40–44
freeborn status, 28, 29
    fictive, 32–33, 113n.55
    names as indications of, 34
freedman class, 27, 28
    barriers to social rise of, 33
    equestrian status grants to, 32
    forged status displays, 31
    naming practices, 33–34
    obligations to former masters by, 32, 33
    prejudice against, 33
    status usurpation by, 29, 34
    wealth displays, 113n.59
free enterprise, 96
Freud, S., 102n.1
Fromm, E., 102n.1

Gabba, E., 71, 74
Gaea, 6
Gagé, Jean, 28, 124n.3
Gaius (jurist), 22
Galba, C. Sulpicius, 32
Gallic War, 129n.25
Gallus, Herennius, 27

Gallus, Q. Roscius, 27
garments. *See* clothing
generational relations, 3–24
    Aristotelian antithesis formulation on,
        18–19
    cleavage in Crete, 20
    cosmogonic rebellion myths, 5–6
    first historical record of conflict, 6
    first massive challenge to older
        generation, 10
    Greek filial obligations, 8–10, 16
    Greek polarization of, 10–19
    in Hellenistic Age, 19–20
    Indian conflict, 20–21
    Jewish honor commandment, 7–8
    parental curses and, 9, 22
    reasons for harmony in, 3–4
    Roman elder respect and, 10, 21–24
    Socratic undermining of, 15
generation gap, 102n.3
genetic basis of behavior, 53
German Historical School of economists,
    98
gerontocratic society, 4–5
Gibbon, Edward, 74
Gnomon of the Idiologus, 36, 39
Golden Rule, 16
gold ring, 27, 33, 113n.55
    gold-plated iron forgeries, 31
"Good Young Man"/"Good Old Man"
    (stock comedic characters), 19, 22
Goths, 40
Gracchi, 90
Granarola, J., 109n.125
graphe paranoias, 14
Gratian, Emperor, 43
"great man" theory, 49
Greece
    democracy in, 10, 13, 15, 16, 17–18, 88
    end as autonomous city-states, 19
    first massive challenge to parental
        authority in, 10
    Hellene status in Roman Egypt, 28,
        36–40, 113n.62
    historiographic human nature
        perspective, 45–49, 130n.2
    honor of parents injunction, 8–10
    polarization of generations in, 11–20,
        21
    Rostovtzeff's economic analysis of, 93–
        95
    See also Hellenes; Hellenistic Age

greed, 46
Greek mythology, 6–7
Greeks. *See* Hellenes
group behavior analysis
    Greek historiography, 47–48
    Roman historiography, 49–50

Haemon, 11–12
handicrafts, 84
Hattusas, 5
Hellenes, 46, 89
    biculturalism of, 80
    preferential status in Roman Empire,
        28, 36–40, 113n.62
    rivalry with Alexandrian Jews, 38–39
    ruling status in Egypt, 28, 36–40, 89
Hellenistic Age, 19–20
    factors in decay of, 94–95
    generational disequilibrium decline in,
        19–20
    historiography characteristic of, 49
    Rostovtzeff's analysis of, 90–92, 94–95,
        100
    sources of wealth, 84, 87, 88
    youth associations, 19–20, 24
Hephaestus, 6
Hera, 6
Heracleopolis, 5
heredity ranks, Roman, 29
Hermocrates, 14
Herodotus, 46, 70, 74
Hesiod, 6, 7
hierarchical social structure, 18, 25–26,
    35–40, 60–61
Hierocles, 8
Hippias, 46
Hippocratic medicine, 45, 46, 47, 48
Hippolytus, 9
Histories (Sallust), 50
historiography
    analysis of Dio's, 70–76, 77–81
    analysis of Rostovtzeff's, 82–100
    generational relations and, 3–4, 17
    Greek human nature perspective, 45–
        49, 130n.2
    "modernizers," 98, 137n.92
    Roman human nature perspective, 49–
        53, 74, 78, 130n.2
History of Rome (Dio), 70–76, 77–81
History of the Peloponnesian War
    (Thucydides), 46–49
Hittites, 5

Hobbes, Thomas, 48
Holmes, T. Rice, 78
Homer, 6–7
honestiores, 41
honor commandment. *See* elder respect
honors, Roman, trafficking in, 43
Hopkins, K., 111n.15
Horace, 23, 24, 29
"household economy" school, 98
How to Write History (Lucian), 51–52, 74
humanistic psychology, 59
human nature, 44, 45–53
  concept invention, 45
  Dio on workings of, 52, 74, 76, 78, 130n.2
  Livy's view of, 50–51
  Rostovtzeff's linkage of class conflict with, 91
  Sallust on Roman primary flaw in, 50
  scientific study of, 53
  Stoic uniform view of, 51
  Tacitus's assessment of, 51
  Thucydides's theory of, 46–48, 50, 130n.2
Hume, David, 45, 53
humiliores, 41
Hurrian myths, 5

iconoclasm, 12
Iliad (Homer), 6–7
illegitimacy, 35, 37
indeterminism, 51
India, generational conflict in, 20–21
individualism, 13, 19
industrial capitalism, 84–85, 86
infamia penalty, 32
ingenuitas grants, 32–33, 113n.55
ingenuus status. *See* freeborn status
initiation ceremonies, 4
"Instruction for King Merika-re" (Egypt), 5
intermarriage, Ptolemaic Egypt, 37
Iotape, 57
Isaac and Oedipus (Wellisch), 102n.1
Isidorus, 115n.83
Isocrates, 8, 15, 16, 19
Italy
  Augustan social stratification in, 28
  first century A.D. economic crisis in, 95
  widespread slave manumissions in, 27
  youth associations in, 24

ius anuli aurei, 31, 32, 33
iustus eques, 32

Jaeger, Werner, 45
Japanese sumptuary laws, 111n.11
Jehovah, 3
Jerusalem, 7–8
Jewish Revolt (115–117 A.D.), 39
Jews
  chosen people belief by, 3
  commandment to honor parents, 7–8
  status in Roman Egypt, 37–39
Job, 8, 12
Josephus, 51, 114n.78
Judea, 57
Julia (grandmother of Augustus), 60
Julian family, 68
Julian Law, 32
Junian Latins, 28
just war, 58
juvenocracy, 13

Kalinga War, 20
Kautsky, K., 137n.92
"Kingship in Heaven" (Hittite text), 5
knights. *See* Equestrian Order
Kumarabi, 5
Kumarabi text, 6–7

Laberius, D., 27
Lacedaemonian reverence, 16
Laius, 7
Laski, H. J., 100
Lasswell, Harold, 64
legal system
  Athenian intergenerational, 14, 17
  Roman birth registration, 35
  Roman intergenerational, 21, 22
  Roman rank recognition, 29
  Roman rank usurpation, 32
  Roman social changes, 27
legions, Roman. *See* military service
Leïtus (theater attendant), 29
Lepidus, 62, 72
Letta, 74
Levi, M. A., 72
Lewis, N., 132n.1
Lex Aelia Sentia (4 A.D.), 35
Lex Licinia Mucia (95 B.C.), 27
Lex Papia Poppaea (9 A.D.), 35
Lex Roscia (67 B.C.), 29

Lex Visellia de Libertinis (24 A.D.), 32
Libanius, 42
liberti dediticii, 28
libertini. See freedman class
libido, 102n.1
Life of Augustus (Nicolaus of Damascus),
    124n.2
Livia (wife of Augustus), 60, 67
Livy, 50–51, 58, 70, 76
    as source for Dio, 71–72
Lucian, 51–52, 74
luxury consumption, 24, 29, 31, 84,
    113n.59
Lycurgan system, 9
Lysias, Claudius, 35
Lysitheos, 107n.80
Lyttian War, 20

Macrinus, Emperor, 34
Maecenas, 29, 71, 79–80, 81
Maevius (clerk), 27
maiestas imminuta charges, 56, 57, 58
manumissions, 27, 28, 35
Manuwald, B., 72, 75–76
Maras (deacon), 31
Marathus, Julius, 61
Marcus Aurelius, Emperor, 35, 75, 76,
    77
Martha (Egyptian woman), 42
Martial, 29–30, 31, 33
Marxism, 98–99
mass production, 83, 84, 93
materialism, 24
Mauryan dynasty, 20
Mead, Margaret, 102n.3
Media Atropatene, 57
medical practice, as historiographic
    analogy, 45, 46, 47, 48
Meleager, 6–7, 9
Menander, 8, 19, 22
Menas, Pompeius, 32
mental incompetence, 14
Meri-ka-re, 5
Mesopotamia, 3
Messalina, Emperor, 35
Messenian War, 9–10
Metis, 6
Meyer, Eduard, 98, 137n.92
Mickwitz, G., 85
middle class, 86–87, 91, 94, 95, 98
Middle Comedy, 8

military service, Roman, 39–44
    Egyptian barriers from, 39–40
    illicit usurpation of status, 25–26, 27,
        40–41
    by slaves, 27, 40
    third century (A.D.) revolution and, 92–
        93
Millar, Fergus, 52, 71, 74, 81, 130n.2
Minos, 7
mistakes, human proneness to, 47
mobility. *See* social mobility
modernizers, 83, 98
Momigliano, A., 110n.1, 133n.7
Mommsen, Theodor, 82
monarchy, 75, 77
monetary uniformity, 81
moral relativity, 12
mos maiorum, 21
mothers, 5–8
Müri, W., 47
Musa, Antonius, 32
Musonius Rufus, 15
Mystalides, 107n.80
myths, 3, 5–7, 9, 11, 17

Naevius, 22
naming practices, 33–34, 113n.62, 113–
    14n.63
Nanneius (bogus knight), 30
nationalism, Roman historiographic, 49,
    50–51
natural rights, 12, 13
naval forces, 40
Near Eastern theogonic myths, 5–6
neoi associations, 19–20, 24
Neopythagorean literature, 8, 9
Neo-Stoicism, 50–51
Nestor, 7
New Comedy, 8, 19, 22
Nichomachean Ethics (Aristotle),
    108n.106
Nicias, 14
Nicolaus of Damascus, 124nn.2, 6
nineteenth-century thought, 98
nonconformity, 18

obedience, filial, 8, 9, 12, 13, 15, 16, 21,
    22
Oceanus (theater attendant), 29
Octavian. *See* Augustus
Octavii family, 60

Octavius, Gaius, 60
Odysseus, 7
Oedipal conflict, 3
Oedipus, 7, 9
"Oedipus Myth, The" (Fromm), 102n.1
Oikenwirtschaft theory, 98
Old Comedy, 13–14
"old democracy," 16
oligarchy, 15, 18, 48
Olympian civil war, 6
"On the Acient Medicine," 45
"On the Constitution" (Thrasymachus), 13
"On the Nature of Man" (Hippocrates), 45–46
"On Truth" (Antiphon), 46
operant behaviorism, 53
oracles, 7
Orosius, 72
Ortega y Gasset, José, 53
ostentation, 29, 31, 113n.59

Pacatus, Claudius, 40
Pallas (freedman), 113n.55
papyri sources, 35–36, 39, 113n.62
Parthian Empire, 57, 78
Pasicles, K. Crassicius, 33
passive resistance, 89
Pater Patriae title, 63
patria potestas, 10, 21–22
patriarchal society, 4–5, 10, 13, 21–22
patricide, 7
Paul, St., 35
Paulus (jurist), 25, 65, 112n.34
peasantry, 92–93, 95
Pédech, Paul, 119n.33
Pelasgus, 11
Pelling, C. B. B., 129n.29
Peloponnesian War, 13, 15, 46–48
Pelops, 9
peregrine status, 30, 34, 35, 115n.84
Periclean Age, 11
Pericles, 10
Perictyone, 9
Perperna, M. (father), 26–27
Perperna, M. (son), 27
Perrhebeians, 7
Persian Empire, 19, 93–94
Persians (Aeschylus), 11
pessimism, 51, 100, 130n.2

petite bourgeoisie, 86, 99
Pharsalus, Battle of, 55
Phasis (equestrian), 30
Pheres, 12
Phidippides (Greek comedic character), 14
Philemon, 8, 19
Philip II, king of Macedon, 62
Philip V, king of Macedon, 49
Philippi, Battle of, 29, 55
Philippus, Lucius Marcius, 60
Philopoemen, Titus Vinius, 32
philosophy of history
   of Dio, 76
   of Rostovtzeff, 82, 98–99
   See also historiography
Phoenicia, 57
Phoenician History (Sanchuniathon), 6
Phoenician myth, 5–6
Phoenix, 6–7, 9
pietas concept, 22
piracy, 52
planned economy, 88–90
Plato, 8, 9, 13, 16–18, 19, 46, 50
Plautus, 22
plebians, 29, 78
Pliny, 31, 40
Pliny the Elder, 32
Plutarch, 49, 51
   on Antony and Cleopatra, 78, 79
   Dio parallels with, 72
   literary methods of, 129n.29
   lost Augustus autobiography and, 59
plutocracy, 28
polis culture, 10, 13, 47–48
political systems
   Dio's analysis of Roman, 80
   generational struggle and, 3, 10–11, 13, 16, 17
   group behavior analyses, 47–50
   personality typologies, 59
poll tax, 36, 38
Polybius, 20, 49, 51, 70, 74
Polynices, 9
Pompey, Gnaeus (the Great), 52, 55, 56, 58, 62
Pompey, Sextus (son), 40, 79
Pompey, Sextus (unrelated consul), 79
Poseidon, 6
Posidonius, 51
Pouncey, Peter R., 46

powers
  given to Augustus, 62–63, 64
  paternal, 10–11, 21–22
power seekers, personality profiles of, 59,
    60–61, 64, 66
Praetorian Guard, 34
predestination, 50–51
prejudice, 25, 33
pre-Socratic philosophers, 45
primordial patricide, 102n.1
Primus, Marcus, 65
princeps title, 24, 63, 75, 77, 79
Pro Archia (Cicero), 111n.15
Proculus, Flavius, 32
Pro Deiotaro (Cicero), 55
Prodicus of Ceos, 45
proedria, 31
progress, concept of, 98
proletariat/proletarianization, 83, 86, 89,
    91, 92, 98
property ownership, 28, 29, 80–81, 84,
    91, 95
prosperity definition, 85–86
Ptah-hotep, 4–5, 12
Ptolemaic Egypt. *See* Egypt
Ptolemy Caesarion, 57
Ptolemy Eurgetes, 90
Ptolemy Philadelphus, 57, 88
Ptolemy VI Philometor, 54–58
public games, 81
purple garments, 30–31
Pythagorean doctrine, 8, 15

rank, usurpation of Roman, 26, 41–44
reason, "deauthoritization" of fathers in
    wake of, 11, 12, 15
reductionism, 45
Remus, 64
Republic (Plato), 13
Res Gestae Divi Augusti, 59, 62, 63, 65,
    68, 72, 124n.7
restlessness, as Roman human flaw,
    50
revolution, Roman (third century A.D.),
    92–93, 96
Rhescoporis of Thrace, 56
Rhodes, 90
Ricardian economics school, 93
right conduct, earliest literary
    formulation of, 4–5
ritual myths, 3
Rivier, Klaus, 47

Roman Empire
  absence of racial/ethnic prejudice in, 25
  Augustan system, 75–76
  Augustus's achievements, 62–69
  biographers of, 51–52
  decline causes, 97–100
  Dio's contemporary economic analysis
      of, 80–81
  Dio's historigraphical achievement, 76,
      77–81
  emperor figures in, 24, 64, 81
  "enlightened emperors" of, 92
  historiographical approaches, 49–53,
      70–76, 77–81, 82–100
  naming practices, 33–34
  parental authority in, 10, 21–22
  provincial policy, 28
  Rostovtzeff's modernist economic
      analysis of, 82–100
  sources of wealth in, 87
  status and status symbols, 25–44
  technological decline during, 85
  third century A.D. revolution, 92–93,
      96
  youth alienation in, 24
  youth associations in, 19–20, 24
Roman Republic
  client rulers and, 55–56, 57
  consensus senatus under, 63
  Dio's narrative of transition from, 70,
      76, 77
  Livy's nostalgia for, 76
  Sallust on ruling class weakness in, 50
  social mobility in last days of, 27–28
  war against Cleopatra, 54–58
  youth dissipation in, 23, 24
Romulus, 62, 64, 68
Rostovtzeff, Michael, 82–100
  capitalist predilection of, 88–89
  confusion of bourgeoisie function by,
      86–88
  definition of prosperity by, 85–86
  fundamental historical doctrine of, 82–
      83, 93, 97–98, 99
  projection of modern economic
      concepts by, 85
Russell, Bertrand, 82

sabotage, 89
Salamis, Battle of, 11
Sallust, 23, 49–50, 51, 52
Sanchuniathon, 6

Sargon I, 3
Sarmentus (freedman), 29
Schwartz, E., 72
"scientific agriculture," 84, 85, 95
Scipio Africanus, 62
Second Servile War, 112n.37
Second Sophistic movement, 74
Second Triumvirate, 30, 54–58, 62, 72, 75, 78
Seleucus, Emperor, 134n.27
self-interest, 46, 48, 74
self-restraint, 23
Senatorial Order
   Augustan stratification system and, 28
   Augustus and, 63
   banned use of military garb by, 40
   closed ranks of, 28, 29, 33
   curial class leakage into, 42–43
   Dio as member of, 76, 77, 78, 80
   Equestrian Order vs., 33, 41
   as "great capitalist," 83–84
   power of families, 27
   Roman youth and, 23, 24
   Sallust's human nature views and, 50
   as sole aristocracy, 33, 41, 42
Seneca, 51, 66
Sententiae (Paulus), 25
Septimius Severus, Emperor, 33, 34, 39, 76
Sergius, 121n.3
Severan Age, 76, 77, 78
Severus Alexander, Emperor, 74, 75
Sherwin-White, A. N., 35
Sicilian War, 78
Sicily, 14, 27
Siculus, Diodorus, 51
silk garments, 30–31
Sinclair, T. A., 103n.13
Sindunians (tribe), 34–35
Skinner, B. F., 53
slave system
   Augustan curbs on, 28
   erosion of parental authority and, 10–11
   military service and, 27, 40
   as Roman economic backbone, 88, 98
   slave forged status-symbol displays, 31
   social change effects of widespread manumissions, 27, 35
Social and Economic History of the Hellenistic World, The (Dio), 133n.9

Social and Economic History of the Roman Empire (Rostovtzeff), 82–100
social class
   alienated Roman youth and, 23–24
   Athenian youth and, 16
   Augustus's early years and, 60–61
   Hellene elite in Egypt, 36–40
   Hellenistic decay and, 95
   Marxian theory on, 98–99
   polarization in later Roman Empire, 41–42
   Roman decline and, 97–98
   Roman economic problems and, 80–81
   Roman intergenerational harmony and, 22
   Roman status and status symbols, 25–44
   Rostovtzeff's view of, 86–87, 90–91, 92
   Sallust's historiographical view of, 50
   third century Roman revolution and, 92
   Thucydides's view of human nature and, 48–49
   See also hierarchical social structure; social mobility; specific classes
socialism, 88
social mobility
   as distinctively Roman, 25, 44
   "enlightened" Roman emperors and, 92
   in last days of republic, 27–28
   as mimimal in later empire, 41–42
   Roman illicit, 25–26
   Ventidius's career as historic paradigm of, 78
sociobiology, 53
Socrates, 13, 15, 106n.66, 107n.79
Solon, 9, 16
sons. See father-son conflict
Sophists, 13, 46, 74
Sophocles, 8, 11–12, 118n.12
Sophronistoi (Restrainers), 16
Soviet Union, 86
Sparta, 9–10
sports clubs, 20
state capitalism, 88
status and status symbols, Roman, 25–44
   conspicuous consumption and, 29, 31, 113n.59
   dress as, 30
   earliest known illegal assumption of, 26–27

status and status symbols, Roman
   (*continued*)
   in Egyptian province, 35–40
   fictive, 33–34
   forged citizenship and, 35
   forged symbols, 31–32
   growth in fraudulent practices, 41–44
   property ownership and, 28
   theatrical seating as, 27, 28, 29, 31
   title proliferation, 41–43
stereotyping, 48, 50–51
Stobaeus, 8
Stoicism, 8, 15
   as Augustan influence, 64–65
   as Roman historiographic influence,
      49, 50, 51
stratification. *See* hierarchical social
   structure
Strepsiades (Greek comedic character), 14
Suetonius, 51, 72, 124n.6
Sulla, Lucius Cornelius (dictator), 27, 55
Sumerian tradition, 5
sumptuary laws, 26, 30–31
Suppliant Women (Aeschylus), 11
Syracuse, 14
Syria, 88

Tacitus, 26, 51, 52, 68, 70
Taras (later Tarentum), 10
Tartarus, 9
taxation, 36, 38, 80–81
technological progress, 85
Telegonus, 7
Temenos, 7
Temple of Janus, 62
Temple of Mars, 68
tenant farmers, 88
Ten Commandments, 7
Terence, 19
Teshub, 5
Theages, 106–7n.79
theater
   generational relations portrayals, 11–
      12, 13–14, 19, 22
   ranked Roman seating, 27, 28, 29, 31,
      32
Thebes, 7
Theodosian Code, 42–43
Theodosius, Emperor, 26, 43–44
Theodosius II, Emperor, 30–31
Theognis, 8

theogonic myths, 5–6
Theogony (Hesiod), 6–7
Theopompus, 119n.33
Theseus, 9
Thetis, 6
Thorianus, G., 28
Thrace, 79
Thrasymachus, 13, 46
Thucydides, 14, 46–49, 53
   Dio compared with, 70
   as Dio model, 51–52, 70, 74, 76,
      130n.2
   on root human characteristics, 46–47,
      50, 130n.2
Thyestes, 9
Tiberius, Emperor, 26, 30, 32, 63, 68
timocracy, 31, 36
toga, 30
trade. *See* commerce
Trajan, Emperor, 40
transfer of methods fallacy, 48
tria nomina, 33
Triopas, 7
Tryphon, 112n.37
Tubero, Q. Aelius, 129n.25
Tulliassians (tribe), 34–35
tunic stripes, 31
Turner, R., 82, 93
tyche, force of, 49, 51
Typhon, 6
Tyrian purple garments, 30–31

Ugaritic text, 6–7
Ulpian (jurist), 112n.34
Universal History (Siculus), 51
upper classes
   Augustus's entry into, 60
   Hellenes in Alexandria and, 36
   Roman decline and, 97–98
   Roman harmonious generational
      relations and, 22
   Roman youth and, 23, 24
   Rostovtzeff's historical perspective on,
      83–84, 89–90, 100
   undermined economic stability of, 80–
      81
   See also aristocracy; Senatorial Order;
      status and status symbols, Roman
Upper Pannonia, 79
Uranus, 6, 17
urban bourgeoisie, 87, 92–93, 95, 96, 97

Vagia Isauricus, P. Servilius, 56
Valentinian, Emperor, 26
Valentinian II, Emperor, 43
Valerian, 43
Valerii Flacci, 26
values, Roman, 23
Velleius, 70
Ventidius, Publius, 78
Vergil, 23, 62
Verres, Gaius, 27
veteran privileges, 40–41
violence, Roman youth and, 24
virtues, Greek and Roman, 64
Visellian Law, 32
Vitruvius, 65, 68

Wahkare-Achthoes II, 5
Walbank, F., 100
wealth
    capitalist interpretation of, 83–84
    concentration in ancient world, 91–92
    distributive inequality in Ptolemaic
        Egypt, 89

Roman ostentatious displays of, 29, 31,
    113n.59
viewed as corrupting Roman youth,
    23
Weber, M., 98, 137n.92
Wellisch, E., 102n.1
Wilson, Edward O., 53
Wilson, Woodrow, 61

Xenophon, 16, 119n.33
Xerxes, 11

youth
    Greek artistic idealization of, 11
    revolt in Athens, 15, 16
    Roman alienation and dissipation of,
        23
    Roman ingrained elder respect by, 22
"youth" (as derogatory term), 14, 22
youth associations, 19–20, 24

Zenarchus, 64
Zeus, 6, 9, 11, 15, 17